Typ/Oxford

OXFORD — 1914

Magdalen Tower, Oxford   J. W. King

At light of dawn,
When the May buds in the hedgerows
White the thorn,
There's a song in Magdalen tower;

Then, as thunder in the blue,
A sound comes breaking through,
And we know it is not thunder as it comes;
We know it is the sound of distant guns.

J. B. L.
1914

OXFORD—1914

by

J. BRETT LANGSTAFF

Illustrated with Facsimiles of Significant Letters

and

Biographical Index

VANTAGE PRESS

NEW YORK • WASHINGTON • HOLLYWOOD

FIRST EDITION

Published by Vantage Press, Inc.
120 West 31st Street, New York 1, N.Y.

Manufactured in the United States of America

Library of Congress Catalog Card Number: 65-19607

DEDICATED

to the Presidents

of

Harvard and Magdalen College

MAY I SAY?

Phyllis Langstaff

Because it has been my privilege, since our marriage, to share with Brett many of the friends herein mentioned, may I say a word of appreciation for the kindnesses this journal recalls? A bright thread runs through this account of daily happenings during a period of deepening distress; it is the hospitality and friendship given so liberally by British people to a youthful stranger. *They* were in trouble — not he. Yet no one said, "Come back some other day when things are easy for us." Instead, they opened their doors at once and said, "Come in and stay."

At first with his own country neutral, Brett could not do more than is recorded in these pages. But when his country had joined its forces with the British and his friends were fighting off the enemy with their backs to the wall, then — though by that time he had been ordained priest, and was therefore forbidden by the Archbishop of Canterbury to join — Brett enlisted in the British army as a fighting man. This he did with the sanction of the American Major Advocate in London and was invalided out in 1918.

When the war was over, Brett remained with his British friends, serving them as a priest, working with them during three years of national reconstruction and learning from them still more of how to live. This was to him of far greater value than the studies leading to his Bachelor of Letters. And perhaps equally developing had been the daily living in Magdalen College which earned him the commendation said to me with some self-satisfaction by his college servant — who I met on our wedding trip — "He won't be any trouble to you, Mam."

FOREWORD

Nothing could be more fitting by way of preface to the journal of an American student resident in Oxford during the first two years of the first World War than the following letter from Edward, Prince of Wales, later to become King of England and finally Duke of Windsor.

Written in his own hand from Headquarters, 14th Corps, British Expeditionary Force, June 29th 1916, it touches on beagle hounds and undergraduate life at Magdalen College, it refers to his cousin, George of Teck, one who figures prominently in the journal, and finally it suggests the military and academic excitement which emanates from this war time record of Oxford.

The "photograph signed" I published with the Prince's sanction years ago in connection with a settlement work in which we both labored. The letters which accompanied it, and the letters of others which illustrate this volume, serve to preserve the rare spirit of their writers. I have thanked them before and do so again.

In sharing with the reader these literary reminders — mingled with personal notes of my own — I seek to introduce him to a group of friends and trust he will give us his friendship as he reads.

J. B. L.

Dear Langstaff,

Many thanks
for your letter; I return
you the photograph signed
as you asked. It's kind
of to suggest sending me a
copy but I have some !!
Well, do I remember that
day's beagling last Nov.!!
I wonder when I shall
get another day? I was
also delighted that they
gave George a commission
in his father's regt. as a he

was so keen.!! I'm very glad to hear you think the beagles will be able to carry on another season by which time one can only hope the war will be nearing its end; but who will be master? Is there anyone left who is keen & likely to do it well? My congratulations on getting a B.Litt. & I wish you the best of luck on your return voyage to New York.!!

I remain,

Yours sincerely

Edward.

EDWARD, PRINCE OF WALES (later King Edward VIII) written from France while on active service with the British Expeditionary Force to Brett Langstaff, referring to the Magdalen beagles which the latter co-mastered with Prince George of Teck. (See index)

CONTENTS

May I Say? by Phyllis Langstaff

FOREWORD

front — Nuneham Park — Harvard alumni at Oxford — Beagle hounds and fellow undergraduates — Varley Roberts, Brightman and Sir Herbert Warren — Work on the dissertation — Another letter *from the trenches* — The Ladies Harcourt and Astor and their hospitals — Lulu Harcourt and the *Lusitania* — Walt Whitman and the author of *Queed* — Winston Churchill and the Dardanelles — Blenheim Palace and its hospital — A bride-to-be in Bath— Meriel Talbot and the Victoria League.

ORIGINAL LETTERS REPRODUCED

1

ENTERING OXFORD
AND THE BEGINNING OF WAR

MY letters home (1914-1916) have just come to light after having been boxed away for a period of about fifty years. Preserved in chronological order by the loving hands of those to whom they were addressed they form a pattern of the first years of the Great War as seen by an American student at Oxford. More than that they make real and live as of today an academic atmosphere which vanished in the wake of total wars to follow.

I well recall how I looked in 1914—a slender youth with fair complexion and unruly blond hair. I must have been twenty five years old but never seemed to be given credit for my years. I had just completed a year of study at the General Theological Seminary in New York. It was an unrewarding year. My Harvard training was too liberal, perhaps, to fit me for such a conservative seminary. Moreover there was a disturbing controversy in churchmanship which centered on the Liturgy. I determined to seek out the highest authorities on the subject and therefore withdrew from the Seminary and made application for admission to Oxford University.

It was the summer of 1914 — when I was vacationing in a little house I had built on the beach at Stony Brook, Long Island — that war was declared in Europe. I had watched a fleet of the New York Yacht Club furling their sails and coming to anchor in Smithtown Bay. Then, as birds frightened by the firing of a gun, the news of war that evening of August 4, 1914, scattered the pleasure boats never to return in the same luxury of a peaceful

world. My immediate question was whether the Oxford colleges
would open, and in spite of reports to the contrary I determined
to sail for England.

A month later from the deck of the *Cameronia* — Twin Screw
Steamer of the Anchor Line — I was writing the first of a series
of letters home, a boy's letter addressed to trusting parents and
an older brother who had come to the pier in New York to see
me off.

"It seemed strange to sail away alone and leave you all on the
dock. If it were not that my cause is so engrossing I should be
mighty lonely. But after a few gulps I settled down to planning
the coming two years which are to mean so much to me and, if
God wills, to a great many other people. How many obstacles
were placed in the way of my going! As long as I have your help
and prayers I shall overcome the obstructions of the future as
those of the past have been overcome. Do not think of me as
sad and lonely, nor as spending my time in pleasure. I go forth
to battle expecting hardship and danger, but like the Greeks, I
go singing.

"There are just twenty passengers on board, but it undoubtedly
makes things more comfortable. An architect from New York
and a music enthusiast of near my own age are my special companions. A dear old Scottish clergyman who is sitting nearby
amusing a little boy and an assistant professor of the Medical
School in Glasgow — these are my acquaintances of the first day.
Then of course there are the ladies."

These excerpts are taken from a letter addressed primarily to
my mother who was taken up with an organization she had started
for British women living in the United States. It was as much
with the hope that I might contribute to the cause in which
England was engaged as it was for my personal career, I feel,
that she consented to my going. My bishop, Burgess of Long
Island, himself a one-time undergraduate of Oxford, complained
that in going I was wasting my time. And the university authorities
gave me little encouragement, especially of being admitted to
Magdalen College which held for us a family tradition.

If the spirit of this letter of fifty years ago sounds quixotic
in our days of regimented service, the reader must remember that
those were the days of heroes who were about to prove their
mettle in voluntary sacrifice for God and country. It is difficult to

explain what appeared as a revival of medieval romanticism impelling men to go forth in defiance of the world, the flesh and the devil if necessary — to right a great wrong. Not animosity against any nation or people, not as it became later in the war *to keep the home fires burning*, but to take one's stand with drawn sword on the side of the right — this was the spirit with which the British entered the war. And I? Well, perhaps I was just 'running with the old machine.'

The next letter which comes to hand was written from that dreary station hotel in Glasgow named after the father of Methuselah. Nothing could have been more depressing. It was long before hostile submarines appeared in the Atlantic, but the danger of German mines made exciting news.

"You cannot imagine the suspense of being without news for eight days of the war toward which we were heading. The trip itself was pleasant. Easy sailing, few people but interesting, excellent accommodations — in short, luxury. But how painted luxury seems when there are hundreds of men being shot every day.

"We passed the U.S. Battleship *Florida* in New York Bay and the British ship *Essex* not far out.

"Now I am spending the night in the St. Enoch Hotel.

"You have probably heard long ago of the cruiser sunk by German mines off the Scottish coast. There is a splendid spirit of patriotism here. The French are held in great esteem. Buttons etc. grouping the allied flags can be seen everywhere.

"Everything is safe so far with me, and I go up to Oxford on the 9:20 tomorrow."

The fact that the *Stars and Stripes* did not appear among the allied flags seemed to be taken for granted. This war began as a European conflict. Although Britain was pleased to have America's approval of her part, certainly for the first year and more there was no evident desire to have the Americans involved as active participants. No one objected to an American student going to Oxford, but no one seemed to care how he got there. Finally I wrote from the City Hotel in Peterborough.

"Here I am in Peterborough. The direct line from Glasgow to Oxford is all broken up by troop trains, and I was sent here to the other side of England in hopes of catching a cross line to Oxford. It did not work, and I have been forced to put up for the night.

"I saw the old cathedral for the first time in the 'pale moon-light' and again early this morning."

This was my first jolt toward realizing what a change in values war brings in its trail. Oxford had become a way-station, a student from a neutral country such as mine had lost potential importance, and what was more, I was beginning to see, the time for contemplating the past or planning for the future must give place to the need for the immediate necessity in the present danger. What a great patient face Peterborough Cathedral presented to a young foreign student at the beginning of a long war. Even with its doors shut it said something to me as I stood before it in the moonlight. Cut in shadowed tracery on its façade I could read more history and philosophy than I would be learning at Oxford, more of the theology that builders and masons had come to appreciate about faith in God cementing men together, more of what it takes to weather the stress and storm over the years. Night came and went, and in the 'dawn's early light' I saw the old cathedral still dreaming of the beauty of holiness and peace on earth.

Finally on the 9th of September I was able to write from Oxford: "After being shunted about I was returned to Rugby from whence I took the train of another road to Oxford.

"Once in Oxford, however, I drove straight to Magdalen to ask for lodgings. Thus I came to my present address, 66 The High Street, which is across the High from Magdalen. Here I pay three shillings a day including a hearty breakfast.

"The next day I went to see the President, but in his place found the Senior Tutor, Mr. Cookson. He was polite, even cordial for he offered me a cup of tea. When I told him that the *specials* were claiming the Russians had been landed in France, he told me in turn a great cock-and-bull story about how the troops had been brought around from Archangel to the north of Scotland and for many nights had been shipped down through England to France. We ran all over the city trying to find the *special* of which I had spoken, but it was not until I had left him in his room that I saw one. I immediately bought a copy and carried it back to him. This is typical of the general excitement which interrupts all business.

"After I had presented all my documents to him he was satisfied that I should come in as a Junior Foreign Student, *if* two half courses at Harvard counted the same as one whole course at

Oxford. This had to be referred to several authorities because the University Statutes said nothing about half courses. Then he decided that I was exempt from *Smalls*, which are the Responsions or entrance examinations, in everything except Greek.

"The enrollment for men coming up next term at Magdalen is a bit overcrowded, perhaps because the Prince of Wales is enrolled, and when the war is over and they all come back there doesn't look as though there would be room for me. This may happen within a couple of months."

In this manner I finally arrived in the dream city of the English intellect. It was not the first time I had passed from the High through the Lodge into old St. Swithin's quad, tunnelled through the dark cloister and come out on the broad expanse of lawn on the far side of which rises that 18th century building where Magdalen dons have for years shivered before little open fires in their high-ceilinged rooms. I had come 'sight seeing' with my tutor, Mr. Hanckel, when I was still a school boy. It hadn't changed. I thought it never would. One thing was certain, they were not prepared to change their way of pronouncing the Greek language to conform with the way I had learned to speak it at Harvard. To effect this adjustment I was packed off to a crammer.

"There was no use protesting with Mr. Cookson," I wrote from Haslemere in Surrey. "I obviously needed a tutor for my elementary Greek exam. So we telegraphed a well known tutor in the south of England, a Mr. Bromley. Then I packed up and rushed to the station. There I sat for five hours watching soldier trains going by every quarter hour. At last one stopped, and I was able to crowd on board.

"The line all the way to London is guarded, especially at bridges and other crossings. As we came nearer Aldershot there were large camps, although it is impossible to see the main Aldershot camp from the train. The harvest seemed to have been taken in and the country looked as prosperous as could be.

"There were many touching scenes where a family or a sweetheart would be saying goodbye perhaps forever to the soldiers. There was very little weeping. None on the part of the men. The soldiers seem to have a grim determined look when they are serious, and a rollicking carefree expression when they are not."

From the railway station I was driven to the residence of Mr. Bromley, just in time for dinner. It was one of those com-

fortable-looking English dwellings built on to an older house not
so comfortable and surrounded by ample grounds maintained for
privacy more than for any landscaping beauty. It bore the unpre-
tentious name, *Inval,* to indicate the obvious — it was in a valley.
Nevertheless, what I did not realize at the time, it had the reputation of being the most regarded institution of its kind in England.
Many a famous career had been saved by the intensive and
timely cramming of the man who was to be my master for the
next ten days. As it introduced me to Oxford, so a perusal of
my contemporary account may fittingly introduce the reader.

"'Upon my word,' said Mr. Bromley coming out into the hall
to greet me and interrupting the formal duties of the English
butler. 'I, I hardly expected you so late. Your coming was so
sudden. I received your telegram and — Come in and —.' Mr.
Bromley is a small, nervous clergyman with grey hair. His speech
is so hurried that he often repeats a word.

"As we entered the dimly lighted drawing-room a sweet-looking
young woman in a black evening gown approached and shook
hands. Maud, for so her father called her, had the same curious
impetuosity in her manner. Conversation slipped along easily
about the tedious trip from Oxford to Haslemere, about her
grandfather, Bishop Courtney, now rector of St. James's Church
in New York, and other conventional first meeting topics.

"The door suddenly opened and the same formal butler
announced the arrival of Miss Dorothy. Miss Dorothy Bromley
was stouter and although she was curt, there was more repose in
her than the rest of the family possessed. She had just returned
from London and had taken care to disguise the fact that she had
come from the country by dressing to suit the urban conventions.

"Finally Mr. Bromley told me that after Buck — this being the
name by which the butler went — had shown me the ways of
the house, he would like to see me again in his study. Whereat
Buck opened the door and excusing myself I left the room. My kit
and steamer rug were carried to the third floor where I was shown
a room of considerable size whose ceiling sloped tent-fashion,
lighted by two small windows. This was with apologies since it
was the only room left. (I afterwards found that it was about as
good as any in the house because all the good sized rooms had
been partitioned off to increase the number of sleeping apartments.) From thence I was led from the *modern* part of the house

in which we were to the *ancient* portion that had been built on to. I think Buck took his idea of the division of the house from the English hymnal. Up a few steps, down a few, along dark corridors where except for the candle Buck carried there was no attempt at lighting, finally into a low ceilinged room which had a small light burning in it.

"I had been following the butler in the most interested way as though I were being shown through the Catacombs. But no sooner had he entered this room for which he had been making a bee line than he doubled over in a deep bow. 'Pardon, your 'iness,' he exclaimed and recoiled upon me so that I was bunted back into the hall again. After a few more exhibits of hewn timber — similar to the primitive construction of our barn in the country — I was shown into the gun room. There I was introduced to the other pupils of the Rev. Mr. Bromley by proclamation of my guide.

"The walls of the gun room were a cheery red. On two sides were large windows and opposite were untidy shelves of books reaching to the ceiling and a large ingle nook with its ancient fireplace. There was a long wooden table in the center of the brick floor.

"It was on this table that the other pupils dressed in dinner coats with their hair glistening were seated. They explained that they had been catching mosquitos and became interested in the difference which I pointed out between English and American varieties of these tormentors. I also sat on the table, and we were soon acquainted.

"*His Highness,* whose privacy I had before broken in upon is the eldest son of the Duke of Teck and thus nephew to Queen Mary. His full title is His Serene Highness Prince George of Teck, but in reality a very decent fellow. Perhaps nineteen years old, light hair and rather tall except that he stoops a bit. His eyes are in such a condition of shortsightedness that he finds it necessary almost to rub his nose against a page he is reading. For this reason he has gone up already twice for *Smalls* without success. Nevertheless he has a grand build for a youth and a courteous manner.

"Then there is Harvey, an overgrown boy who has still another year before he will go up to Magdalen. He hates noise and except when he is alone rarely says a word. His father is a *knight* and evidently has a large estate in South Devon. Also the son of a successful Belgian merchant named Buysee who had at one time manufactured chicory in Jersey City. Again, a couple of rollicking fellows who are planning a gay army life, Frith and Bewicke. Finally, Trafford, a tall dark-haired fellow who wants to be a doctor in South Africa, and a stupid little chubby chap whose delight is to catch fish from the lake in front of the house with his tennis racket."

This suddenly intimate introduction into the lives of men — some of whom were to be my life-long friends — was to be typical of my two years ahead at Oxford. The fact that I was older by five years or more than most of my new companions seemed to make little difference. The fact that I was as unknown to them and their ways as they were to mine invited interest, perhaps, but more than that, it removed the *class* and *set* barriers which might have kept us at a polite distance. The reader may have some Freudian analysis in mind, and if so, I can assure him it was neither in my mind nor in the minds of the men I came know. Doubtless the unsettled times — when everything took on an accelerated pace — had much to do with it. The times, however, had nothing to do with the swift orderly movement of Mr. Bromley's establishment, as will be seen by my immediate account.

"The order of the day is this. Bath at seven in a large tub of painted tin, in a room at the other end of the house. (There is no key or other means of locking the door.) A bath, i.e. if the Rev. Mr. Bromley, or 'the old man', as he was popularly styled, is not there before you.

"From 8 to 8:30 with the old man. Then a gong, assembly in the dining room, Bible reading and prayers, short grace, and then breakfast. The last syllable uttered is the signal for starting the meal. I immediately seize the bread in the shape of one of those round English loaves and furiously hasten to slice it. No sooner than I am half way through the business when the oatmeal starts to be passed. Between passing milk and sugar from one side to the other I manage to gobble half my porridge. But then when the meat starts to come, it seems wisest to get up and take your plate to the side table and start something new. Before one has more than begun that, it is marmalade, please? bread, please? butter, please? jam, please? until Miss Bromley who sits at the end of the table — after an ominous pause — rises to leave the room.

"There is a period of do-as-you-will after breakfast before the four hour work schedule begins. In the middle of the morning —

at what I call beer and pretzel time — Buck brings in a pitcher of water, not too cold of course, and biscuits and apples. It is generally my fate to have an hour with a Mr. Scudamore. This queer little man who had gone through Oxford, and now trembles in the service of Mr. Bromley, is probably typical of the old fashioned English tutor. His teeth are uncared for — as is common among the middle class here — and his face is a caricature. I tell him what we are to do and then he hears me decline or follows my translation in the *Anabasis*. Sometimes he asserts himself by questioning some remote origin. And then he spends fifteen minutes in searching through *Liddell and Scott* for something that his certainty at the start shows he has no question about. He teaches in the cottage, a little brick-and-stone structure which was probably built for a root cellar several hundred years ago.

"On the second day Tunnicliffe came. So quiet was he that I am sure nobody was conscious of his arrival any more than they will be of his departure. He is tall, light hair and blue eyes and in all a fine looking fellow. There is a delightful taste and 'swag' about the way he wears his clothes. He is lodged across the hall from me, and whether it is that the sun shines in his room and not in mine, although he is six years my junior, we have become great friends and take a delight in the humorous side of our present situation.

"Harvey, Tunnicliffe and myself go on long walks through the surrounding country. Long aisles of tree arched lanes, paved with a mosaic of sun spots and separated from the fields by hedge-topped sod-banks; winding village streets whose flower decked cottages all but crowd one from the sidewalks; and finally the wild rolling hills of purple heather dotted here and there with green furze or broom. Here is the setting for many of the thrilling scenes of Conan Doyle's detective stories. Here can be seen in reality the simple country life which lends such charm to the tales of Romola and Adam Bede. And in the distant views and shady nooks one can trace some of the later fancies of the great poet laureate. For here are the homes of Conan Doyle, of George Eliot and of Lord Tennyson. The Tennyson residence is especially attractive. I walked up and down the little terraces and through the gardens until the overlooker wished to know if I 'owned the place.'

"Thus life goes on at *Inval* and from all appearances will go on until the end of time — at any rate as long as punctuality can be observed — for, as Buck, the butler, continues to inform each new comer, *Punctuality is the essence of politeness."*

In about a fortnight's time I had to return to Oxford for the examinations. During that time I had come to appreciate the crammer famed for putting men through the entrance exams of Sandhurst, Cambridge and Oxford — "without doubt an excellent teacher," I wrote, "the best I ever had." My last record at Haslemere was on 11th September 1914 saying, "I leave here on Tuesday morning for Oxford. The Greek exams come on Wednesday morning in the Sheldonian Theatre. There goes the 10 o'clock bell for evening prayer in the dining room. Goodnight!"

"I paid the Revd. Mr. Bromley his 10 guineas and started on Tuesday morning for Oxford," I wrote my brother from *66 The High.* "When I arrived at the above address — which by the way is considered to be the best and most reasonable *diggs* in town — I learned from Tunnicliffe that there were only 146 out of a usual 600 up for entrance exams. The examinations, however, seemed to be harder than usual.

"I was to appear in a dark suit and white dress tie — without which I should not have been allowed to take my *Smalls* — at the Sheldonian Theatre at 9:30 Wednesday morning. The Sheldonian and Divinity Halls are reserved for expected wounded British soldiers and perhaps German prisoners. Tunnicliffe had called on his Rector-to-be the night before his first exam and the Rector had told him that his dark brown suit would not be dark enough. This, even after he explained that he did not have another with him. The result was that he was forced to spend a good part of the night and the next morning hunting for a ready-made suit that would be dark enough.

"The ancient carvings of seals and coats of arms, the wonderful pulpit from which some graduating speech is delivered — I know them all by heart. Especially the painted ceiling where floating cherubs draw back the red plush curtains to disclose a marvelous tableau of wisdom, taking care to avoid unveiling the answers to questions put before you. The examination papers are in large pamphlet form. A question, or part of a question, printed on each page, and then space left for the answer to be written below."

As I saw it in those days, the university examinations were to prove my ability for research studies while the college tests were to satisfy the Magdalen dons that I would make a congenial member of their academic group and a scholastic credit to the college.

"Once more I battle at the gates of Magdalen," I wrote on September 24th from what I had learned to call my *diggs* at 66 High Street, Oxford. "It is easily the hardest college to enter in Oxford, but it must be done. Yesterday I took the two Greek exams for which I had been studying at Mr. Bromley's. Although I sailed through 2½ hrs. of translation, I fear the results of my hour exam in the grammar. I will write you at length when I am enough settled to have my typewriter sent up from the station."

I had come out of the mill rather well at Haslemere. Clare Cookson, who sent me there, learned a lot more about me through his friend Bromley than I was aware of. I had stood the test administered by a group of critical English school boys. I must have had certain characteristics unacceptable to them — my horned glasses, my creased trousers and my inexcusable lack of a dinner jacket. If so, they were probably allowed for as 'American,' but thanks to my Anglo-American upbringing in Brooklyn they were evidently not too bad. At any rate, with certain of them I was accepted as a friend.

"While waiting for the reports of our exams I went around to see George Teck where he has been put up in the famous rooms of his 'noble cousin,' H.R.H. the P. of W. The heir to the throne is much esteemed because he is breaking a precedent by having rooms in college just like any other undergraduate. His grandfather, Edward VII, did have rooms at Christ Church but he really lived by himself in a house in Oxford. The Prince of Wales' are the only undergraduate rooms I have seen so far, but — well mine will not be like them if I can help it."

This was my first personal contact with 'royalty.' The *spirit of* 1776 all over again with *Yankee Doodle Dandie* running up and down my spine, for here were descendants of George III. Behind the ermine curtain I was to have a glimpse of the gilded cage in which the heir to the British crown must live. In this sample of total democracy — of which I came to believe the Royal Family was the only complete exponent — I was not then aware of the hands which held the laurel wreath. It was not for me to overhear the diplomatic conversations between national and university heads which placed a special tutor in a room below the royal apartment and a particular undergraduate to live across the entry hall. I did not learn until later that the architect Edward Warren, whose brother was president of Magdalen, carefully planned the artistic details of these college rooms. Certainly I had no reason to know that Queen Mary herself in the course of a final inspection of her son's academic abode — pausing before a print of Van Dyke's *Three Heads of Charles* — advised Mr. Warren that it must be removed from the wall because of the possible effect it might have on the Prince's character. However, I was impressed.

"The royal rooms on the side of *The Cloister* facing the famous Magdalen tower are, perhaps, two suites thrown into one," I surmised. "I went through the dining room into the drawing room. There must be a study and a bed room and bath. Probably some decorator has done the whole business, for it is no more like what you would expect in a man's college rooms than a boudoir in a business office. Delicate water colours and engravings, pale tinted rugs and wall paper, and flowered cretonne furniture covering. I may be a bit unjust, but it certainly would not be tolerated at Harvard. My, what a 'rough-house' would make of it!

"I had an interesting but short call because I had taken Tunnicliffe with me and he was afraid of disturbing His Serene Highness. There is an aura that surrounds the throne."

Now that I recall my rooms in the ancient Holworthy Hall at Harvard, they dated from Puritan days but they were not as puritanical as I was leading myself to believe. I and my roommate, Gilbert Elliott, had separate bed rooms, and the windows of our large common study looked down the length of the Yard through a grove of graceful elms. Also President Lowell had just installed for each suite modern showers and toilet fixtures which would have astonished the Prince of Wales himself. To be sure, in spite of a few comfortable chairs and a piano, our study in the Harvard Yard presented a business like appearance with telephones and typewriters, etc. Indeed it was equipped for business, for it was from there that I organized twenty nine territorial clubs which later, President Lowell said, first suggested to him the idea of dividing the college into the present *Houses*.

"Well," I was finally able to report, "Monday the names were posted. Poor Teck and Tunnicliffe had flunked, but Johannes B. Langstaff appeared as clear as day. Mr. Bromley writes me, 'I am delighted. To tell you the truth I did not think it was possible

May 16, 1914

Dear Sir

I am greatly indebted to you for sending me a copy
of your "Harvard of Today from the Undergraduate Point of
View". It is, I am sure, a valuable addition to our Harvard
literature.

Yours most truly

Joseph H. Choate

Mr. John Brett Langstaff

JOSEPH H. CHOATE (Ambassador to Court of St. James) who lived in
the Holworthy rooms later occupied by Brett Langstaff at Harvard and
writes him, 1914, regarding his first publication.

in so short a time.' Pres. Warren admitted it was 'greatly to my
credit,' and Mr. Cookson — the Senior Tutor and most important
of them all — said that it 'was a proof that the age of miracles
had *not* passed.' But with all this I am not at all pleased at the
small consideration given my Harvard degree."

The fact that I passed was really rather a miracle because,
although I had read most of the Greek classics, I was always poor
at Greek composition. More than that, I was panicky in examinations from my earliest childhood. I constantly wanted to argue
with the examiner and evade his questions even when I knew the
answers. Personally, I should never have any misgivings about
believing in miracles — I seem to have been brought up by them.

Whatever satisfaction I had in having cleared my first hurdle
I was definitely saddened by the prospect I had looked forward
to being blighted by Teck's failure to make the entrance. We were
potential friends from the start. His exalted position in the British
social order meant little to me so that we met on the level.

On October 2nd I noted, "Prince George lent me some books
and in sending them back I enclosed my *Harvard of Today*. I also
typed a wee note and told him he ought to come to America. This

was his reply scrawled over four pages, from The George Hotel, Amesbury.

" 'My dear Langstaff. Thank you very much for the book, which you sent. I am absolutely delighted with it. I was quite annoyed when I heard that I had failed. I think poor old Bromley will be rather knocked up. Of course in your letter you never said if you had passed or not, but I do hope you have.

" 'I shall be here until the regiment goes, which, I think, is not far off now. I have an awfully busy time. We start riding at about 8:30 till 12:30 to see the regiment out drilling on the plain. We have just come back here from the camp, where we spend most of our day.

" 'Thanking you again for the book, Yours ever, George of Teck.'

"The regiment Teck refers to is that which his father the Duke is drilling at Salisbury."

My next hurdle was what I have referred to as the college tests. What I most dreaded was being examined verbally. It seems strange that I never had oral examinations at Harvard or Columbia. They are so much the thing in these days. If I failed I might still have become a student of the university and live anywhere within a mile radius. This is the genius of Oxford's collegiate structure. The university gives the examinations and grants the degrees. The colleges prepare undergraduates by providing them with tutors and the necessary instructors. The independence of each separate college has enabled them to develop their own peculiar atmosphere — and I was about to discover that Magdalen was the most peculiar of the lot.

Accordingly I wrote, "After all my success at passing the university entrance exams, I am now required by Magdalen College to be examined in Greek prose on sight (viva voce) and an essay in English and some part of the Bible. This is a complete surprise. It may be my undoing!

"I think I shall offer the Epistle of St. James for this Matriculation exam, since that is the most difficult Greek in the New Testament. As for my Greek and Latin viva voce exams, I have never been examined that way and I shall have to use my wits."

During all these days of testing I continued to lodge at 66 *The High*. With my two recent friends gone I was left with a desperate feeling of loneliness. Oxford was not a happy city in those early days of the war. Her curving streets and winding alley ways were to me unattractive and bewildering. People seeing me sitting solitary in a restaurant seemed to be wondering why I did not join up with the army. Then a new friend came into my life.

It was through the landlady of my diggs. She had taken me to her boosom in a Bardell-Pickwickian sense, and during the process of feather-dusting around my room when I was trying to study she suggested that if I were lonely there was another American in the room below who seemed awfully alone. Her eyes were big with sympathy for my sensitive face drawn with the tense strain under which I was laboring. I could not choose but follow her down. Her timid knock, and a not too welcoming voice from within, brought me into the presence of a trim little man who with exquisite politesse offered me an over-stuffed chair similar to one I had upstairs.

After a few introductory remarks I realized I was face-to-face with the great Spanish-American philosopher-poet, George Santayana. I should have recognized his round face with gimlet eyes and a neat little mustache, but I had come to Harvard just as he was abandoning the faculty he had helped to make famous. He was just past fifty years, keenly alert to current events, and welcomed the sort of friendship I was only too happy to give. This was the beginning of an intimate association which was to interpret the new life about me.

"One especially interesting thing about my diggs," I wrote my brother who had studied under him at Harvard, "is that Professor Santayana is staying for a few weeks below me. We go out to tea occasionally, and he has loaned me several books on the deeper reasons of the war. As you probably agree the Bernhardi book is bigoted military rot but natural in an army officer." After further dissertation my letter referred to an Oxford scholar whom I came to know and regard in the months to come. "Dr. Sanday has put out a rather weak reply to some of these attacks in which he claims that the war has been caused by the tendencies of so small a part of the Prussian people that it makes little difference even if their grievances are legitimate."

It was a satisfaction to show Santayana my *Harvard of Today* in which he took much interest, especially in its preface written by the former president, Charles W. Eliot. It was being brought out under the direction of the men who were in the process of starting

the Harvard University Press. "My book seems to be just coming
before the public," I wrote home. "When W. R. Thayer sends me
the number of the Graduate Magazine that has my preface in it,
please read it and send it on." This was a bond in common with
'Santy' — as one called him — and led to more personal things.

"I was mighty glum last night. You know how glum I can get.
If it had not been that Prof. Santayana — who knows both sides,
i.e. what I have been through and what I am up against — explained things to me I don't know what I should have done.
Probably I should have made a mistake.

"Here is the proposition. I am not entering a college such as
our American colleges. It is rather a club in the university. A

                              Asticoù, Maine,

                                   August 7, 1913.

Dear Mr. Langstaff:

          I send you herewith the Preface
you wished for the publication entitled "Student
Life at Harvard"; and I also return the manuscript
for the volume which you mailed to me on the 20th of
July last. Please send me galley proofs of the Preface.

     Hoping that this undertaking of the Harvard
Federation of Territorial Clubs will be well
carried out and prove thoroughly successful, I am,

                              Sincerely yours,

                              Charles W. Eliot

Enclosures.

CHARLES W. ELIOT (President of Harvard University) letter enclosing
          preface written at request of Brett Langstaff.

group of men who can live and study together congenially. And Magdalen is the choicest of the Oxford clubs.

"It seems hard that I who stood out against the 'Gold Coast' clubs at Harvard should now be trying to enter one at Oxford. I will let you know all the trials and worries I have undergone when I am settled inside. Scofield Thayer and Govy Hoffman, two of my classmates at Harvard, have been here in Magdalen for a year.

"Prof. Santayana and I are planning to walk out to Iffley this afternoon and take tea there. In spite of my difficulties everything is beautiful and wonderful, and I am working hard." Subsequent letters picked up with enthusiasm my affectionate regard for this man who was at that time counted the greatest mind in Europe. "I take great delight in George Santayana living in the room below me. We considered him outstanding in the Harvard galaxy which numbered Royce, Munsterberg, William James and other such philosophers. Why he resigned his professorship at Harvard two years ago — something about Socratic unsettling of the youth — and then R. B. Perry, whose lectures I attended, was given precedence over him? Anyway, he stimulates me a lot."

A comparative study of the beginnings of wars would probably show that the battle of minds which preceded the war in 1914 was something peculiar to the type of "cold" war which continues to distress the world. Wars in the past can be ascribed to jealousy among rulers and to economic causes — even to religious fanaticism — but total war in its modern sense seems to involve a conflict of ideologies. Certainly the university atmosphere into which I had entered was charged with the bellicose spirit of the time — howbeit on an intellectual level.

"Santayana's views on the German situation are wonderfully interesting. He said the other night that he wondered in the natural rejection of German philosophy which will follow the war, whether people would recognize that French philosophy (probably referring to Bergson and his followers) was based on German thought and reject that also. I was not a Bergson enthusiast but I did study under him.

"Among the books Santy lent me there is a small volume entitled *Germany and England* by R. A. Cram, pub. by John Murray. It is especially valuable in setting forth the ideas of Heinrich von Treitschke whose writing although unfamiliar to me has evidently had the greatest influence in present-day Germany. He points out that the two nations which have a natural genius for empire are Germany and England. The difficulty is that whereas England has secured her empire and is now engaged in the peaceful pursuit of uniting its several parts, Germany has still to acquire her territory and consequently has an emperor who must fight to create his empire. Is it fair, he asks, that England — who has *made her pile* — should now call the war game off and live in peaceful luxury on her conquered profits?

"Treitschke insists on the inherited right for Germanic empire and upholds the ideal of the *Will to Rule*. Cram is an enthusiastic admirer of Treitschke, and where he goes on to say, 'Almost the last time we see Treitschke, those noble features of his lit up...', Professor Santayana has put in the margin: 'I heard him in Berlin: he was fat, flabby and violent, with a horrible impediment in his speech caused by the fact that he could not — lucky fellow — hear himself talk.' (He was deaf.)

"The average man here is impatient to be at the front. He talks against the German barbarism with a most barbaric desire for revenge. Consequently all day they drill and practice bugle calls down in the meadows. The crowds gather and cheer when the wounded are brought in to the Examination Halls which are being used as a hospital. And, in short, everything is WAR!

"All this has its religious significance which is of special interest to me. As Cram points out, the Germans by accepting Christianity lost the opportunity of creating their own religion, and it is not till now — when the writings of Nietzsche bring German thought back to the state it was in during the reign of Alaric — that Germany is free to form a religion by which she can truly live."

The night the first ambulance rolled up the High to deposit their human freight in the university building where in due time they would deposit me, I was standing alone — feeling terribly alone — in the watching crowd. It was the civilians' first shock of tragic realism from the front. In the glare of the street lights the people seemed to be holding their breath in anxious silence. Then suddenly they broke forth. Their first greeting to the wounded soldiers was more of a cry, or a shout, than a cheer. As I returned to my diggs I was grateful that I had a wise counselor as a friend.

It was now October, and I noted that "Professor Santayana and I strolled for a great distance down the Thames. We passed the Iffley church and took tea on the river bank. He said, among

other things, that William James — when somebody would come
to him with a theory of his own — would catch a suggestion from
what this person said. Then developing the idea silently in his
own mind — which would be entirely foreign to what his ques-
tioner was saying — James would seemingly agree in everything.
He would then advise his visitor to go away and develop the
thought — meaning James' own idea rather than what his visitor
had been expressing. Thereafter, William James would pin his
own idea to the man who had tried to suggest something entirely
different. Santayana was a pupil and friend of the pragmatist —
or absolute realist as he later became."

What a pity I did not have a course with Santayana at Harvard.
He finally told me the reason he left Harvard and subsequently
refused a chair at the Sorbonne. He was tired of "pushing men
through a sieve of examination" and preferred to be in the position
of a master drawing disciples after him. I was now one of those
disciples evidently, and I was fortunate. What I was not conscious
of was that parts of these peripatetic lectures which I listened to
so attentively as we sauntered down the tow path toward Iffley,
would later appear in one of Santayana's books under the title of
SOLILOQUIES 1914.

Perhaps it was Santy's impatience with examinations that made
him sympathetic with my ordeal which he compared with his
experience in Germany. "The German universities," I wrote home,
"before the war were far more generous and hospitable to foreigners than Oxford is being to me. Thus there has always been
more good feeling between German and American scholars. This
probably led the Germans — whose scholars hold a real power
in the state — to think that they had the sympathies of the United
States more than they have found to be the case.

"Professor Santayana and I walked to Heddington yesterday.
Harvey, whom I made friends with at Haslemere, comes to tea
this afternoon. It will be good to see somebody I know again.
Except for Santy, I've been alone a long while."

Then finally on October 7th I could write, "I have finished my
last exam today. They asked me to offer some of my theological
work, and so I picked out the most difficult passages of the New
Testament. They did their part in making the exam hard. And I
think I returned the ball by passing it very well.

"The 'enemy' seemed to weaken last night when Pres. Warren

c/o Brown Shipley & C°
123 Pall Mall. S.W.1
Paris, Oct. 11, 1922.

Dear Kraystaff

Thank you very much
for sending me an invitation
to the Presentation of Lord
Coppenfield's Library to the
Browning Gift Society. It
proves that you're someone
else), have appreciated my
praises of Dickens. His books
were a great solace to me
during the war, when I would
then practically for the first
time. I am also glad to
know that you are active
and already in a Presidential

chair.

In my own occupation
there has been no great
change; and I am trying
to improve the thinking
(though afternoons) book
in practising all all the
philosophical and other
works which I have had
in petto for years. The
first volume (my
system of philosophy,
solving all the riddles
of the universe by proving
that there are no riddles
is already in the press.

I hope to return to England in the spring of next year, after a two ... absence, and to see and (perhaps) hear you.

Sorry Hoffman and his wife were in Paris a year ago, and very kindly looked me up. I have had a letter from Peter Warren, and Raymond Mortimer is at this moment in the same hotel in which I have been living, and we have lived lunch together at the Café de la Régence today. You see that my pleasant associations with the Oxford are still alive.

Yours sincerely,

Santayana

PROFESSOR GEORGE SANTAYANA (philosopher and poet) written to Brett Langstaff 1922, in which he refers to The Children's Libraries Movement, the Oxford reading-party and his own writing.

tried to be very sure about my receiving notice of the examination
and led the porter to think that he had sent me a note which I
did not receive. When I went to ask the President about it he was
very cordial. Even the butler who opened the door was much
more pleasant than when I had called before. The President told
me not to worry too much about the exam next day.

"Some of the tests were mighty stiff. A long poetical passage
from Ovid and a difficult part of Socrates' *Apologia.* Also a three
hour test in Latin prose which nearly killed me."

After my tests in the dining hall at Magdalen I would wander
about in hope of picking up an acquaintance with some undergraduate come up early for some reason. "I noticed this morning
as I was coming out that the man who was putting up the names
of next year's tenants at the bottom of each stairway had just
posted the name, *Prince Geo. of Teck.* I suppose they intend to let
him have another try at responsions after he is in college some
time. I am glad I shall have an opportunity of seeing something
more of him."

Students from overseas were apt to be the first arrivals. I was
delighted to be joined by old friends, Francis Butler Thwing whose
father was president of Western Reserve University and George
Gifford who years later became a professor at Tufts. "Who should
I meet this noon while I was looking for something to eat," I
exclaimed, "but George Gifford. He is a Harvard man of my 1913
Class who took a Rhodes Scholarship and came to Balliol a year
ago. He tells me that Francis Thwing, another of our class-mates,
is to be at New College this coming year.

"Tunnicliffe has sent me a telegram asking me to meet him at
the station at four o'clock. He comes up to take his *Matric* at
Exeter. I had dinner last night at the hotel in Oxford with Harvey
and a friend of his who came up to keep him company. Harvey is
a very fine good sort, but he is not coming up this term.

"In an essay Magdalen gave me to write I had the opportunity
of saying that the Germans, unlike the proud English scholars who
look down on American learning, had welcomed students from
America. This may not have been a politic thing to say, but I
just had to. In some ways the English are absurdly bigoted. I
can see, however, that I am going to get what I am after and what
I could not get in America.

"At last — October 8th — the bursar has let me see the rooms where I may — if the privilege of studying in the royal college is granted me — be able to study. They seem most gorgeous affairs for one person. I hardly hoped to be put in *Cloisters,* for that seems the most desirable place of all. My idea that the Prince of Wales' rooms were a double set thrown into one was because of its size. But there are many sets of three rooms each.

"The suite I have been assigned (if admitted) is No. 3 First Floor Right. Goodness knows the furniture, especially the rug, is handsome. I will have to take it over. If I wanted to put furniture of my own in, it would be necessary for me to have that which is now in my rooms stored. Moreover if I had any furniture in my room which the bursar did not approve, he could force me to take it out. Here is the floor plan of the rooms I saw this morning.

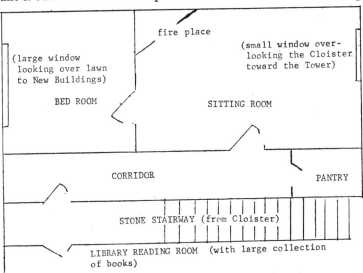

"P.S. Although I have had part of my goods taken over to these Cloister rooms, the committee which decides my admission to the college does not meet until five this afternoon. It will probably let me know my fate tomorrow."

I came to think of this ancient cloister as sheltering hundreds of generations of eager students such as I. Much as an old setting-hen covers the eggs placed in her nest, the cloister would take us under its eaves even if one were only a china nest-egg. She was probably complaining at my critical attitude toward my new surroundings, but it would be some comfort to her to feel me pecking away at the shell which was merely my protective covering of provincial inhibitions. And if I did hatch out to be a duck instead of a chicken? What then? The farmer would always furnish more eggs.

"Magdalen College, Oxford, England — 9th October 1914 — Here I am at last, domiciled at least, in Magdalen. I was most anxious to live in the Cloisters. Not because that was the abode of princes but because it was the most attractive part of the college, in short it is what people think of when they say, *Magdalen.* Also I understand Mother's father lived here. The only rooms which overlook the quad are those on the first floor, i.e. one flight up. One side of the quad is taken up with the Dining Hall and Chapel, and another by rooms which do not seem to be open to students. Then, out of the other two sides there has to come the Junior Common Room, called the *J.C.R.,* and the large Scientific Library next to me." I came later to know that the side "not open to students" contained the official guest apartment, the president's drawing room and the college library.

"This leaves only a few students' rooms from which one looks on to the greensward of the cloister. On the side facing east is Prince George of Teck, Scofield Thayer of Harvard 1913 and another fellow whom I don't know yet. On the side facing south is H.R.H. the Prince of Wales, Lord Stanley (the Earl of Derby's son) and Langstaff (son of John Elliot Langstaff Esqre, M.D., U.S.A.). How can I afford it? For the year, which includes the privilege of staying here the entire time if one chooses, the rent is 22 pounds ($110). That is an average between the maximum and minimum charges for rooms here, and it seems to me very little.

"Don't forget, when you think it over, I may stay here reading when the town is deserted and dreary. I plan to be constantly in my rooms and I will not have a lot of fellows wearing them out by entertainments. They are rooms I would never have had a chance at under ordinary circumstances, but when there are only 50 men out of an usual 150, rooms are vacant which otherwise would be in great demand. The son of the Poet Laureate, Robert Bridges, was in these rooms last and took the highest honors in his work."

My description of the luxurious furniture which I had to purchase from the college; "a most comfortable bed which many of the other rooms do not seem to be blessed with — they had to put in a new one since the former one was taken out for the military hospital — and particularly the carpeting, thick napped so that you sink down in it as you step on it," all was recorded in enthusiastic detail. It was really a comparative small apartment, in post war days to be furnished in a modern way for a college guest. Even what I called my "toilet china (the Royal Worcester nonplumbing sort), on a stand and under the bed," is now happily supplanted.

Perhaps with a thought of encouraging undergraduates to write home, Magdalen had a custom — I suppose it was a general custom — of sending to your room a gift of the finest letter paper bearing the college address. My observation was, "Looks as though I were not going to be sent away."

"My view from the study is perfect. Right in front stands a little stone king looking out at other more grotesque figures around the quad. Rising above the battlements and pinnacles of dining hall and chapel is the great tower with its four vanes and four crosses. With all this it seems to me an ideal room for the hard study I plan. Its location will make it possible for me to exert less effort to know men I may want to know than if I were off in some corner of the college. With only one other room on my stairway below, I can shut myself off when I think wise and yet be in the midst. Moreover, the rooms are so pleasantly situated that it would be no hardship to stay here during some of the vacs.

"The scout says my typewriter looks 'natty', but I don't think it goes well on this 'swank' writing paper." It was an old Oliver portable — not old at the time — and it apparently created a sensation as an American innovation. I was fortunate to have fallen into the hands of a good 'scout.' These college servants were the real preceptors of undergraduates. I was to learn the wisdom of always asking his advice since he was the one man who knew for sure how a man should live in college. His name was Hunt — known only by this surname — and I needed his encouragement sorely in a new mire of 'despond' through which I was about to wade.

"This morning I was summoned to the Senior Tutor's room in New Builders. There sat my Mr. Cookson slumped down in his Minty chair with feet stretched out toward the little open fire

and a glass of whisky conveniently by his side. He is short, stout
and at his best a cheerie sort of don but always sarcastic. His
round face continually puffing a pipe was unusually red and serious
on this occasion.

"'Now, Mr. Langstaff, we must settle this business. The *matri-
culations* comes in two hours and if you are to matriculate it will
be necessary for you to take *moderations.*' (Mods are rather difficult exams in Classics and Logic which take at least two terms
of hard study and which must be passed if the student is to continue
in college. They are a necessary step to the degree of B.A.)

"'But, Sir,' I objected, 'I am a Senior Foreign Student and...'

"'We have discussed all this before,' was his retort, 'and it simply
comes to the question of taking these exams or leaving the college.
You are by no means a Foreign Student, etc.'

"It dazed me for a while. I knew from my talks with other men
that if I were to attempt to take the exams he referred to my time
would be wasted and I would end by becoming discouraged.
Cookson was waiting for a reply.

"'Let me have time to think it over,' was my plea.

"He saw no reason why I should have any more time to think.
It was a matter of yes or no. But finally he gave me two hours to
bring back the answer. If I said I would not be willing to study
these two terms with a tutor and pass the exams I would of course
be unable to go up for matric.

"I grabbed my belongings and bolted for the door, down the
stairs, out on the lawn and over to my rooms. Then with my
Harvard diploma and my Oxford handbook I started for the
Registrar's office. The registrar did not come in for some time
and every moment was so precious! At last when he came I got
from him a slip of paper saying that I was a Junior Foreign Student
and had his reassurance that my degree was sufficient evidence
that I had enough education to permit my taking some special
subject for a B.Litt. degree.

"With this I hastened back to the president with whom I had
not talked over my course before. He was in and very genial. I told
him that what I wanted to specialize in was the Prayer Book. (My
reasons for this I will give in a later letter at more length.) As a
subject I suggested the doctrine of the Holy Eucharist as found
in the Collects or something of that sort. My idea was that whatever
the special subject was it would lead to a thorough study of the

Book of Common Prayer. He rather advised that it would be better for me to keep away from doctrine while I was still a student. He was right too. History seemed to him better. Such as the history of some part of the Prayer Book. Then I told him Cookson insisted on my taking Mods and would not hear of my studying a special subject. The president thought I might take part of the Mods and let that suffice.

"With this I rushed to Brightman, a don who is the author of good liturgical books and seems to be at the head of the theological department in Magdalen. Canon Brightman is also short and stout with a completely bald head and a soft, slow way of speaking. He said that Mr. Cookson had been talking with him and it would be necessary for me to take Mods. I pointed out that in this case it would be almost impossible for any American to proceed to advanced studies in England, i.e. if he had taken a degree and attended a seminary in America as I had.

"He quietly inquired what my degree said I knew and when I related to him the number of subjects I had taken at Harvard (there was a long list under our elective system) he was amused, saying that in England they never attempted to read in more than one subject. But, he said, sit down and prove it. Whereupon he handed me a German theological work which is, as you know, written in the hardest German and asked me to translate it. Then a French book on some technical subject. And so on with books and probings on all sorts of minute questions until I told him I had to go to Mr. Cookson. Then he spread his hands in an attitude of despair and said, 'You see you don't know anything after all.'

"With the registrar's slip of paper and with all President Warren had said I persuaded Cookson to be more reasonable. Finally he took me back to Canon Brightman and proposed that since I was not, in his opinion, ready to go into any special subject, I should read generally for a term and then take up my studies for the B.Litt. Brightman agreed, and it was settled.

"When the Senior Tutor of Magdalen College called out the names of the entering class of the year 1914 for matriculation before the Vice Chancellor in the Great Divinity Hall, it was really not necessary for him to mention the name of Langstaff because I was writing it down on the record book before he came to it. But call it he did, and that was the way I came to be admitted to Magdalen."

2

MY FIRST TERM — 1914

NOW that I had won my academic battle with Oxford and scaled the walls of Magdalen, I contemplated under Santayana's influence the new world which surrounded me. I had to remember that the world to which I had committed myself was limited to a mile radius of Oxford University. It was an academic world such as was being destroyed in Europe. There were nine professors come from the ill-fated Louvain University, one of the first targets of the German army after scrapping its treaty and invading Belgium. I would know some of them later when I went up to Dr. Osler's. Lady Osler was raising money in America to rebuild the library destroyed by the invaders and to carry on the university in exile. President Lowell offered a lectureship at Harvard to one of the refugee professors. These were evidences of the great war of ideologies. There was indignation in America expressed in Wilsonian terms, but in Europe there was fighting with the Germans winning.

I learned that 1,400 Oxford undergraduates had volunteered and been accepted in the army, and another 400 had not come back to college. This would mean a loss to the colleges of about $500,000. Then there were the German Rhodes scholars and a lot more students who had been enrolled from Germany — they were now being suspected of having been spies. The vice-chancellor, whom I came to know later, roundly denied this, but there would have to be more proof if the increasing bitterness was to be ameliorated.

I was caught up with the rising tide of indignation. I did not write home about it, but I made every effort to join the Officers Training Corps which was drilling one or two hours every morning.

46

However, my family were sure to have read the official ruling, as published in the American papers—that Kitchener's volunteer army "must be British subjects of pure European descent." So, there was little more that I could do than 'carry on.' The ideology that was Anglo-American had to be preserved as well as fought for.

"I have just come back from one of our daily evensong vespers in the chapel," I wrote. "The tone quality of the boy choir is superb. And anthems I know any choirmaster would consider too difficult with us are rendered marvelously—often without organ accompaniment. I make a point of attending regularly, although I am sometimes the only student there. A heavy stone screen separates the visiting congregation from the choir stalls—lighted by 54 candles in elaborate brass brackets—where the robed dons and undergraduates of Magdalen sit with the vested choir.

"The reredos is a mass of niched saints, and directly over the simple altar is a painting of Christ Bearing the Cross. The whole effect is so sincere and beautiful, I look for six o'clock with much satisfaction.

"I never before felt myself going ahead so fast toward the ideals I have aimed at all my life. I now hear from the president that my one time French professor at Harvard, Sumichrast,—now returned to England— and Ben Greet—now stopping with his sister Clare in Oxfordshire—both came to my rescue with letters recommending my admission to Magdalen."

The fact that my feeble soprano voice was for years part of of the choir of the old St. John's Church in Brooklyn made me the more appreciative of the Magdalen choir which under masters such as Stainer and Roberts had long maintained an international reputation. I felt I was strengthening my roots at the same time that I was extending my branches. This was healthy growth and in time gave me confidence to reach higher and wider. With all this natural religious instinct, there was never any danger of my becoming pious.

"Life is made more intense by the sadness about, for two thirds of the splendid men who were here have gone and all the able bodied who are left are drilling to take commissions which will be left open by officers who are killed or wounded. Far from distracting, this makes my work more real than I have ever felt it before.

"I have just come back from a vigorous row on the river with

Pye-Smith, an Eton fellow. To be sure, I nearly upset the craft but it was great sport and I learned a lot. It is the best exercise and the most typical of Oxford that is now to be had. Can you picture me in black shoes and stockings, white shorts, black coat and a long knitted scarf? This last article of black and white — the Magdalen colors — seems to be worn on all occasions.

"The barges are a good ten minutes walk by the side of a winding stream arched over with trees. This stream which is known as the Cher, contracted from Cherwell, empties into a rather large river for these parts called the Isis which is really the upper part of the Thames. Along the college side of the Isis are anchored some twenty gayly painted house-boats called barges. These are provided by the several colleges for their crews. They are divided into a comfortable lounge with an open fire and rooms for changing and bathing — their roofs form a deck with chairs for watching what goes on on the river. Owing to the scarcity of men we have combined with New College and Univ., i.e. University College. The way we start rowing is for two of us to go out in a heavy boat with a coach as 'cox' in the stern steering and shouting at us.

"As for work, I am reading Duchesne's *Origines de Cult Chrétien* as a basis for my liturgical study and I am writing an essay on *War and Poetry* using the Psalms as my example. It keeps me very busy, and the thing is I am so contented when I am busy."

I must have had a naturally happy disposition. There are snapshots showing me with a broad grin which I know is suddenly going to burst into loud, infectious laughter — I say infectious because then everybody around would start laughing, not at me but at nothing at all. I had good legs for rowing, they told me, but I needed development in the arms and chest. At Harvard *the river* had meant for me mostly canoeing down the Charles to the rough waters of 'the basin' or up the bosky Asabeth where Emerson and Hawthorn had lived — so the experience on the Isis was all new to me. What we were seriously trying to do was to preserve the continuity of a great rowing tradition at Oxford. We felt it was important for undergraduates who had gone to the front — at any rate comforting — to feel the Oxford life they once enjoyed and to which they hoped to return was still carrying on. There was a close association between the colleges and the armed forces.

"Teck stopped me today to tell me that his father had come back from France with some sort of fever and was going to

Windsor. Teck was going to see him so I suggested asking his father why the generous donations of horses and fodder, etc., which my mother was able to secure for the British government had been turned down.

"As for horses, Teck said that there were plenty of four-year-olds which were being worked up for service and in the line of fodder there was no need. Blankets, however, have been advertised for here in Oxford for some time and I believe the reply was enough to fill the demand."

My academic goal was always before me. So much so that I sent home a "picture-postcard showing a man in long black gown wearing a blue hood with white fur lining" and suggested it was "a picture of me returning home after two or three years. Then in another seven years — according to the statutes — I should be able to get this turned into a D.Litt. outfit. For the present I am taking lectures on history and exegesis, but I have not decided what the subject of my dissertation will be.

"My plan of making a small and select circle of friends is working out well. There is no difficulty about getting along with all the fellows, but I feel that after I leave for America there will be little use in acquaintances at such a distance, either for them or for me. Teck, I have told you about. Then there is a man named Howard, large, light-haired, and another named Pye-Smith, small and dark-haired, and both friends of Prince George's at Eton. The grandfather of the first was Lord Strathcona and the father of the second was the late head of Guy's Hospital in London. We get on well, although I am older. In a few months when this war is over and the men return to live in the college rooms reserved for them, I shall come to know them all better."

This making of friends was taking on a new significance for me. I had made plenty of intimate companions while studying in America. I recall with affection that group of Harvard friends set on learning how to speak effectively in public. We entertained at dinner in the tower of Memorial Hall almost every eminent orator who visited the university — from Woodrow Wilson to William Jennings Bryan — and as an after-dinner speech made him tell us undergraduates how he did it. Our staff which edited the HARVARD ILLUSTRATED MAGAZINE was small enough to be close and companionable. And so it went, with the Harvard Memorial Society, the Conversazione, the Dramatic Club and half a dozen other groups whose common working interest made for pleasurable companionship until that graduation day when our academic ship touched the shores of the outer world and we dispersed.

Now I was about to make friends after the Oxford manner, more deliberately with the idea of a lasting personal relationship. This was not going to be easy for me. It is an American characteristic, perhaps, to have faith in groups rather than in individual persons. My experience in England seemed to be proving the contrary, and I felt that if I could measure up to it this might be the reward — rather than any degree — for having gone to Oxford. The times were ripe. Dangerous adventure, magnified idealism, but chiefly the fact that in the depleted state of the colleges the few of us who remained were going to be thrown closely together. This meant not only undergraduates but also the dons — all of us together as never possible under normal conditions. And here was an early example.

"Dr. Roberts, our choirmaster, asked me to stop after service the other night and with great care explained to me the bad musical grammar which my singing an octave lower than the choir boys was creating. It was only the hymns, but you know how I like to sing. He was mighty courteous about it and invited me to come

HARVARD UNIVERSITY FOOTBALL ASSOCIATION
CAMBRIDGE, MASS.

ROBERT T. P. STORER, '14, CAPTAIN   GEORGE F. PLIMPTON, '14, MANAGER

Holworthy 16

June 1,1914.

Dear Langstaff;

Thank you very much for the copy of HARVARD OF TODAY. It is a blame good piece of work and should help out a lot among the various schools.

Ill do what I can to distribute the book around.

Sincerely,

Robert T. P. Storer

ROBERT TREAT PAINE STORER (Harvard football captain) written Brett Langstaff 1914.

up in the organ loft over the rood screen and sit with him there during service.

"Several days after that I went up in the loft and waited for him. When he had managed to climb up — his bulk is such that he just manages to squeeze through the stone passageway and his lameness adds to the difficulty — and discovered me standing there in the shadow, he came over and said, 'Now just what is your name?' Upon my telling him he asked further whether I was one of 'that Teck lot.' Then he explained. He had understood that I was Prince George of Teck and if that were the case he wanted to make his 'humble apologies' for having spoken to me about my singing.

"I protested that Prince George and I were friends and went about together. I was merely a commoner. He seemed relieved. That settled, he took me over to the organ and we sat on the bench side by side while he played the service.

"Later, as we were descending the winding stairway he inquired what part of England I came from, and on learning I was an American he nearly collapsed. However, he was pleased with America because they played so much of his music. J. Varley Roberts is his name. It seemed familiar to me although at the time I did not appreciate that he was the author of some of the anthems which I had sung often as a choirboy. He has the highest Oxford honors and his choir is considered the best in the kingdom."

My entering experience with probably the most popular composer of Anglican Church music of his day made me sensitive to the limitations under which members of the Royal family were forced to live. The aura which surrounded them seemed to prevent a normal approach of loyal subjects even when that approach was invited by the royalty themselves. This traditional 'apartness' not only demanded self-sacrifice on the part of the royal individual but it also meant he was deprived of the stimulation and moral support which a commoner derived from a normal circle of friends. The fact that I was a foreigner in England might have tended to lower that barrier and perhaps accounted in part for the friendly relation which had sprung up between myself and the Queen's nephew. But this was merely one of the new phases of Oxford which I was learning to accept.

"My rowing is doing me a world of good," I wrote. "Somehow a regular exercise such as rowing which requires a continuous

concentration of purpose makes for like regularity in one's studies.
I am certainly learning to study on my own. The lecture system
is not overdone so that there is time, and indeed necessity, for
reading and developing oneself. Then, too, the seriousness of the
war spurs one on. Many of the wounded 'allies' are due in Oxford
from the late activity in the north.

"I have had wonderful opportunities before but never had the
chance for advancement offered itself so much as now. My day
goes like this," I noted on October 26th. "A fifteen minute stroll
around Addison's Walk, the Dean's prayers in Chapel, *breaker*
of porridge, coffee, toast and jam in JCR, study till a ten o'clock
lecture, back again and study till Hunt (my scout) comes with
my bread and cheese for lunch, dress in my shorts, stockings,
scarf, etc., run down the bank of the Cher to the barge, row down
the Isis to Iffley and back, run home, study till five, go out to tea
or have somebody in for tea, make and eat tea and biscuits till
six, attend musical service in the Chapel (sometimes in the loft
with Dr. Roberts), dinner in Hall at seven with Teck and some
other interesting men, perhaps coffee for a short while in one of
the undergraduates' rooms directly after dinner, back to No. 3
Cloisters for more study, and then to bed.

"You can see I am not taking too many lectures. My tutor is
the Canon F. E. Brightman with whom I consulted before entering
college. It is his idea that going to lectures and accumulating facts
is all very well for reference, but they need to be referred to and
made part of oneself. This I am trying to do under his direction. I
have not yet decided on a topic for my B.Litt. dissertation."

This was a complete reversal in the method of learning from
what I had become accustomed to in America. As a student there
I had been informed by lecture or assigned reading and then
tested on my comprehension by a system of examinations. I recall
Canon Brightman's dry way of asking me on my first official visit
with him if I had read the Statutes. When I nodded, without
realizing what that would entail, he replied, "Well, then, you know
that I do not have to tell you anything until you ask me some
sensible question. In the meantime we might as well talk about
that amazing country from which you come." This did not faze
me as much as it might had I not in mind Bishop Rhinelander's
telling me that Oxford in his experience as an American undergraduate was "a kindergarten of scholarship." This intensified

my feeling of isolation, and I reached eagerly for any friend from home.

"I saw by the paper that Vincent Astor was visiting his mother in Grosvenor Square and since social affairs are said to be rather dull in London I invited him out here to meet Teck at lunch in my rooms — included his wife too. I looked forward to a simple but important lunch party, but I have a note from his mother to say that Vincent sailed last week.

"I found great reserve among the men I wished to know here, but by showing an equal reserve myself things have turned out all right. In the case of Teck, for example, I spoke to him only when I happened to be near him. I never called on him unless he asked me and I asked him to come and see me only once. As a result, night before last when I chanced to be walking down the cloister with him, instead of turning up his own stairway he kept right along with me — even then I did not say come up, as one would naturally — but he came up to my room where we had a wonderful time for the rest of the evening looking over *The New York Times* which had just arrived from home. By the way, those war pictures in the *Supplement* are far better than anything we receive here.

"The other day I went to an informal prayer gathering of enthusiastic men around Canon Streeter in Queen's Coll. The trouble is these men not only feel that the formal service is of no use to them but they also are convinced that other people are mad to try to worship in a liturgical way."

By November 2nd my acquaintance was widening out so that I could write, "You remember my telling you of Phil Pye-Smith whose father was head of Guy's Hospital? He went to have lunch with his father's friend, Sir William Osler, last Sunday. I had told him of my father having known Osler when they were boys in Canada, and he relayed it to Sir William. The result was that Dr. Osler asked him to bring me out to Norham Gardens where the Oslers have an ample house and garden. We went. An interesting company of guests around the large luncheon table which was cluttered with reference books before the animated conversation ended. Sir William, full of fun, said his uncle was vicar of the church at York Mills when my father's uncle was physician for most of that part of Yonge Street (north of Toronto).

"As I expected in the beginning, the college costs here will

certainly not be more than what they were at Harvard. The cost
of entertaining, such as was done in pre-war days, could be very
high if one went into it extravagantly, but the 'battels' which have
come in so far show the board bill to be just about $5 per week.
The food in Magdalen is noted for its excellence too.

"I am now discovering that the man who has been appointed
my tutor is the great authority in *Liturgics* — which is important
to me since what I am intending to specialize in is the Prayer
Book. I find him referred to constantly by such an author as
Duchesne. But he is a strange little chap — pale flabby face and
bald head, with a wabbly gate and a disconcerting way of thinking a long while before speaking. He will take an age of knowing.

"There seems little use of my telling you any war stories for
they are sure to be contradicted before they reach you. Everything
is military here. One feels in the midst of it all. I had tea with
some Belgian officers yesterday. Their description of the bomb
dropping on Antwerp was terrifying."

This violation of the treaty with Belgium which the German
Kaiser was reputed to have called a 'scrap of paper' was having
an inflammatory effect on American opinion and led to the slogan
of *'brave Belge.'* However, many in England considered emotional
reports of refugees — such as that to which my letter refers —
were over-dramatized, and widespread sympathy with the German
people was outspoken among loyal British subjects. As the war
continued this began to lessen, but for the present, undergraduates
felt free to argue for or against the war.

Two days later I was writing, "My tutor turns out to be a
greater authority on liturgics, both eastern and western, than I
first supposed. Now that I am getting to know him better in our
private conferences I find he is a wonderful teacher free from all
petty conventions that his subject might suggest. He sends me to
certain lectures and gives me certain books to read, and when we
meet in his room in New Builders between 9:30 and 12:00 we
discuss them.

"The feel of these old college buildings in this time of national
crisis is deeply religious. The Dean's Prayers in the morning and
the wonderful choral evensong continue to be my regular times
for going to chapel, while the preachers at the University Church
— where Archbishop Cranmer made his recantation — are an education in themselves. As to the 'atmosphere of Oxford,' you know

what that is. To live actually in the midst of it enriches the effect tenfold.

"Another valuable influence for me is the acquaintance with men whose lives have been so different from my own. There is here something — it must be in the training of the public schools before they come up — that I am sure we do not have at home. To associate with these men and come to know what one might call their spirit of manly gentleness means a great deal." One remarkable difference I observed was the far higher regard of the English pupil for his master. This is carried over into college and at times amuses me.

"I met the vice chancellor of the university (Thomas Strong) by accident yesterday as I was coming up from rowing. It was only when I had caught up with him on the path by the Cher that I recognized him as the don who stood before the matriculation group in the Divinity Hall where he — after a short Latin speech — had doffed his mortarboard by way of acknowledging us as new students of Oxford University. Overawed, I slackened my pace to let him go ahead. Embarrassed, the vice chancellor did the same thing for the same purpose. Then we both increased our pace and again slackened. There was nothing for it but for me to say, 'How do you do, Sir?' His reply was, 'Have we been introduced?' To this I answered, 'But yes, Sir, at matriculation in the Divinity Schools.' This evidently covered the formality of an introduction because we then continued walking together in a most friendly way. He recalled Bishop Rhinelander who was his one time pupil at Christ Church. Among other things, he said that 150 wounded had come in, and that he had given them the run of Tom Quad. I told him about my mother's work with the Daughters of the Empire and he was duly impressed."

It was difficult for me to comprehend how a university — having no president such as I was accustomed to at Columbia and at Harvard — was presided over instead by a chancellor whom I was never to lay eyes on and a vice chancellor which office rotated with the heads of the several colleges; the dean of Christ Church being the incumbent for the time. Although the set up differed it seemed to prove satisfactory in both cases. I resolved not to try to change it. Also I had to understand that my new friend 'Tommy' Strong, as dean served in the same capacity for Christ Church as our President Warren did for Magdalen. Other colleges, I was to learn, gave different titles to their presiding officers.

My journal from Magdalen on the 13th of November read, "I will take for the theme of my dissertation something like the history of the Holy Communion in the Book of Common Prayer. I shall also read generally so that I will not miss the other subjects which I might have received at the General Seminary in New York if I had continued there. Since the important part of my work is with my tutor, Mr. Brightman, I am very happy. He is not only a big man in reputation but he is big in character. However, there his bigness ends.

"It is wet and rainy, but somehow one gets used to it. When the sun does come out it looks right in my window and seems to make up for all the gloom.

"We were rowing full tilt in a four-oared shell this afternoon when suddenly there was a crash and a shower of splinters. We had struck another shell broadside. By the way, we don't have sliding seats and I am sore in the place I was taught to sit on, so sore that I feel as though I were on a pin cushion without the cushion. The provoking part is that it does not affect the seat of the boat at all. We are working up for a race with some school down the river.

"Do you happen to have seen the last volume of the Cyclopedia of American Biography with Mother's picture, etc.? If not please look in the New York Public Library and tell me what you think of it. It should be a very handsome publication.

"As for the war and us, between the two evils of German bombs from above and over 2,000 rough soldiers suddenly billeted in the town of Oxford, authorities decided to risk the former and turn on the street lights."

The military aspect of soldiers crowding the High took me back in my history reading to the days when Charles First made his headquarters in Oxford. The city seemed always to have been a strategic point because of its central position in relation to the coastal ports. As for the roughness of the soldiers, I didn't know it then, but the day was to come when I too would wear the uniform of a British *Tommy*.

"Today (November 15th) it was announced that our president, Herbert Warren, was to be a Knight Commander of the Victorian

Order. This seems to be an order which includes the loyal subjects who are responsible for the education of the Prince of Wales.

"Teck and several other fellows have asked me where I was going to spend Christmas, but it was not until this afternoon that Banner — the man who lives under me, next to the rooms reserved for Hansell, the P. of W.'s personal tutor — invited me to go home with him. He lives in Bournemouth, as far as I know a fashionable suburb of London, and if his people are as interesting as he is I shall have a splendid Christmas Day. His mother is a Canadian. Although he has invited me for practically the entire six weeks, I shall of course not stay so long.

"Professor de Sumichrast has also written saying that he would be happy to have me in his home at Christmas. Most of my vacation, however, will be spent here in my rooms. I have a lot of reading to keep me very busy. Considering the fact that there will be few of my friends here much after Christmas I have thought to ask the two people I should most like to entertain, James Bryce and George Reid, to come out and have lunch or tea with me. The term ends in three weeks time."

To the casual reader it might seem presumption that a twenty-five-year-old junior foreign student should think of entertaining the diplomats mentioned in my letter. At Harvard representing some undergraduate activity I made my own personal contact with Sir James Bryce when he was there lecturing. But then, he and his wife were friends of my parents, added to which Lady Bryce was the first honorary president of the Daughters of the Empire when they were at the embassy in Washington. As for Sir George Reid, I could count on his not having forgotten the afternoon he and his lady and all his staff came out to Harvard with the request that he might meet A. Lawrence Lowell because of Lowell's reputation as an authority on English government. For this reason — although it seemed unprecedented in our Harvard annals — the president of the university came to my undergraduate rooms. I clearly recalled in the course of their conversation Lowell asking the High Commissioner for Australia what his people would do if the British navy were unable to protect them from invasion by an enemy, and Sir George replying without hesitation, "We would seek the aid of the United States."

The 19th came and my Magdalen journal read, "Things look

HARVARD UNIVERSITY
CAMBRIDGE

September 26,1912.

Dear Mr Langstaff:-

         I will certainly be
at your room between four and five
o'clock to-morrow to meet Sir George
and Lady Reid.

            Yours very truly,

            A. Lawrence Lowell.

Mr J.B. Langstaff ·

Note of acceptance from A. Lawrence Lowell, President of Harvard University, written to Brett Langstaff regarding Sir George Reid, High Commissioner for Australia.

more Military every day. Twenty officers are billeted in Magdalen and some of the colleges are filled with *Tommies*. I have a Colonel Justice — an amusing suggestion of civil and military authority — in Lord Stanley's rooms next to mine. One of my best friends, the Hon. Arthur Howard — whom I've mentioned before — was the first to leave. I am keeping some things for him in case he returns, but chances are 1 to 100 that he will never come back. Teck and I went to the play together this afternoon. He will probably be the next to leave. And then the third of the 'muscateers', as I call them, Phil Pye-Smith.

"Recently I learned that Addison, the essayist, lived just about where my room is. At the time, this second story was built of wood but shortly after Addison's time it was rebuilt in stone. It is all very wonderful and historic, but the feeling comes mighty often that I wish home were a bit nearer. This will be my first Christmas away from home."

To be sure, Joseph Addison, whose spirit I could feel hovering around my rooms in *cloisters,* lived between 1672 and 1719. But I knew a lot about his way of thinking from reading his poems and essays published in the *Spectator.* I sometimes wondered what he might have written of a youth from those far away colonies who had now come to Oxford claiming that he had once helped to edit a paper known as the *Spectator* at Columbia. Yet he died before Columbia College was born! Nevertheless, my father's fore-fathers were Englishmen also, first settlers in the recent chartered Colony of New Jersey seven years before Addison was born. For almost 250 years they lived as British subjects in America—U.S.A. or Canada — until a month after I was born in the City of Brook-lyn. I liked to think Addison might have perceived something mutual in our cloistered studies at Magdalen. At any rate, he would have understood our family interest in the present British cause.

"Well, then, your mother is really a very great person!" said President Warren after he had read Ambassador Spring-Rice's commendation of the *War Relief Fund* in the New York Post. Then he went on to observe that Sir Cecil Spring-Rice was an undergraduate when he himself was at Oxford as an undergraduate, and they had been close friends. Indeed President Warren considered Sir Cecil one of the most brilliant scholars of his time.

"The result of all this enthusiasm was that the next day I

received an invitation from Mrs. Warren for lunch on Sunday. I
still need this sort of introduction to help me over the barriers of
cautious acquaintanceship.

"I don't know where I will go for Christmas Day. I hardly think
I shall go to the Duke of Teck's because the other night when
George was here in my room and asked me where I intended to
spend Christmas he explained that their house in London was so
filled now that it would be necessary for their Russian maid to
be put up somewhere in the neighborhood when he went home. In
all events I shall go to London for a few days about Christmas
and probably stay here the rest of the time."

I was not to find London the calm, ordered city which I remembered from my last visit which was in the summer of 1908. Those
were the plush days of Edward the Peacemaker and I was a school
boy sight-seeing with my tutor. Now, although no bombs had been
dropped on the crowded streets, Zeppelins were floating about
and threatening. If I did go home with any of my Oxford friends
I knew I would find their families deep in war work. There was
a determined spirit which would naturally require sacrifice of the
usual festivities of the season in order to see this war through.
However, everyone seemed confident that the war could not go
on much longer.

"With every mail from home the report of Mother's war work
spreads. I think I shall have to go into the British navy and be
assigned to the Mediterranean squadron in order to get a share
of the plum puddings she is sending over for their Christmas
dinners. As for the knitted scarves, I suppose they will go to the
fleet which is guarding our eastern coast. When you work for
'dear old England' you are certainly helping a brave nation. Things
may be in a hubbub now but if anything should put England
under we in America would take a swiftish trip back to barbarism.
Mother should be able to start twenty new chapters of her Daughters of the Empire on the enthusiasm of this unhappy war.

"They have a Belgian Day here now for raising money to make
the homeless refugees comfortable. The idea is much the same as
the Alexandra Day except that little Belgian flags are being sold
by girls in the streets. The English are outdoing themselves in
being hospitable to these harassed people. One feels that the
refugees are in many cases being made more comfortable than
the English can afford to be themselves. But it is commendable.

"Delmar Banner, whom I have referred to as living in the room below me, has been turned down by the military as physically unfit, but he is really good to know — artistically stimulating. I shall accept his invitation to spend Christmas at his home in Bournemouth, i.e. from the Day to near New Year's Day. Arthur Howard is off. He had invited me to lunch several times and I had not time to return his courtesy. He is tall, well-built, with teasing humor and natural consideration, but not what one associates with his late grandfather, Strathcona. I am keeping his pet crocodile for him. (It's wood with a pendulum which wags its tail and opens its jaws.)

"These are momentous days, but a more testing time, I fear, is about to come. England will, many think, be invaded. I must be here when that happens. I shan't do much good but I shan't be in the way. I could be of service.

"I went to lunch in the president's 'Lodgings' with Sir Herbert and his Lady, and they didn't seem any different than just the other day when one called them Mr. and Mrs. Warren. This title, he feels, is conferred upon our college for taking care of the Prince of Wales during the past two years. Also I called on the Hon. Mrs. Matheson whose husband is a tutor at New College. He and Sir Herbert were friends of Sir Cecil Spring-Rice at Balliol. Sir Herbert asked me to call because of our connection with the Spring-Rices in Washington. Mrs. Matheson is a dear old Scots lady with pure white hair. They were very courteous and asked me to come any Sunday."

I felt benefited by these personal contacts with foreigners — for they were foreign to me as I probably seemed to them — especially with the President of Magdalen. From his build one might imagine that he was an impressive man in his youth. Now, he was handsome, if by that one did not mean good-looking. He had small, calculating eyes. And his thick lips could shape themselves into an engaging smile, if it were not for something wrong about his teeth. Also he had a game leg — gout they said — which must have given him sharp pains because when he moved it I could notice twinges in his face.

On the occasion of this first of many meals at *The Lodgings,* the butler ushered me into a little study just to the left of the entrance door. There I found my host seated. He was cordial but did not rise. He evidently avoided standing. Then he took me quite informally into the long dining room whose windows looked out into an enclosed garden. There I found Lady Warren waiting. She seemed at first a demure little woman, but before long I found her very positive on Catholic practices in the Church of England. They were both the butt of many undergraduate yarns filled with mimicry and amusing exaggeration.

"You ask for a description of the Prince of Wales. Naturally I am in a position to see him unofficially but anything he does or says is strictly 'off the record' and I hesitate to set it down here. I can assure you, however, H. R. H. looks like his pictures — i.e. he looks the part. Although surprisingly short in stature, he is well proportioned and carries himself well. What you have heard about his attractive personality in undoubtedly true. When he returns to college after the close of war I hope to have the opportunity of knowing him better.

"I went to see the copy of Holman Hunt's *Christ at the Gate* in Keble College this afternoon with a *General Theological* man whose bishop sent him over here to recuperate. You may remember the original painting on a column in St. Paul's, London. Here it is set in a little chapel by itself so that it is more possible to study it.

"In the library which is just next door to my rooms I have often noticed a theological student. Now he persists in coming in here. You see it is cold in the big library and he lives somewhere at the end of the world. He not only came here this afternoon but when he went away he left the table pulled out and covered with his books, etc., ready for work at night. When he returned I was merrily typing this letter. They're not used to typewriters over here — at least in Oxford — and he could not stand the noise. Then he asked me to suggest some other friend's room to which he could go. And I proposed Prince George's across the Cloister. He didn't dare, so he said. Teck came in shortly after my self-imposed guest had departed and said he wished the man had come, adding that I was to send for him if the man bothered me again."

The right to privacy was a sacred tradition at Oxford, as I was coming to know. *Sporting your oak*, which referred to shutting the heavy oak door with a handle only on the inside (the door hinged immediately outside your apartment door) was a sign that the inmate was not to be disturbed. From this it might be thought that I was easy-going and too polite except that I can recall vividly the first night I decided my friend Teck had lingered in my rooms too long for the good of my studies. When he refused to go, I resorted to force. Jacob's tussle with the angel was not to be compared with the wrestling match which followed. Complete exhaustion on both sides determined the need for mutual retirement. It was the first real "rough-house" I had had since I left Harvard. The overturned furniture and general dishevelled condition of my "sitter" presented a problem in discretion for my scout when he appeared with my hot water the next morning.

On November 27th my journal recorded, "Yesterday was Thanksgiving, and we Americans celebrated it with a service. Dr. Brown, the President of Union Theological Seminary in New York, conducted it. Curious that people about here can not get it out of their heads that it is anything but a celebration of the American Independence. Admitted our family never does much about Thanksgiving in Brooklyn, nevertheless I let my nostalgia take me back to the New England banquets I enjoyed with the Charlie Edgars in Brookline on that day.

"Perhaps it is this that has decided me also to have a feast. Not for Thanksgiving exactly but in appreciation of the men I have come to know best at Magdalen. They are men who will probably not return till after the war and perhaps not then. These will be the guests. George Teck, Phil Pye-Smith, Archer Tunnicliffe, Delmar Banner and our American cousin Ridgely Lytle. I wish I could have included Arthur Howard for we were almost friends in the sense that I am coming to recognize that term. I had also hoped to have for this festive occasion — as I think I mentioned before — either Lord Bryce or the Australian Commissioner with their respective wives. They have written, however, that they will come, but later in the year. So, there will be six of us at 1:15 in my rooms on Sunday next. I'll let you know how it comes off.

"Cardinal Wolsey, who was bursar of Magdalen when our famous tower was built, endured the trial and enjoyed the advantages which are mine today. He was born in the same month with me (March) and only about four and a half centuries before me. He studied as an undergraduate here with the financial aid of no one but his parents, as, thanks to you, I am doing. He was ordained at the same age I hope to be, but then he did a lot of things which I trust I shall never be called upon to do either for church or state."

Three days later I could write, "It is over. My Thanksgiving-Christmas first and perhaps final feast is over.

"My attractive room looking out on the Cloister I have described before, but this is how the table was. A large mahogany dining table, without cloth or doilies. Laid with the historic silver of Magdalen College. Handsome silver tankards of the 14th and 15th centuries and every other conceivable silver table equipment, each piece engraved with its date and special historic connection. If it were proper to mention money in connection with invaluable things, I should say that the silver on the table was worth a thousand dollars. This was my silver, I was made to feel, because I was a member of Magdalen. Then in the centre I arranged a mass of asters — bronze in the middle and fading out to a brilliant yellow on the edge — although flowers, inexpensive as they are, I seldom see used as a table decoration here.

"Of the courses, the first was soup. Soup in a silver tureen. Then came chopped meat sort of stuck together with jelly and pastry over the top, in short a jelly meat pie. With this was served salad. Then came a compote of fruit with the famous Magdalen meringues and cream. The luncheon concluded with the usual cheese, bread and butter. During the whole meal lemonade was shot from syphons into the aforementioned mugs. (I call them mugs because, unlike our silver tumblers at home, they have handles. And I said lemonade, not that we don't drink stronger beverages later in the day or night.) Then — yes, still more — we left the table, and although we went only to the other end of the room which was not far, we had coffee served in beautiful little cups which I borrowed from Lord Derby's son next door. This together with cigarettes and *sweeties* ended the eating part.

"One thing probably a bit out of the usual with such student luncheons was the fact that we had grace to start with. Then we started the fun. Teck was feeling sleepy because of the night operations which had kept the O.T.C. men up most of the preceding night, but I have never seen him in such an unbuttoned mood. Even Lytle blossomed out in great shape. The dignity of the occasion, for it was an occasion, was never lost, but there was not the slightest hitch or stiffness. It was important as a farewell party since there seems little chance of any of these men returning after the Vac."

My menu gave little warning of food shortage and rations to come. The flat silver was of course what was regularly used in hall and the tankards were many of them gifts to the college by undergraduates of the past. What was remarkable — especially as viewed from two score and ten years later — was the quality of the college servants who served as our scouts. My "Hunt" was a gentle natured, responsible man whose privilege of serving was inherited and whose entire life was dedicated without question to doing for all Magdalen undergraduates committed to his care what he was then doing for me. In many imperceptible ways he would guide my ways of living and for the rest of my life I would not be able to forget his critical eye. As he folded my clothes and put them in the bureau drawers or laid them out for me to put on, I knew he was right. I was his *gentleman*. His was the responsibility of a groom to a race horse. He knew what I should eat and when I should exercise and he had a pride in seeing me properly groomed when I went out. I became conscious that partly for his sake I must win the race that was set before me. This sort of self-respecting service was to pass away with the peace times to come.

"The papers have just arrived from home. (December 7th.) It was good to see the account of the Yale game. My, I would like to have gone to New Haven for it! What gloom for the poor Elis especially at the opening of their new *Bowl*. We don't play football that way here, of course, but the Oxford men were interested.

"Besides the two weeks at Bournemouth with Banner I can now count on spending about the same time in London with Pye-Smith and Tunnicliffe. The Duke of Teck has been forced to move out of the city because of his health so that perhaps I shall see nothing of George during the Vac. Nevertheless these visits will take up my time until next term. While I am stopping with these men I shall study because they themselves have to do the same.

"All this visiting is going to require dress clothes. My scout agrees that my present outfit is in a very sad state. Thus I have arranged to purchase a dress suit — coat, trousers and vest, i.e. a waistcoat — and a dinner coat, i.e. a Tuxedo, of the same material. All this I can have for eight pounds and one shilling, half the price it would cost me at home. I enclose a sample of the cloth which matches the sac suit I purchased in London some six years ago."

The fact that I was to have the chance of getting to know Philip Pye-Smith better by spending two weeks with him in London meant a lot to me at the time. I did not think to analyze what it was that made him so attractive. He was not tall nor remarkably short. As far as I knew he had not excelled in any sport but seemed in all acceptable. His great shock of black hair was groomed only on occasions, and yet he had a trim stance which kept one aware of his alert mind. The clear brown eyes looking frankly at you beneath heavily marked eyebrows were a further indication of this. Not too large a nose but a generous mouth and well defined. In his prominent chin a dimple. Yet the personality of this lad of nineteen years was not fully written in his face. He was the sort of man one could love without becoming sentimental or queer, and apparently he had an affectionate regard for me who was almost six years his senior.

"I have just returned from lunch at Sir William Osler's. It was great! Not only were Sir William and Lady Osler most pleased to see me but they seemed offended that my father had not sent me there before. In fact they made me promise to make up for my 'bad treatment' next term. I think I am supposed to come every Sunday, but of course that won't do. Phil Pye-Smith was the fellow who took me there and introduced me. He is also going to take me in a few minutes to the famous scholar at Christ Church, Dr. Sanday, who was a friend of his father. I omitted to say that sitting directly across from me at the Oslers', on Lady O's right, was the also famous Canon of Durham, Hensley Henson.

"I asked the Canon after lunch if he considered the war a religious war. His reply was that it was not a religious war in the sense of its being the contention of churches as Catholic or Protestant, but it was becoming more and more evident that it was a conflict of religious ideals. He went on to say that the Christian ideal of the family as an institution gave nations a religious significance which was opposed to the domineering policy of the German emperor. He seemed to think that the religion of Islam was so split up by the various descendants of Mohamet that in case of trouble one of these could be selected by the Allies and backed up by political power. In this way they could easily win the majority of the *faithful*. He seemed to consider that the political had come to be associated with the religious in Turkey. If the political were won over, the religious would follow naturally."

My final letter from Magdalen (12th December 1914) read, "I go to London tomorrow afternoon with Pye-Smith to stay with him at 26 Hyde Park Square. There I plan to remain for some five days and from there I shall either go and visit Tunnicliffe or I shall take a room in a house where a Harvard classmate of mine, Lee Ustick, is lodging during his visit to London. Later I shall see Professor de Sumichrast and Ben Greet. Also Miss Meriel Talbot has asked me to call.

"Did I tell you I had a letter from our Spanish cousin Estelle Longstaffe who is traveling in South America? She sent me the enclosed picture of herself and her eldest daughter and said how sorry she was that her house on the Thames was closed because otherwise I should have been welcome to go there for the Vac. There are lots of promises for the good times she suggests giving me when they return to England."

3

CHRISTMAS VACATION, 1914

MY letter of the 13th announcing, "Well, here I am in London again after six years," suggested a comparison between the peaceful past of Edwardian days and the precarious present facing the possibility of enemy invasion. Headlined reports regarding floating mines and Zeppelins — with an enemy navy poised across the North Sea — were only beginning to rouse the people to a sense of danger. Any thought of a Spanish armada or a battle of Trafalgar belonged to the realms of romantic history and had no place in the practical affairs of modern life. Therefore business and pleasure — stimulated to be sure by the *phony* war across the channel — continued as usual.

English society was still patterned along class lines and the upper classes dominated. Because of this it was their responsibility to provide for the security of Britain. It accounted for the volunteering for military service on the part of Oxford undergraduates as in keeping with their class obligation. The cultured home in which I was now a guest was — according to my hostess' own estimation — upper middle. But to me as an American witnessing this ordered society in action it was strangely interesting. I accepted it as the English status quo and took care to respect it as best as I could.

Two days after my arriving at 26 Hyde Park Square my journal read, "I have just come back from the Coliseum with Arthur Howard and Phil Pye-Smith. A splendid variety play. H. B. Irving in one of Conan Doyle's one-act plays, Vesta Tilly in the character of a *Tommy* and again as a gay undergraduate who had just come down from Oxford where she had drunk 'ginger ales with the Prince of Wales.' She gives a lilt to her songs, and in her boy costume she cuts quite a figure.

68

"It was really Arthur Howard's party and we dined at his house before going to the theatre. I sat on Lady Strathcona's right. Mr. Howard — her husband, you remember — was at dinner also and especially interesting to me because he had played football on the McGill team against Harvard. They have one of those spacious houses on the north side of Grosvenor Square. The excellent dinner was served with quiet dignity. There seems to be a style here of dressing a table by having a silver or gold trophy, such as the vase presented to Mother by the women of Long Island, in the centre of the table empty, and at intervals down the length of the table short cut flowers in small glass jars."

Table decoration — even for the simplest home dinner — had a peculiar significance for me probably because I had grown up in a family which seldom had time or occasion to sit down together except around the dinner table. To have a rare specimen of Georgian silver, such as I saw at the Howards', to serve as a centre piece for this family circle was ideal. The only piece we had at home to compare with it was the vase I mention as presented to my mother at the time of her *Midwinter Fete* in recognition of her part in saving the charity foundation of the diocese of Long Island from being shut down by foreclosure. Her dramatic charity benefits into which I was inevitably drawn as a boy were having the effect now of making me feel at home in a foreign society which seemed to justify itself by the charitable causes it sponsored. The time would come when I myself would produce in Devonshire House, Piccadilly, a charitable show which the newspaper of the day hailed as "the greatest social and literary event of recent years."

My letters were now addressed from 7 Gordon Square where I had gone to be near my Harvard friend whose home I had visited in St. Louis, Missouri.

"I spent from Saturday to Thursday at the Pye-Smiths', and a wonderful time I have had. I have seen what mother saw when she was here at the coronation — the insides of things.

"We went out for dinner most every night and the rest of the time we had the comforts of a well run English home. It is one of those typical Georgian houses at the end of a tree-lined square with seven servants and a hostess as comfortably informal as my own mother. 'Mrs. Pye' — as the Howards call her — is a widow, short, stout and active. Kindly humour marks her spirit to which is added a lot of common sense. She lives for her only son, and

fortunately he is the sort of man who doesn't spoil. Picture her
in a large square drawing-room behind a temptingly laden tea
table. The floor is centered with a great rug of royal purple standing out against the white painted floor boards on all sides. Long
windows face the square and the other sides are hung with heavily
framed paintings.

"I took Phil to dine at the Tunnicliffes' on Wednesday. Archer
himself is forced to go away for sometime in connection with his
joining the army so that he had to cancel his invitation to have
me stop with him. But Lee Ustick is staying here in a nice board
and lodging place near our old Torrington Square and he arranged
to have me in the room over him. We are having a cosey time
talking over his father with whom I stayed in St. Louis and our
many Harvard friends.

"I dine with the Sumichrasts tonight, lunch tomorrow with our
cousin, Dr. Longstaff, in Putney Heath, and listen to a lot of
speculation as to where this war is going to land us."

I never attended any of Professor de Sumichrast's French classes
at Harvard, but the way I came to know him personally was when
I went to a luncheon at the Brookline Country Club to represent
my mother as president of the Daughters of the Empire. 'Sumi' — as
one came to call him — was giving the party to have the officers
of the Victoria League in Boston meet Miss Meriel Talbot, secretary of the League in London. It was the first time I was to see a
woman smoke. As a pleasant gesture when the professor opened
his cigarette case after lunch on the terrace, he offered it to the
distinguished guest. To the amazement of the other ladies and to
the horror of the members of that exclusive club, Miss Talbot
took a cigarette and held it for Sumi to light it. This he had to do,
and all the other ladies had to follow suit. Even I didn't smoke
in those days.

"Ustick and I went to take dinner with the Sumichrasts. They
are comfortably located in a largish house in Ealing. The professor
gave an enthusiastic lecture at a nearby hall afterward which
probably did something for the recruiting in the district. It is
curious what people need to make them wake up and take an
interest in the present danger to their country. Sumi recited a
poem in a dramatic way which quite took the house. His slides
were excellent and ended with pictures of the Scarborough disaster
which occurred the day before. I must say that he got some of

his effects unjustly, but when you are trying to persuade a man to kill other men there is little use in enlarging upon the splendid character of the enemy. Granted the end is just — as I feel sure it is in the present struggle — the means must be allowed for, I suppose."

It was difficult for me and my contemporaries to understand why the German fleet made this feeble surprise attack on the East Coast of England. Later it was revealed that the Germans had planned to make a far more formidable assault and cripple British merchant shipping, but they found the British fleet on the alert. Bottled up in their own harbor the Germans had to make some show of offense. To this end they sent some ships to scatter floating mines as best they could in the North Sea. The three cruisers which fired on Hartlepool and Scarborough damaged a few hotels and churches as well as occasional laborer's cottages, but the casualties were slight. It did arouse resentment even in America, as I read in my papers from home. They condemned it as being useless destruction. Certainly it helped my friend Sumi and others who were recruiting in England.

My next letter (24th December 1914) showed that I was stopping with the Banners in their residence, "Brooklands," on Branksome Wood Road in Bournemouth.

"I do hope the unfortunate disaster off the east coast of this tight little isle did not make you worry about me. Although I am on the coast at the present moment it is the south coast so that the German ships would have to get through the well guarded English Channel before they could damage our resort hotels. The shelling of Hartlepool made exciting news, however, so that it is suggested darkening the ocean front windows. Personally I feel I am in no more danger than you are in New York. Even with the *Emden* on the high seas most of us are preserved from ill chances.

"Even now I don't seem to have time to tell you fully of my visit with the widow of the late vice-chancellor of Guy's and her son, Phil Pye-Smith. He and I spent the day seeing old sights I could recall from my 1908 trip. He is a fascinating little fellow, about eighteen, whom I hope I can keep on knowing for a long time.

"Before coming to Bournemouth I went out to lunch with our cousins the George Blundell Longstaffs. Theirs is a large rambling

stone house with ample grounds on the edge of Putney Heath.
While waiting in a small reception room I remarked on a realistic
picture of tropic foliage directly above the fireplace. Upon closer
observation I discovered it was a glass window looking out into
a great conservatory on the other side of the wall. I wore my
'topper' and morning coat and did my best to represent our branch
of the family bush.

"Dr. Longstaff — a most genial, intelligent gentleman, remembered mother and made me immediately at home. He said that
his great grandfather who lived in the north riding of Yorkshire
was called Langstaff and when he came down to the south of
England everybody pronounced *lang* with an *o* sound. Thus he
conformed and allowed his name to be written Longstaff. I have
the same experience but will not change the spelling. The doctor
is an M.D. and a Fellow of London University but has never
practiced medicine. One of his sons commands the flagship of
the Australian fleet and the other is in the army. The doctor's
brother financed the Scott expedition to the South Pole with the
result that the mountain nearest the pole is called Mount Longstaff.
We walked about his six-acre garden and Mrs. Longstaff showed
me the rare snails she raises for the Kensington Museum. They
were very kind to me and insisted I make their house my home
in London."

Wherever one went the chief topic of conversation was the
war. Dr. Longstaff said, "This war is an evil obsession," and yet
he could add, "It is a great satisfaction to a father to feel that
his only boys are doing their best in the cause, not only of their
country, but of right and justice. The saddest thing to me is the
way in which a great nation has ostentatiously thrown religion to
the winds." He told me that he was "daily expecting to have
cavalry horses billeted here."

There were many stories of how the people in the "devastated"
area of the east coast were taking the attack. One told of a Territorial officer hurrying down one of the main streets to the front
when a typical British workman with a basket of tools over his
shoulder, stopped him: "Aye, sir," said the workman with great
emphasis, "This kind of thing would never have happened if we
had a Conservative government in power!" Another citizen, much
excited, hurried into his garage to tell the driver to get ready at
once to take the family away. He found the driver quietly polish-

ing the brass trimmings on the automobile. With an old man's satisfaction he looked up from his task and observed, "Ah, Master George, they've coom! Ah've always said they'd coom, and they've coom!" And there was the old lady, living on South Cliff, who picked up a gun on hearing the bombardment and hurried out to the sea front anxious to have a shot at the enemy.

So it was in the early days, the reactions to the hostilities in Europe differed according to one's position in life. Some thought it an exciting inconvenience. Some saw in it an Armageddon of religious or cultural ideologies. The press found in it welcome headlines for selling their papers. Diplomats and military were brought into the public eye as never before. In some parts it was termed a "phony" war. No one anywhere understood it yet as a "total" war. As for the Banners with whom I was stopping, they were a delicate, nervous and wealthy family with investments probably at a safe distance in Canada. They found the war dreadfully upsetting but since their only son was outspoken in his sympathy for the Germans and preferred to take the stand of aggressive neutrality, the subject was avoided as far as possible.

"The Banners are giving me a splendid time at their stately residence on Branksome Wood Road. They have a couple of motors and a well appointed establishment designed for comfort and security. Mrs. Banner was a Miss Tiffin of Montreal and is always well dressed and attractive whatever the hour. Mr. Banner, as other men I have come across in England, seems to have loads of time on his hands. Certainly there is nothing he could do for me that he does not do.

"My beautiful bed room with a great bay window looking down the leafy valley to the sea, the delicious meals—in all these houses I visit it seems a dinner party every night—the soft-spoken servants and, pervading all, the cultured hospitality of my hosts; everything would be ideal if there were not a war going on at the same time. I have a good spirited horse to ride and Delmar and I go on many a walk by the sea. The lights along the coast are all darkened and people are being ordered to keep their blinds shut because of possible bombardment.

"I went to call on the sister of Mother's secretary, Mrs. Edward Francis. She with her husband and daughter are stopping at one of the luxurious hotels. Over the tea cups we discussed the war and the weather. Also a pushing little American acquaintance of

Mrs. Banner's came in to call. She made a point of having come in Lady Reid's motor. When I remarked that I had met Lady Reid she turned to Mrs. Banner in wild enthusiasm and exclaimed that I was an old friend of Lady Reid's. Afterwards I explained to Mrs. Banner that I was not responsible for the Australian Commissioner's wife, that it was her husband I really knew. Some days later Lady Reid came to rest in Bournemouth. And one day while I was walking down a hill with Delmar a motor stopped half way up, there was a feminine scream, and the little Mrs. American Friend jumped out and rushed down after us. We were dragged back to meet Lady Reid. Of course she remembered coming to tea with me at Harvard, and since there was a particularly opinionated young man with whom I had argued the night before at dinner sitting in the car I was delighted when Lady Reid asked me, "How is the President?" The man thought, of course, that she meant the President of the United States instead of the far greater man who had come to my rooms at Harvard to meet Sir George. I promised to call, but since Sir George is in Egypt cheering up the Australian troops now guarding the Suez I postponed the call."

About this time I received a letter dated December 27, 1914, from my friend Phil Pye-Smith in which he said, "I was gazetted on the 22nd to the 11th (Service) Battn of the King's (Liverpool) Regt which is now at Farnham and was just what I wanted—I only wish poor old Teck could have come with me. But I have got to report on Fri. next to the Adjt at Oxford for a 'course of instruction' which I believe lasts a month and may be in Oxford. If so I shall see you all for the last fortnight. Cookers wrote me such a nice letter about it and Tunnicliffe is coming to tea today, I hope, also Arthur Howard.

"By the way Kirby sent me an agonised postcard wanting to know your address so I have sent it him—he has piles of letters awaiting you at Magdalen.

"Give my 'love' to Banner & tell him that Cookers told me in his letter that Banner had done extraordinarily well in the *History Previous*. Mind you call here on your way through London even if I am away.

"All good wishes for 1915—I am yrs affect, Phil Pye-Smith."

My New Year's letter from Bournemouth read, "Here beginneth

the year which is to mean so much to all of us—for better or for worse! I continue having a luxurious time here at the Banners. Hot water bottles to make my bed warm, a constant fire in my room, a box of biscuits for between times, morning tea as well as afternoon tea if I wish it, cocoa before retiring, horseback rides, motoring, concerts—you know how it is. We have just returned from a long ride out by the New Forest. Soldiers drilling all over the hills and marching on the roads. We stopped to speak with some of them and found we could not understand a word of their county dialect; Somerset or some such talk.

"And now Lady Strathcona has asked me to come to their town house on Grosvenor Square for my last week. I fear Arthur Howard has been gazetted, however. If so perhaps I'll stop at Dr. Longstaff's or with the Pomeroy-Burtons who have just written me a most cordial letter. But better, I will return to Magdalen and my box-from-home—which I hear awaits me there—and start work again. I would rather visit the Howards when Arthur is there."

By this time it seemed to me the hope of any swift conclusion of the war was gone. The fall of Antwerp and the ruthless invasion in defiance of international treaties had not secured coastal bases with which the Germans planned to menace the Channel. The battle of the Marne and Ypres had proved nothing decisive for either side. The Turks had allied themselves with the Austro-German side and were, I understood, having a hard time at the hands of the Russians. Zeppelins with their bombs were being viewed with terror when sighted but were easily driven off by frail bi-planes sent up by the Allies. As for the United States—nothing but more "notes" of protest from our President, Woodrow Wilson. My next letter was from London.

"Just arrived from Bournemouth. Don't want to let you think I had too much of a carefree party at Christmas. It was a quiet time and very little like the joyful frolic we used to have at home.

"I came directly to Grosvenor Square. The nearest thing we have like it in New York is the block of old houses on the north side of Washington Square. Arthur Howard was waiting for me, and was I glad to see him! The family here, beside the doctor and Lady Strathcona, are the eldest son Donald (grad. of Cambridge), Harry (grad. last year of Magdalen) and Arthur (my friend).

Also The Hon. Edith Howard and an older sister Frances whom
I haven't met. This is 'not to speak of the dogs,' Winkie, Jock and
Cockles.

"I am allotted the late Lord Strathcona's desk by the window
of a large basement room. This is the place where the Canadian
patriarch liked to do all his writing in spite of the fact that people
on the pavement in front of the house could stare down through
the iron railing of the area and watch him working. He evidently
desired to be one with the *man on the street* and there are many
tales of his democratic ways. The guest room above the drawing
room is also assigned to me. One of the luxuries I appreciate is
running water and my own tub.

"I cannot describe every detail of my visit here but they make
me one of the family. If I want to stay out late I have but to say
or if I wish to bring somebody back to lunch it is not necessary
to mention it beforehand—in short I am home. And it is very like
our adjustable home in Brooklyn. Everyone is busy doing things
for other people, and meals etc. are made to fit the convenience
of the household. While I sat reading in the boudoir (a sort of
general living room) one night, and Lady Strathcona was scratch-
ing away with her pen at her writing table, I seemed to forget the
thousands of miles overseas and thought for a moment it was
Mother writing letters in our library at home.

"Arthur is busy all day drilling his men. Each morning we go
to the front window and watch the long brown line led by a band
march through the square to Hyde Park. Today Arthur is taking
them up Bond Street for the sake of recruits. There was a mixup
about his being gazetted owing largely, it seems, to the fact that
our cousin Lord Esher—who is at the head of the Territorials—
is very old. Harry Howard came home from some place on the
coast where he was drilling with a cyclist corps. The eldest son
also came back from the front in France. He looked more as
though he had returned from a health resort, but then over there
one must keep healthy to live, so they say. With the father I have
had many long talks about Jefferson Davis and General Lee who
went to stay with the Howards in Montreal after our Civil War.
He knows the history of the U.S.A. backwards.

"I have just received news of Uncle Gari's engagement to
Josephine Chadwick. Edith Howard found it in the Post and
accused me of the act. Who is the lady? Her father is 'Colonel' of

what is counted a very fine regiment, and they live in Bath. Should I fish them out, or mind my own business?"

The batch of mail accumulated in Oxford during my absence numbered "71 letters from all sorts of interesting people." They were forwarded by the porter of the Magdalen Lodge and I received them finally at Grosvenor Square. One from my mother contained a note written to her by Lady Brittain whose husband has been largely responsible for carrying on the Anglo-American society known as *The Pilgrims*. "By some strange coincidence," Lady Brittain wrote, "my young brother was staying with me when your letter arrived this week, to see all he could of our eldest brother who was home from the Front on five days leave. He has been at Magdalen for three months, and knows your son quite well. I told him to ask your son to look us up when he is in London. When writing him you might mention Robert Harvey. He is very young but they are all chums in College. Oxford is very empty now."

Several of the letters were from the faculty of Harvard University. "I have heard from more than one source how the university has been depleted this year and how all the older students have gone or are going to the war," wrote LeBaron Briggs, dean of the university and head of Radcliffe College. "Our young Englishman, Lionel—otherwise known as *Johnny*—Harvard, is drilling with the militia here and will, I understand, enlist in England as soon as he graduates." This collateral descendant of the John Harvard who founded Harvard College, was one of my close friends and I looked forward to seeing him when he came over. Also a letter from the president of Harvard saying, "I am delighted to hear that you found what you wanted at Magdalen; although, of course, one does not get what one would get in ordinary times at Oxford. Nevertheless, the experience of being there during this war must be of immense interest. It is most certainly one of the greatest periods in the world's history. Wishing you a very Happy New Year, A. Lawrence Lowell."

The dean of Harvard College, Byron Hurlbut, was another of my correspondents and wrote, "Your experience is certainly exceptional in the highest degree, and I hope that you are taking the time to keep a very careful journal of Oxford life in these days, for it will be valuable. If you haven't provided yourself with a great supply of durable paper (Note, I say durable and I mean

HARVARD COLLEGE

OFFICE OF THE DEAN
    4 UNIVERSITY HALL
                                CAMBRIDGE, MASSACHUSETTS
                                December 28, 1914.

Dear Brett Langstaff,

       It was a great pleasure to Mrs. Hurlbut
and me to receive your Christmas greeting, and to learn
that you find your life at Oxford so happy and interesting
despite the changed conditions there.   Your experience
is certainly exceptional in the highest degree, and I hope
that you are taking the time to keep a very careful journal
of Oxford life in these days, for it will be valuable.
if you haven't already provided yourself with a great supply
of durable paper, (Note, I say durable and I mean durable;
don't buy cheap stuff) get something that will last, and take
ample time each day, (and you will have to take firm resolution with this) to write down your experiences.

       Mrs. Hurlbut joins me in wishing you every
success.

                Sincerely yours,

                  B. S. Hurlbut.

J. Brett Langstaff, Esq.

BYRON SATTERLEE HURLBUT (Dean of Harvard College), written
   1914, urging Brett Langstaff to keep the "journal" here recorded.

Brunsdale, Mass.
December 20, 1925.

Dear Mr. Langstaff,

Thank you for your kind card of remembrance with the appreciative and helpful verses dedicated to you.

With all good Christmas wishes, I am

Yours sincerely

Rev. J. Brett Langstaff & · B. R. Briggs

LE BARON RUSSELL BRIGGS (Dean of Harvard University) referring to "verses" written by Lauchlan MacLean Watt.

durable; don't buy cheap stuff), get something that will last, and take ample time each day (and you will have to take firm resolution with this), to write down your experiences. Mrs. Hurlbut joins me in wishing you every success." And Professor Bliss

Perry's letter was in the same vein: "You could not have gone to
Oxford at a time more memorable and inspiring, and I hope that
your stay will reward you to the full limit to your ambitions for it."

Finally from England there were letters of hospitality and good
wishes, one especially from Prince George in answer to a query
I had made on behalf of my mother. It seems George's grandmother (Adelaide Duchess of Teck) had sponsored as her favorite
charity The Needlework Guild which supplied new garments to
the needy. Of The Needlework Guild of America — a branch of
the above started by Lady Wolverton — my mother had been
president for more than twenty years. Now, recently a new organization of similar name had sprung up in Canada being organized
by Miss Catherine Merritt (later Lady Pellatt) and since it had
the personal patronage of George's aunt (Queen Mary) — being
called Queen Mary's Needlework Guild—much confusion was
resulting.

From 4 Devonshire Place, London, Prince George of Teck
wrote, "I have been away up in Derbyshire for Xmas and as all
my family except me caught influenza up there we only got back
yesterday. I understand that Miss Merritt has authority to form
branches for Queen Mary's Needlework Guild in Canada. Please
give my blessing to Pye-Smith and Howard. As I have not found
a friendly Colonel we shall probably meet on Friday."

From Grosvenor Square on the 5th of January my journal
continued. "Early Service and *breaker* and 11 o'clock at St.
Mark's, North Audley Street. The Duchess of Teck was there
again in the pew in front of us. There is a peculiar charm about
this congregation, probably the most generally aristocratic in
London. The multitude of graces and marks of character make
themselves felt without ostentation, while the fact that most of the
worshipers represent titled families makes the titles themselves
appear more reasonable and not just socially *upish.*

"Lady Strathcona and I walked across Hyde Park to see John
Buller, her year old grandchild and his mother Frances Kitson.
Jim Kitson is an officer in the Navy. Then I hurried down to St.
Paul's to hear the Archbishop. I secured a chair and in a few
minutes a lady came and stood beside me, so I gave her my seat
and joined the heroic figures of a nearby tomb. The Archbishop
stormed away. Told the people to push and pray and keep a stiff
upper lip.

Dec 26. '14

**5 CLEMENT CIRCLE,
CAMBRIDGE.**

[handwritten letter]

Dear Mr. Langstaff:

I am delighted to hear that you are so happily situated at Magdalen College. You could not have gone to Oxford at a time more memorable and inspiring and I hope that your stay will reward you to the full limit of your ambitions for it.

With the best Holiday greetings

Sincerely yours

Bliss Perry

Letter from Bliss Perry, Professor of English Literature at Harvard
University, written to Brett Langstaff referring to Oxford in 1914 as
"memorable and inspiring."

"After the cathedral service I taxied to Lambeth Palace to make a promised call — there's no direct way of getting there by bus or tube and it was too dark to walk, I thought. I made my way through the court yards, up the broad staircase and into the drawing room. While I was sitting there alone except for a steaming kettle, in came a youngish cleric who informed me that he had brought the Archbishop's 'clothes' (by which he meant his robes), but that he and Mrs. Davidson were walking and would not arrive till six. (May I observe it was a comfort to know that, if the Archbishop chose to send his clothes ahead and walk home without them, darkness covered the earth and would doubtless cover him also.) The young cleric's name was G. K. Bell, and since he had just come down from Oxford there was much to talk of.

"Then came a little lady who seemed perhaps Mrs. D's sister. She had been reading the recently published *Life of Lord Strathcona* in which she was greatly disappointed. So I told her how Lord Strathcona, through modesty as much as anything, had repeatedly refused during his life time to allow such a volume to be written (even by the Duke of Argyll who could have done it well), and to make certain he had ordered all his papers to be destroyed. How a political hackwriter had petitioned after Lord S's death to be allowed access to his papers for the purpose of compiling a biography. How the family had informed him of the Baron's wish in the matter. How this writer had gone to men in Canada who were—perhaps—not conscious of doing anything but honour to the *Empire Builder* in giving their recollections of his part in creating the *C. P. R.* and the Bank of Montreal. In short this writer had pieced together bits of rumour and gossip to make his publication sell as a third class thriller.

"By the time I had got that far in my tale several other members of the Palace household and a Mrs. Montagu who had been one of Phillips Brooks' great friends in England had come in. They all seemed to know of me, for why I can not tell. So when Mrs. Davidson finally arrived it was to find me halfway through tea and as much at home as if I had been in Brooklyn. She kindly sent for the Archbishop.

"His Grace was a bit tired, but we sat on a couple of uncomfortable chairs and had a splendid talk for about 20 minutes. I wanted his reasons for preventing the clergy going to the war as regular officers and soldiers, but there were too many ladies for real shop talk. I was about to go, but he said he hoped to see me again and made off before me. It must have been 7 o'clock before I started to take leave and then Mrs. Davidson thoughtfully suggested I must see the Palace. So Mr. Bell was detailed to show me about.

"The oldest part is the Tower where the Lollards were imprisoned and under this is the porch through which Wickcliffe, Cranmer, Laud and the rest often had passed from the river into the Chapel. In this Chapel which was redecorated by Archbishop Tait, Mrs. Davidson's father, are many relics of the church's history. The crypt had been unearthed by Mr. Caroe, an architect whom I met at Dr. Longstaff's, and there I saw certain valuable paintings hiding from possible bombs and carefully watched over by a small oil stove. But you know about the spacious Palace from having been there.

"We made our way back to the drawing room where I took final leave of the ladies. Mr. Bell came down to the door, helped me on with my cape-coat and saw me out — now that I come to look back on it, rather an unusual way to be shown out of a palace. But he was a splendid fellow and promised to come and see me in Oxford."

That same Rev. G. K. Bell who was so courteous to me was to have a distinguished and active career as Bishop of Chichester and a leader in Anglo-American relations. As for my warm reception at Lambeth Palace, I would have understood it better if I had seen the archbishop's wife writing my mother on January 7th, "I shall be very pleased to make friends with your son when an opportunity occurs, and am glad you sent me his address. I will write him.

"Thank you for your great sympathy in our time of intense anxiety. It helps more than I can say to feel our American friends are sharing it with us. It is a very great time though a sad one and I do trust and pray will lead us out into something better."

As for the archbishop, Randall Davidson, I was to see him later in the course of my own career, especially when I defied his orders and enlisted in the Scots Guards as a fighting man. I used to wonder how it was he came to know so much about far away parts of the world — more of British colonies, it was said than any other member of Parliament. I came to attribute this in part to his giving such personal attention to returned missionaries and foreign visitors, even such as myself, because it afforded him an immediate source of information. He would often have them in his library alone and taking out a book on the particular part of the world from which they had just come he would say, "The last report I had from there was such and such. Now," he would go on, "what is the condition today as you found it?" The changes noted by his visitor would then be carefully recorded in the margins of the book. When the visitor had been dismissed and the book replaced on its shelf the information was accessible for future reference. In rank the Archbishop of Canterbury comes next to the Royal Family itself, but aside from this, Randall Cantuar was one of the great statesmen of his time.

The journal continued from Grosvenor Square: "I had promised Arthur Pomeroy-Burton to be at *The Old Mansion,* Frognal, at tea time and stay for dinner. He had stipulated I should not dress so I could go directly from Lambeth in my morning coat and topper. The wrong tube station, an ignorance of people of one part of London as to any other part of town, Zeppelin gloom, in short the *powers of darkness* had combined with the archbishop to make me late. But I arrived in time for cocktails.

"Among the guests I met a society-painter type, a successful song writer, a reciter of E. W. Wilcox, a lady who sang at concerts and the Princess Eristoff who was enthusiastic about the part the Cossacks were playing in the Russian advance on East Prussia and Galicia — a different atmosphere from what I had left at Lambeth. The house seemed an important old residence a bit crowded with encroaching neighbors. I could not help wishing the noisy crowd would all go and leave me to talk with my hostess who is an aunt of Ward Melville's and a charming person.

"Mr Burton was not there. Gone shooting or something with Lord Northcliffe. I fear Mr. Burton is responsible for that sheet, the Daily Mail, so detested by respectable people now for its attack on Lord Kitchener and its pessimism generally. Journalism is on a low scale in more than a social sense here in England. I shall not speak of this visit when I return to Grosvenor Square, but Mrs. Burton made me promise to make *The Old Mansion* a home spot on my vacs in London. Certainly it was a pleasant reminder of the Melvilles and our other neighbors on Long Island.

"One of Lady Strathcona's closest friends, General McGrigor, came to lunch today. He had just been talking to the *Times* correspondent, and their opinion was that this slow trench fighting would continue until May and then more aggressive measures would be taken. He is rather short but he has two rows of medals. Donald Howard also came home from the front in time for lunch."

The father of this Sir James McGrigor was, I have been told, in an important way responsible for Lord Strathcona going out with the Hudson Bay Company when the future baron was a poor working lad in Scotland. It is a fine example of inherited friendship. The general's information was correct in forecasting the spring offensive which was to come a little sooner than expected.

Lady Pomeroy-Burton — as she came to be styled in time because of her husband's controlling position in the Harmsworth Press — had had a word from her sister, Mrs. Frank Melville, — our country places were near each other in Stony Brook, Long Island — regarding my coming to England. My association with Ward Melville in bringing out the student daily at Columbia College may have interested the Burtons.

Among my mother's letters forwarded to me in London was one written by Lady Ebury from Moor Park, Rickmansworth, saying, "I have written to your son but I fear I can do nothing further at present. Our life is a very very anxious one. We have two sons in the Army and all the conditions of existence are altered — all our men servants have enlisted, horses taken for the army. Everyone is immersed in work all day.

"I hope when the happy time of peace comes I may meet your son. He will find a very different existence here to what it used to be. We none of us think of anything but the war or do anything but war from day to day doing what we can for those splendid Sailors and Soldiers of ours."

And another to my mother from the Countess of Jersey added to the picture of England at war. "I am so sorry that owing to Lord Jersey's health we have to go to the South of France immediately after the New Year and therefore I fear that I shall have no chance of seeing your son at present. I will note his address in case I have a chance of seeing him after our return — and will also let Miss Talbot know that he will be at Oxford. I am much interested to hear of the splendid work of the Chapters of the Daughters of the Empire. The sympathy of our kindred living in America is very valuable and cheering to us all in these anxious

times. We have no fear as to the ultimate result but the struggle
is hard meantime."

Miss Talbot was secretary of the important organization of
which Lady Jersey was president and as such showed herself a
remarkable woman. Later she was to be given the title of Dame
of the British Empire for her services especially in organizing the
young women of England to work on the land in place of farm
hands who had joined the forces.

On January 13th came my last letter from Grosvenor Square,
saying, "I have just returned from seeing Miss Victoria-League-
Secretary Meriel Talbot. She may have heard of my being here
through the Sumichrasts who are all down with the *flu;* anyway
she wrote asking me to call. She is the most business-like busy
woman I have met over here, but even then she seems up to her
ears in war work. I should say over her ears. Nevertheless, as I
saw her with papers piled high, a bit untidy and her nose rather
red, she seemed in control.

"I told Miss Talbot of my mother's work with the Daughters. I
tell everybody. Regarding the nurses they sent over here, it is
provoking to hear of three of them (the nurses) going back to
America. You must think there is a confusion in army regulations.
I could give you many examples to show how true this is. But this
is where a person with Miss Talbot's ability helps. She seems to
think the American nurses expected too much. Miss Talbot said
that with the Victoria League their chief occupation now is distributing information and through the medium of meetings and
pamphlets coordinating the public with the government's effort to
protect their interests.

"Miss Talbot remembered our party at the Brookline Country
Club, though I didn't mention the smoking. She kindly offered to
write the well known Oxford theologian, Scott-Holland, to introduce
me as her friend."

I left London with a sense of privilege that in a country where
people were sacrificing the peace and security of their homes
for the cause of justice I, as an American, was granted the sanctum
of Oxford for research and contemplation. It was with a great
appreciation of the families from which my fellow undergraduates
had come, and a deeper sense of responsibility for the work in
which I was engaged that I took up my studies again at Magdalen.

4

MY SECOND TERM, 1915

AFTER a series of unexpected experiences during the *Xmas Vac* I returned to my cloister rooms in Magdalen with a clearer understanding of my opportunity as a Junior Foreign Student. Officially I had been enrolled as such at Oxford but unofficially I had been accepted by widely varying groups of people who had not only offered me the hospitality of their homes but also had opened to me their minds on matters in which I had neither the presumption nor the knowledge to question. In the studious atmosphere of my cloister I could now check over so called "facts" which were being implanted on the public mind by newspapers and popular expression. There were corrections which I did not feel at the time free to commit to writing, and certainly not using as my authority private conversations and personal observations I had been allowed in the homes of my new friends.

One fact was that the slogan, *brave Belge,* which had impelled so many Oxford undergraduates to enlist was not the cause of the war. The civil war in Holland in 1830 which had resulted in the independence of Belgium was not to be laid at England's door, but soon after the nationality of Belgium was recognized England had played a leading part in the treaty which forced France and Germany to accept it as a buffer state. This England had done because the new nation across the channel was indeed at her door. These facts I had from my study of history. Now the violation of this treaty destroyed this protective area behind which England had felt more secure in extending her colonial empire during the Victorian era. Thus in coming to the aid of Belgium, England was primarily concerned with defending her own bulwark. The school-boy idea of protecting the small boy against the German bully could still be used in recruiting, but the potential threat of a German-dominated Belgium seemed cause enough for England's entrance into the war.

It seemed clear from my informants at the time that if France had not taken strategic precaution to reassure England that she would respect the sovereignty of Belgium, England might have remained neutral or even taken sides with Germany whose ultimatum had promised the reinstatement of Belgian independence after the war. Friendly relations with France — as established under the influence of Edward VII — might have given cause for the Kaiser's complaint of "encirclement," but Edward was dead and the new king had reestablished the family relationship with his Teutonic cousins. All this made sense in the resentment my friend Banner had at the fact that we were fighting England's natural allies, the Germans.

My first letter home from Magdalen was dated January 31, 1915, and read, "Even if you did not have a Christmas tree you did not have the anxiety that the people in this part of the world had. All the men here were in the coast defense trenches on Xmas Day. All the way up the eastern coast they were looking for a German attack. The men who had Xmas leave to come back from France were held over. I hardly think many people realized it was Xmas at all.

"Here is a version of the *Sister Susie* rhyme which was being sung in London:

> "Mother's sitting, knitting little mittens for the navy,
> Bertha's busy bathing baby Belgian refugees,
> Sarah's shaming shirkers making guernseys for the Ghurkas,
> Oh what busy bees, all sewing, oh such busy bees!

> Maggie, Moll and Maud are making mufflers for the Marines
> While Winnie winds the wool when they begin,
> Sister Cissie's knitting socks and Susie's sewing shirts —
> Still poor papa props his pants up with a pin.

"It is good to know that there are some in America working at war relief. Everybody is doing it here. Teck came back from spending his vac with the Duchess of Devonshire and he brought with him a little wooden business with pegs on it whereby he was able to knit scarfs. He said the whole household was at it.

I did a bit of relief business myself while I was at the Howards'. The Duchess of Somerset came for tea and told Lady Strathcona that she wanted some bed-jackets for her new hospital. The next day while Lady S was out looking for the jackets I went to call on Mrs. Pye-Smith. Mrs. Lee Smith, Mrs. Pye's sister, was there and said "bed-jackets?", she had 18 specially good ones which she wanted to be sure would be well used. So I arranged that she should send them to Lady S. And when I came back to Grosvenor Square I found Lady S had been hunting all day in vain and it was a satisfaction to be able to say that I had arranged to have 18 of the best sent to her immediately. Mr. Howard seemed to think that this might be considered a breach of neutrality.

"Arthur Howard has lent me his bike (bicycle) for the 18 months he will probably be away, or for the duration of the war."

The opportunities I had been given for studying the war from different angles in the contrasting homes in which I had visited during the vac might seem lost when I returned to the university. But there was one home in Oxford in which I was now to become an intimate member of the family which gave me a chance of meeting and talking with many of the important persons who came to England from Canada. This was the residence of Sir William Osler in Norham Gardens which — thanks to Arthur Howard's bike — was conveniently near Magdalen. As Regius Professor of Medicine Sir William had an established position in England. In America the reputation he had acquired while teaching at Johns Hopkins in Baltimore had gained him recognition in the world of medical science, but as a Canadian from McGill University where his career had commenced he had a lasting place in the hearts of all who lived north of the United States border. Osler was a great man in every sense of the word and was accepted as such in his own time. Therefore his winsome personality and the disarming way he had of expressing it made him the subject of many stories some of which were embarrassingly misinterpreted.

"Lady Osler sent for me to come to luncheon yesterday," my journal for January 17th read. "All the Wright 'girls' were there, Dr. Mallock and a stupid Canadian in uniform — or maybe he was just war-fagged. Sir William told a story in that serious manner of his which holds one's attention as though what he was saying were all true. One time, he said, there was a man who came to him from the Woodbury facial place with the sad complaint that he had gone there to have his face filled out for the sake of the girl he wanted to marry. It seems she had called him a 'living skeleton' and refused to marry him because of the way he looked. Although the wax injected by the facial people succeeded in rounding out his face, every time he smiled there were evident three distinct sections in each cheek. You see he was so thin, Osler explained, that he had to have the wax injected in that way. My wide-eyed concern about the solution of the man's problem was relieved by Sir William's assuring me that he sent the man to the hospital where it was gouged out from the inside. My credulity gave great amusement to the table full of guests but I have an idea that most of them believed it while Sir William was telling the story. The way he tells these stories is tremendous."

The modern, large-windowed house in Norham Gardens was to become for me a place of relaxation from concentrated study at Magdalen. The library well furnished with rare books and the living room always furnished with unusual people — both rooms looking out over a terraced garden at the rear of the house — this indeed was a fitting setting for the most renowned physician of his day. Osler was short and trim, often wore a red bow-tie, and had an agile way of moving about these rooms. His marked enthusiasm was not the overpowering sort but rather the infectious type which easily transferred itself to an individual or spread through an audience.

Lord Strathcona had much to do with prying him out of his well established American chair — in which he was looked on as the *father* of the Johns Hopkins hospital in Baltimore — and bringing him to Oxford as Regius Professor of Medicine. The extended luncheon table at Norham Gardens would always sparkle with repartee and one seldom left it without seeing it piled with reference books brought in from the library in high excitement to support one side or the other of an important argument. Units of physicians and surgeons came from the United States and Canada for observation and to assist in special war hospitals. Many a problem in hospital administration was solved at Norham Gardens in consultation with Osler, for as he kept up with the last word in medical discovery so he was keen to apply the modern methods of financing. Certainly as far as university financing went the English methods seemed to me antiquated judging from my first bill from our college bursar.

On January 23rd I sent home my first *battels* with the needed explanation. "Enclosed you will find my Battels Bill for the first term. The *Buttery* includes milk, butter, cheese, etc., which I have for lunch. *Kitchen* is chiefly dinners in Hall. *Plateman and Waiters,* a regular charge. *J. C. R. Subscription* entitles one to other things such as breakfast, the morning papers, etc. *Table-cloths,* etc., another regular charge for things used in Hall at dinner. *Porter's Note* is the cost of posting letters, etc. The porter functions in the college Lodge which is a sort of 'outer office' for any member of Magdalen whether in residence or not. *Univ. Dues* are paid by the college to the university for each person as long as he remains a member of the college.

"*Argent* is the charge made for the silver we use in Hall or when we have four or more people to meals in our rooms. This silver is kept at an extraordinary high polish by nothing but scouts rubbing it with their fingers. On an ancient tankard the man next to me in Hall had last night I found the name of one Henry Brett. It was dated 1779 and bore the arms of the college and of the donor. I also had called to my attention that an honor man about 100 years ago was named William Meredith. *Room Rent* is paid in thirds by means of these Bills. When I asked the bursar, Mr. Benecke, regarding *Bedmakers,* he replied in a surprised way, 'Well, someone must take care of the flower-beds.' I believe it covers the cost of all servants, boots, bath and of course my scout, Hunt. Added to this is the smaller bill enclosed from the J. C. R. for my breakfasts, occasional boxes of biscuits, tea, sugar, etc."

In the letter which contained these bills I mentioned another household through whose hospitality I was able to study further the cataclysmic events which were shaping a new world about me. "I take lunch with the Harcourts," I wrote, "thanks to Mother's letter to them, and in the evening I return to have supper with Mrs. Meechen, wife of the Warden of St. Edward's School. This last at the suggestion of Mr. Ferguson, her brother. Teck says I must bicycle to Nuneham Park on Arthur Howard's bike."

I was beginning to think of the war as a great test placed before Oxford's undergraduate body. It had all the seriousness — to me as a student — of a final examination. Whether my Oxford companions now in active service came through "with honors", would be a decisive factor in the outcome of this war. Into the complacency of the university's traditional way of life had been dropped a bomb shell which might mean total destruction of a great cultural tradition. At this point England's survival as a nation might depend on the stamina of these inexperienced boys who were volunteering to die, if necessary, in defense of their country. The details of their experience in training camp and at the front came as strange and exciting news so that their letters home were passed around and read with consuming interest. In the meantime "business as usual" whether in commerce or college had to be carried on in order to preserve the continuity of what the boys were fighting for. This was in itself a hard test for us who were left at home. But the soldiers' letters were a spurring incentive for us to carry on and "keep the home fires burning."

"Here is a bit of a letter from the front which will give you an idea of what our men are up against," I wrote on the 24th and enclosed the following letter.

" 'After I left you I went back on board again and supervised the issuing of jackknives to all the men and saw they got rations. Then about 4:15 we pushed off. . . . We crossed on the *Minnesotta,* a cattle boat which was not as luxurious as it might have been. We had about 800 men and 11 officers on board, but there was no accommodation at all. I slept on the floor of the only cabin in the ship and woke up next morning at 5 a.m. to find that we had arrived off Havre. We were however too late for the tide, so had to cruise about off the bar for twelve hours till 5 in the afternoon, not being allowed to anchor for fear of submarines. It was rather choppy, and a good many people were ill, but I am glad to say I kept well. I counted 56 other steamers round about us, most of them bringing stores over, I expect.

" 'We had our first dose of bully beef and biscuits while on the ship, which was all we could get. Tuesday afternoon the pilot came on board, and at 5 p.m. we crossed the bar and started our trip up the Seine. We came all the way up to Rouen in the steamer, arriving at 10 o'clock on Wednesday morning, but did not disembark till 8. Then we marched about three miles up to this camp which is a huge affair.

" 'It has rained every day for two months, except Xmas Day, so you can imagine the road and mud. We are in tents but they are quite snug as the weather is very mild. They have got an officer's mess here where we get fed and pay three francs a day extra. It is hard to imagine that we are on active service, everything goes on just as usual. There are a great many Indians about who seem to do all the odd jobs and fatigues. My draft of the Cheshires have been warned for the front and may go any hour. When you write please do as I hear the other fellows are having done, namely enclose in each letter a handkerchief. . . . I hear there have been practically no shots fired since the New Year; they seem to have had a sort of truce.' "

Such a letter from an English school boy who had recently been admitted to Oxford and then immediately enlisted in the armed forces was typical of hundreds of others. The quiet way in which such a youth could adjust himself to the severe demands of active military service amazed me. The training made it clear that a soldier was committed to killing the enemy and preserving the life of his comrades and himself. Yet even in the fighting area a clean handkerchief or some sweets from home counted as important. Talking it over with Santayana and others I came to the conclusion that the discipline of the public schools — aimed at equipping a man with self-control under any circumstances — was largely accountable.

The lack of preparation in equipment stood out in such small matters as the enlisted man's appreciation of the gift of a muffler. Mufflers were counted in civilian life as essential for protection against wet and cold under ordinary circumstances. For this reason everybody began knitting mufflers. Why were they not provided by the government? Here again I had competent advisors to point out that Britain was the only European nation which did not have universal military service and that the government, the liberals especially, had no thought of becoming involved in a war. Of this I was to hear more when I had the privilege of conversing with the members of the Asquith cabinet who came for weekend conferences at Nuneham Park.

In response to my mother's shipping me a large case of supplies for my friends in the armed forces I wrote from Magdalen on January 27th, "Things are happening in bunches so that it is hard to find time to write it all down and send it off to you. I must thank you for the box. Quantities of mufflers, plum puddings and candies, the last of these the men are sure to love. There is so little variety in sweets here.

"I may have told you that the Harcourts asked me to Sunday lunch at their country place about six miles from here. I drove out

to Nuneham, as it is called, in a motor with George Fortescue
who left me at the Harcourts' front door and went on to a place
further out. It cost me 6 shillings and I walked back after a
delicious lunch and several stimulating conversations.

"I do not remember whether you went out to Nuneham when
you were here. It is a famous show place. Gates after gates had to
be opened to let us in and the last pair of elaborate iron gates
swung open without anybody appearing at all. A large part of
the house is given over now to a hospital for Belgians. The head
nurse was there and she told me that she had just refused the
charge of the *Hospital of the King of the Belgians* somewhere in
England. Her reason was that the Belgian refugees had become
so disagreeable and unmanageable. This is coming to be popular
sentiment. They act like poor relations who come and sit down
on you and then take it for granted that everything you can do
for them is a duty on your part which entails no thanks from them.
The ones I've seen are a stodgy sort of folk of the lower class.

"I gathered from talking with other guests at Nuneham that
since the present Belgian nation was practically an English creation
there was an obligation. Further it was expedient for the English
to have the good will of their neighbors across the channel after
hostilities ceased. This prompted the English to offer the refugees
the best of their hospitality — the former maid sat and gossiped
in the boudoir and the butcher smoked the best cigars in the
house. Of course it was not expected to go on that way for long.
And the poor Belgians can not be blamed for the continuation
of the war. Much the same thing is happening with the East Indians
who are here in hospitals. One can easily see where there will be
trouble when and if they go back to India. An English official
now in India said to one of the guests at Nuneham who has just
come on from the Far East that he hoped none of these Indians
would return because of the trouble they would bring with them.

"But the vast Georgian manor of Nuneham Park, filled with
art treasures, from which broad terraces go down, down, down in
grassy steps to the Thames river, seems established forever. And
the view up the valley to Oxford where one sees the tower where
I live! Then the large retinue of servants, many of whom live in
houses which form a village on the edge of the Park. There the
massive gates of the main entrance seem guarded with white
peacocks. And within the gates the variety of animals is unbe-

lievable. Guinea pigs and rabbits, pheasant of the most extraordinary rarity, doves, etc. Emus which chase you as you walk through the meadows, kangaroos which become dangerous when they become too tame because they scratch with their front paws, wee prairie dogs sitting on their mounds, a duck which always guards the kennel of a dog it brought up when a small puppy, and a howling collection of different breeds of canine. Many of these are gifts made to the Minister for the Colonies. But there are no elephants!"

The journal goes on to record how I not only walked back to Oxford but "continued on out to St. Edward's School for boys where I took supper with the family of the Warden." The reason why I went by taxi to lunch with the Harcourts and walked bravely back to Oxford needs explanation. It was many years since I had ridden a bicycle. Only George Teck could have persuaded me to mount that beautiful *Sunbeam* geared to Arthur Howard's long legs and start after him down the crowded Iffley Road. When I found I could not manage the English brakes I rolled slowly up to a standing cart horse and taking hold of the animal's nose succeeded in dismounting, much to the astonishment of the driver. My final discouragement was the Heddington Hill where I lost control again and went sailing at a terrific speed that might have rivalled John Gilpin himself. That was why the taxi."

"I naturally see a good deal of Teck and like him the more I come to know him. He has a clear outspoken manner and is a noble stature of a man. If it were not for his nearsightedness he would of course have been one of the first to go to France or wherever his country needed him. When he was dining *en famille* with the King the other day the good monarch was describing his trip to France, of which you may have read. He said President Poincaré came to greet him in a queer costume; a fur hat, green clothes and leggins. The King is evidently quite a stickler in his royal household but along with it he must have a sense of humor."

I was finding that being a *stickler* for form was a natural un-American instinct because my letter concluded, "What I must have before I am accepted for the candidacy for the degree of Bachelor of Letters for which I am reading is a birth certificate. You remember I could not secure one before I left because the Board of Health in Brooklyn said they were not able to grant one since they had no evidence of my having been born. One is fined in this

part of the world if births are not registered." It took some time
for my parents to secure the witness of the widow of a Dr. Kissam
who helped to bring me into the world. On this authority I was
duly registered as having been born on March 22, 1889, at 7:30
p.m. As they laughingly said, I escaped the great blizzard but I
was late for dinner.

On February 3rd my journal read, "I took my Greek Testament
to Dean's Prayers this morning. It is helpful practice to follow the
Lesson in the Greek text. Then I had *breaker* and hustled out to
lecers. One on Church History and a second on English Church
Orders. This latter, a review of monastic life, deals with the growing tendency in America and I feel it will be useful to know how
it operated at a time when it was generally approved in England.

"When I was coming back Dick Graham caught me and took
me to a little midday prayer meeting which is held by the fellows
every day in the chapter room of the University Church in the
High. Just a reading of the Scripture, silent prayer for some ten
minutes and ending with the Lord's Prayer. Such a service comes
very well at noon in the midst of a superactivated existence created
by war demands and the deep stirrings of a constantly changing
code of life. For the sake of the few who seek the advice of God
the country may be saved."

In the face of all that was foreign in the British reaction —
especially in time of crisis — it was reassuring for an American
student to talk things over with fellow students from America.
Thus the journal goes on to note, "I came back to my room for
my bread and butter and cheese and honey, and then went to
Scofield Thayer's room across the Cloister. He had just been
entertaining another Harvard classmate, Francis Butler-Thwing
(as he now calls himself since the trouble with his father). Francis
has become naturalized as an English citizen in order to spend
the rest of his active life in the British army. Any heavy brain
work such as he was noted for at Harvard might risk a recurrence
of his illness and therefore it is perhaps the best thing for him. He
is a delightful person with a literary genius."

Francis Butler-Thwing, whose father was president of Western
Reserve University and whose cousin, Nicholas Murray Butler,
was president of Columbia, had suffered a mental breakdown
during his senior year at Harvard. He could not forgive his father
for committing him to an asylum but he did return to Harvard and

took his degree with honors. I had been his close friend through it all and would continue to be during the tragic days which lay before him.

"Francis wants to make a social thing of it. To this end he trained with the Coldstream Guards for sometime at his own expense, but in the end they would not have him. He asked me to use my influence with Prince George, but I go rather easy in that line. I did, however, mention to Teck that Francis wanted to meet the commander of the London regiment. He thought B-T's voice was against him — thought he spoke with a sort of north-country English accent. Voice seems to count so much. It is taken to be one of the ear marks of refinement.

"What a curious thing English refinement is! It is acknowledged by everybody that there is a class of gentlemen which is different from ordinary people, and the term gentleman does not include polite trades-people. I think in America we make the same distinction but we are too embarrassed to come right out and say it. With us it seems a snobbish matter, with them it is merely a fact. As for Royalty, Mrs. Harcourt said the other day at lunch that she would rather be anything than a petty royalty. To be king or queen or nothing. There is a great deal in that. Her husband is referred to as *the first commoner.* Harcourt and Morgan, what a combination of two powerful families, the one English and the other American. The Harcourts are a credit to both.

"We three Harvard men of the Class of 1913 took a long walk out toward Heddington where I believe Matthew Arnold specially loved to walk. Francis and Scofield Thayer had seen something of our ambassador in London. Mr. Page told Scofield that there seemed to be no place in London society for the daughter of an ambassador. He spoke rather as though he had depended on his daughter — who was president of her class at Bryn Mawr and generally popular — to carry off the social end of his diplomatic duties because of his wife's disqualifications. But when he was invited out his wife and not his daughter is asked to come along too. Somebody at Sir William Osler's last Sunday said that our American embassy in London was now employing 1,200 clerks, etc. By the way, Sir William is planning to go out with a Canadian contingent and his son, Revere, with him."

It is pleasant now to recall walking with my two so different Harvard friends arm in arm along the country by-way where so

many undergraduates had walked before, discussing the American
ambassador's problem. It was not merely to maintain our American neutrality, as we saw it, but to survey the prospect which lay
ahead — as it were over the brow of the hill we then climbed. The
hills about Oxford University should be preserved as a national
park if the mind which the colleges have nurtured in past generations is to continue to dream dreams and see visions. Both of my
companions were in time to suffer for their mental tensity but
they were true to their dreams. As for the ambassador, Walter
Hines Page, he was destined to perform worthy service at the
Court of St. James's, and his wife in her genuine, homey manner
was to win the hearts of the British people.

"I came back," the journal continued, and "got through some
good work on the Sarum. To hear choral evensong coming from
the chapel across the cloister lends enchantment to these old buildings. The chapel and hall raise their lighted windows high above
the dark arches of the cloister as though they were part of a
stage setting. And as it were a back drop behind and above all
— with one side bright from the glare of hidden street lamps —
rises the Magdalen tower.

"I went to *hall*. Teck had gone to have a spree with his sisters
in London. Talked with Ginsberg, our Hebrew, on whether the
semicircular canals or the muscles are more important in keeping
the balance of the body. I thought the former. He had been told
to read a book by Prof. Parker of Harvard. I well remember when
I went to Parker and tried to have him raise my grade B+ to an
A, that he told me if he changed it at all he would make it a C+,
a grade for which he was famous. There is almost a sadistic quality
in the disciplining mind of a professor.

"Humphrey Vernon asked me to have coffee with him, but I
had promised to go down the High with Banner to see why my
hyacinth bulbs had not come. Three honey jars with a bulb in
each I had ordered for my desk — all for one *bob*. I wondered
whether my scout would approve. But he tells me the poet-laureate's
son did something of the sort when he was living in these rooms
before me.

"Came back and did some more good work. This Sarum liturgy
is a sort of Baedeker guide which was necessary when there were
so many different books of prayer in use in England. Hough came
in. He had an ancestor years ago who was president of Magdalen.

Said he wished they used the first Prayer Book now. That is progress if your face is on the other side of your head! Long argument. Went to bed a bit after eleven."

The flower stands of Oxford were a glory in themselves, and a constant temptation. There was a relationship, in my undergraduate mind, between the potential bulbs on my college desk and the full blown lilies on our Magdalen shield. I was fortunate in having the companionship of such an artistic soul as Delmar Banner, and I congratulate myself today in having recognized his talent. In time he was to become one of the outstanding portrait painters of England. I put in more than one good word for his artistic career with his father who was set on his son going into some sort of civil service.

I was beginning to understand the general acceptance of a traditional pattern of war. There were battle areas where hostile armies fought under international laws and there were noncombatant areas where civilians continued to live under a recognized immunity and a reasonable security from enemy attack. The fact that Germany had violated these traditional rulings was counted barbaric and to the history student at Oxford it bracketed them with the hordes of Huns who had overrun Europe in the same lawless manner. But since the Germans had stooped to an alliance with the "terrible Turk" they had seemingly given up all thought of abiding by the code of western civilization. Nor was it surprising to hear that they were proclaiming a culture of their own. Nevertheless, the moral and intellectual nature of the English people must not be warped by compromising with the new standards set up by the enemy. Conscription belonged to a military state, and the idea of *total war* was inconceivable. Therefore, as the journal recorded we carried on.

"Dean's Prayers again this morning. (4th February 1915.) This short service with no music which Brighters (Canon F. E. Brightman, my tutor) arranged is like a shower bath for the soul. It doesn't take long and you come away clean and refreshed. Then to Lock's lecture on the Thessalonians and to one on the Old Testament Theology by a rather affected young D. D. named Simpson. I cut Dr. Sanday this morning because I was anxious to get something else done at my desk.

"Just before lunch Teck came in. He had a capital time in London at the Pantomime. It seems the moment when one of the

actors on the stage cried, 'Hark, the royal steps,' something let
loose behind the scenes and went tumbling down with a loud
noise. George and his sister went into roars of laughter — and no
one else did. I wonder if his aunt, the queen, would have had the
same sense of humor.

"It seems Teck had received a letter from Francis Butler-
Thwing which I had advised Francis to write. I may not have
told you that Francis wanted the Prince to use his influence in
helping him get into the Brigade of Guard. Teck blamed the whole
thing on me and said I should have to write the reply for him. So
I was in the position of answering my own letter.

"I had my lunch. Then I started out with Banner to pay a bill
for framing. He had had some of his watercolors framed for his
room, and since he had given me a large watercolor he did of
Freiberg cathedral which everybody admires I wanted to have it
also framed. With that and a sensitive engraving of Magdalen
from Heddington Hill my part of the bill came to nearly a pound.
But it was Thursday and all the shops were closed. Therefore we
took out Howard's bicycle for another try. It is so long since I
rode one of these contraptions that I rather forget how to
dismount. I think I told you what a mess I made of it with Teck.
But Banner showed me how he did it, and I soon caught on. The
roads are good after one gets away from the city."

The 6th of February "turned out to be a wonderful blue and
white morning" (blue sky and white clouds) and Teck and I
decided we would go with the beagling party. Teck asked me to
come to an early lunch with him. But the scout did not bring it
till it was too late and therefore we took sandwiches instead. About
15 of us took the break at the foot of Queen's Lane. We arrived
in Abingdon in the first part of the afternoon. The little hounds
were let loose, and finally we struck a scent and all started running. While I was trudging over the rough fields I ate my sandwiches. As a result my stomach was feeling a bit upset when
after an hour or two we made a *kill*. The hare had taken to the
water and was drowned. When they had cut off the *mask* and
pads they threw the carcass to the beagles. It was a miserably
bloody sight and did not help to settle my luncheon at all. They
surprised me by pushing a bleeding foot of the hare into my
hand because I was *in at the kill*. I shall have it mounted and
send it home to you."

Some people like to hunt, others like to fish, and it was the latter which I preferred. Nevertheless, this Magdalen-New College pack of beagles had to be kept going for the men who would return from the front. After all the bloodshed they would have experienced in their fighting abroad it was hard for me to understand how they would still like to hunt when they came home. However, for my part the exercise did me good and I was to find in it a hearty kind of companionship with men which I could never have come to enjoy in any other way. I was beginning to note that these English youths who were exhilarated by having their crew win on the river, or their side excell on the cricket field were not so keen about defeating their opponent in single combat. What did give them satisfaction in personal contest was pitting themselves against nature — men against the sea, men scaling a steep mountain side, even men trying to match their skill and endurance against the sly fox or this hare. This seemed to interpret in part their attitude toward the trench warfare in which they were engaged. They would come back from France triumphant that they had been able to endure the cold and the wet and the mental and physical strain of it all. They had won the battle against hostile elements of nature. This meant more to the individual Britisher than killing the Germans — always remembering that they did want their side to win the war.

It was Lincoln's Birthday 1915, a reminder of what some Englishman called *the most gallant war of history*. And, for the time I was experiencing, this was in England a gallant war of volunteer crusaders. It gave a new significance to day-to-day living at home. "The most thrilling time I have had since last I wrote was last night with Dr. Varley Roberts," my journal continued. "He calls himself an 'organ grinder' and I think he hankers after a title or some such recognition as was accorded his predecessor, Sir John Stainer. But he has written, *Seek Ye the Lord* and about 70 other popular anthems and is about as well known as any of our Magdalen choir masters. He asked me to call, and I took with me an old *Order of Mass — 1521* which I am copying out on my typewriter. He explained the music in a most fascinating way. I wish I had time to tell you. He is dead set against the revival of the ancient way of singing the chants without *mensibus cantorum*. Brighters is on the other side. I agree with both of them separately.

Sept. 11 1914

Dear Brett.

I am delighted to
have your letter. & congrat:
ulate you on the achieve:
ment of this real step.
A _padre_ in the "Devil's
own " is indeed a
piquant but promising
paradox. And I hope &
trust. it is the beginning
of really valuable service.
What do you do

between while ? If you
come here come & see us.
We are just back. for
good.
Lady Warren joins in
every good wish.
The last time I wrote to
Garland's Hotel was to Dr.
Van Dyke. I think this
'n'. should be changed to
'l.' suggest shall I. the
manager
             Yours v sincerely
                 Herbert Warren

Letter from Sir Herbert Warren, President of Magdalen College, to Brett
Langstaff on the occasion of the latter's enlisting in the Artists Rifles,
and referring to the author, Henry Van Dyke.

"I took advantage of a rainy afternoon to call on Sir Herbert Warren last Sunday. Undergraduates are expected to do this once in a long while. He lays such stress on little personal matters that it becomes rather embarrassing. Mostly the guests sit and talk generalities. When they run out of these there is an awful silence for minutes at a time.

"Sir Herbert is a genial old soul, however, and his good nature leads to many traditional stories with fictitious trimmings. The other day he called me across the street and insisted on knowing how I knew the Warden of St. Edward's and his brother-in-law Foxton Ferguson. Then, when I told him that I had walked 15 miles from Nuneham to St. Edward's, he was much pleased to find that I was much stronger than I looked. What a contrast he is to President Lowell! I have had another letter from Dean Hurlbut in which he bids me tell the English I meet the feeling of the majority of the Americans, i.e. 'Our hearts are with them in the struggle.'

"My work is progressing well. Prince George read an entire Liturgy off for me while I typed it last night. I don't suppose I shall always have princes to read my services for me. We worked all night (till 12) at it."

I was now beginning to grasp the new learning — or new method of learning, if you will — with which Oxford was imbuing me. It was as though I were discovering the rudiments or principles of learning for the first time, and I was exhilarated by the freedom it gave one. For four years I had argued against socialist minded students at Harvard who were starting a Fabian movement in America. During my recent period of training at the General Theological Seminary in New York I had fought against the reactionary attitude of a Catholic minded faculty who were indoctrinating seminarians with the discipline of tradition. Both these movements seemed prescribed with codal limits which stifled the normal breathing of the spirit and confused the student's intellect. Now at Oxford I was being given the liberty of working out my own ideas with the aid of tutors, original source material and, above all, I was given time. I was learning to be patient with myself as long I was persevering.

"My work is still progressing," I wrote on February 14th. "I have long rolls of *kitchen paper* on which I am pasting in columns the versions of the *Order for Holy Communion* — from the ancient

Latin to the present English, Scottish and American — typed out
by myself with the aid of Teck. It is exceedingly interesting to
work from original copies. At one time the only known copy of
the first *English Ordo* belonged to the Pres. of Magdalen. I have
all the precious books right here on my table to work from.

"I went *biking* with Teck day before yesterday. He showed me
how to get on by the pedal. It meant getting on and off about
50 times. He was so important about it that when — a short time
after — he started down the Nuneham hill and could not control
his own brakes but was run away with by his machine, I had the
laugh on him. I came back by myself through the most picturesque
little villages I have ever seen. On the way I met a bunch of *O. T.
Corps* fellows who were practicing map-reading. My reason for
returning early was to go to tea with an American, Norman Nash.

"Nash and I went to hear Dr. Scott Holland on the Fourth
Gospel after tea. Dr. H. has a theory of which I shall say more
when I have learned more. We then went to a book shop. Norman
had bought a certain set of books for 15/ and then we found the
same thing — except it was not in a large paper edition — for 7/6
in another shop. He was terribly put out because he prided himself on bargains in books. It was a set of three volumes in good
condition pub 1837 with illustrations of Oxford, so I bought them.

"There are great talks about serving in Serbia. It is a temptation. But my personal resolution now is that these are my trenches
here in Magdalen and it is my duty to stick to them and study
for my own battles to come."

My reference to a rising sympathy in England for the Serbs
indicated that the reports of the fall and recapture of Belgrade
were being talked of by government people at Nuneham. The
bombardment of the unfortified Serbian capital they considered
inexcusable, an act of vandalism. It was unprovoked and seemed
to serve no military purpose. Of the 700 buildings struck by bombs,
shell or shrapnel, I learned, only 60 were State property. The fact
that among these were the university — which was the heart of
Serbian culture — and the museum which housed priceless relics
of Rome and Macedon, strengthened my faith in Santayana's idea
that the war was basically a contest of ideologies. Also foreign lega-
tions, hospitals and pharmacies — all suffered in the Austro-
Hungarian lust for revenge. The university was said to be so badly
hit that the building with its classrooms, laboratories, libraries and

workshops, was completely demolished. I could not help feeling that this might have been Oxford itself, if the enemy had its way.

The following day my journal noted, "I have just come back from an exhausting tramp into the country with Humphrey Vernon who is getting in shape for long marches. We went out by train a bit and then struck off into the country toward the village of Dorcester. Then back. Tea at Clifton Hampden. Took the train at Culham, and arrived home in time for chapel.

"There is a swarm of people up for *smalls*. The idea now is to pass this entrance exam — which you remember they made me take part of when I came here first — and then enlist in the armed forces. For some reason the university seems to encourage this.

"Our aunt-to-be Chadwick has written me several times and as a result I am going out to Bath to see and be seen as soon as I get a chance this vac. Miss Chadwick's father had already died, the old colonel was 86.

"A cute little girl — daughter of a professor — joined us when we were beagling the other day. She persuaded a couple of us to bring her back to tea a bit early, and as we were rollicking down the road making believe we were Belgians by speaking French to those we met, we came across a photographer. He snapped us dancing hand in hand with our feet in the air. (What will the professor say?) I'll send you the picture together with a couple of other snaps of the Prince of Wales and Prince George out beagling — and also the pad I mentioned before.

"I have just dined with the President and Lady Warren. Banner went along and two other fellows. Sir Herbert had recently dined with Lord Fisher in London. The latter had remarked that the submarine had seen its day and that now the Admiralty knew what the German submarines were like they could deal with them in the future. The 'Pree' had also sat next to Sir John Jellicoe at one of the King's dinners. It seems John Ruskin had been very keen on making practical use of the undergraduates' exercising, rather than have it wasted merely in sport. And when Ruskin was a professor here, a number of his students including Sir Herbert assisted in constructing a road under the direction of the art critic. Good dinner but we stayed only a short time. The president's residence, with its leaded glass window bulging out into the cloister, is beautifully appointed. The official guest rooms adjoining this have their little windows also baying out over the cloister. There the *Pree* told me that among others Theodore Roosevelt had slept. Ever since he read the ambassador's commendation of the D.B.E. in America the Pree makes some reference to it. This time he observed that my mother was certainly *a true daughter of the Empire,* and hoped she would some day come over here.

"Went to call on Cookson with Banner after dinner. HE SAYS I MUST HAVE MY BIRTH CERTIFICATE! The next meeting of the Board is March first. I am getting to see that a lot of *Cooker's* browbeating and sarcasm is meant in fun. It seemed pretty cruel at first. Here is his new story of the war. An officer announced to some of the English soldiers in France that the French would retreat in a certain place at a certain time. Arrangements were made for letting them back. They turned out to be Germans in French uniform and did considerable damage behind the lines. Whoo said it was troo!!"

The very fact that this and many other such stories could be related to a keenly interested audience at home without producing a feeling of resentment at the trickery and unfairness of the enemy indicated an attitude toward war which was to change after the first two years. At the time I found it difficult to understand. Someone tried to explain to me that it was like a game of chess — a game which was used at military colleges such as Sandhurst to train students in strategy — and therefore you deliberately deceived your opponent. And if the high command found it expedient to sacrifice the lives of one of their units, it was nothing different from sacrificing a pawn or a knight. Such sacrifice was justified if it gained a position on the board. In playing this game of war it was expected that many pieces would be lost. The object was to win the war. My friend Banner rather sided with the pacifists. But to me it seemed that the men who enlisted voluntarily gave their lives right then and there. The sacrifice was according to the individual's own free will. If he were killed, the supreme sacrifice was his. And if it were made to preserve his honor and integrity, it was justified.

On February 18th I copied an excerpt from a friend's letter and sent it home saying, "Here is part of a letter from the trenches, almost. I don't give his name because I have not his permission to relay it, but he is an officer younger than myself who has recently gone out.

" 'The day after I wrote you we moved further north into new billets, so as to be in a more convenient spot for the firing line if required. The whole brigade was on the road at 7:30 a.m. last Monday morning, and we marched solidly with a few short halts, till 1 p.m. Our company headed the column and my platoon happened to be the first of the company with the consequence that I was right in front, marching right behind the general and his staff. It was quite a fine day but the roads were covered with a thick mud and loose stones, and we had to march in great coats and full equipment which was rather hard work. A good many fell out, especially among the natives. We only covered about 15 miles altogether but of course when it is such a big body of troops you can only move slowly.

" 'Even though we are supposed to be resting in our billets the time is fully occupied in keeping the men fit and teaching them all sorts of things. For instance I have been machine gunning all week: learning all the mechanism, taking it to pieces, and putting it together again, learning how to repair it and fire it.

" 'The idea is that we are now going to have six machine guns per battalion instead of the previous two, so as to cope with the Germans. Really it is the most extraordinary warfare and so antiquated. There are parties of men, some learning hand bomb throwing, others bomb gunning and others catapulting. The bomb throwers have to get out of the trenches and then throw their hand grenades into the enemy's trench. They go off with a pretty good bang but the effect is very local. Then the bomb gun party, which I was watching at their practice this afternoon, have a funny little drain-pipe for a gun, with a small hole in the bottom through which they light the fuse with an ordinary match. Its extreme range is 250 yards, and you can see the bomb coming as it turns over and over in the air, and then explodes with a terrific bang. It is filled with lots of jagged iron and broken glass and makes a pretty big hole in the ground, but is also very local. Then the catapult: 3 straight boards and a very strong spring, hurls the ordinary hand bombs. Quite like Roman warfare, isn't it? We see aeroplanes every day reconnoitering and hear the guns booming incessantly. I believe both sides are running rather short of ammunition.

" 'Our time for the trenches has come at last and I shall probably be in them by the time that you get this. We move out of here early, about 2 p.m. The part I don't like is that I hear the trenches are *full* of water, in places up to your waist, and last time two fellows fell into holes made by shells and went into mud and water up to their necks. We have to stay in about 12 hours at a time and then come out and seize as much hot rum and water as we can; I only hope it does not freeze as they say it did last time.

" 'They seem to think out here that as soon as the weather clears up definitely and when K's army arrives, they will make a big dash somewhere and play for a grand slam, after which the war may drag on till next September with a kind of guerrilla warfare and will then end.' "

My personal reaction to this letter from the trenches was contained in the opening of my next writing home. "There seems little we can do here for the self-sacrificing men we hope will return someday, unless it be to hold things together so that there will be an Oxford for them to come back to. I have sent your mufflers etc. off to Phil Pye-Smith who has some fifty men under him at Farnham, Surrey. His mother took a house near him and had Phil and some of his fellow officers billeted on her.

"The photographic reproduction of my birth certificate (just arrived from the U.S.A.) quite mystified the dons here who had only seen the process used for manuscripts. I am now fully registered as a candidate for the degree of B.Litt. which I should receive two years after the day I came here. The subject of my course as approved by the Board of Theology is as follows: 'The Order for the Administration of the Lord's Supper or Holy Communion, as set forth in the prayer books of the Church of England, of the Church of Scotland and of the Episcopal Church in the United States of America.'

"Several letters have come from Canada. Aunt Minn Macklem with whom we spent those delightful summers on Arthur's Island in the Georgian Bay. And Uncle Edwin's wife with messages to the girl in Bath whom his brother is going to marry. What times we boys had during summer vacations at the homestead in Yonge Street where Uncle Gari now has his hospital! And again Dora Denison has also written from Toronto. She seems to be very happy and says her brother, Edgar, is with the *Patricias*. A Canadian officer at the Harcourts yesterday said that the casualties among the *Pats* in the recent engagement were heavy. If anything goes wrong with Edgar perhaps I can get the

Harcourts to take him in at Nuneham, for it serves as a good hospital for convalescents. Personally I have never felt healthier in my life. People are constantly telling me how well I look. I wish everybody could be the same — especially the men at the front."

The use of these great country houses for the wounded entailed not alone the expense of upkeep by the owners but also a personal supervision. The Viscountess Harcourt — as she was in time to be — was doing this in an efficient way. Lady Astor — to whose hospital in her Cliveden mansion Sir William Osler often spoke of going — was doing the same thing. Visiting with the patients made an extra reason for my frequent visits to Nuneham Park and afforded an opportunity of coming to know the Harcourts in a personal way. The fact that I was a youthful student from a neutral but well-wishing country seemed to relieve the tense atmosphere of the restless group of convalescent soldiers.

"While most of the fellows were out beagling," I noted on February 21st, "I was giving a tea to some of the convalescents from Nuneham. Mrs. Harcourt had said that the reason she and Mr. H could not have tea with me at Oxford was that when they come down for the weekends they feel they have to give their time to the patients at the Park. Thus I concluded the best way for me to reciprocate for the hospitality they have shown me would be to help them entertain the patients by having them at Magdalen. Therefore I planned a tea in my rooms and invited as many of the patients as could come. And this is how it went.

"Banner helped me decorate my rooms. Everything that was gorgeous in his rooms plus everything gorgeous in my rooms did make an artistic effect. Among other things he lent me a huge bunch of white lilies and lots of tulips.

"First came the fellows who had refrained from beagling to assist in the entertainment — Dick Graham, Bateson and Robert Harvey. Then from Nuneham came Mrs. Alexander, the head nurse at the hospital who comes from South Africa and knows our friends the Scotscurvings. With her came Commandant Giron, a Belgian of the rank of *Major,* in his uniform. He goes to the front on Monday. Also Dr. Scrimger who goes out with the rest of the Canadian contingent this week. Then Mme. Clavel who is governess for the Harcourts' children, and Commandant Tourney. And finally, the president, Sir Herbert Warren. To have the president come to an undergraduate's rooms was an unheard of break in the custom of Magdalen just as it was at Harvard when President Lowell came. But Sir Herbert was really the life of the party. He lost all his usual stiffness and milled about quite merrily.

"The party went off smoothly and I feel that it accomplished a lot, besides the fact that it helped in the general cause. They all went to chapel afterwards and finally motored away delighted.

"Today, Sunday, after calling on the Hon. Mrs. Matheson of whom I have spoken before, I went on to the Oslers'. I met Revere on the way and he said he was coming up to see me sometime after *hall*. Lady O was in, also Mrs. Maxmuller and others. Sir W came in later. I may go to France to do some war work during the *long vac*. I will write more of it."

It was pathetic to observe the bewilderment and concern with which the dons were contemplating their college now that practically the entire student body had been snatched away from under them. For generations the structure of college life had been built on the assumption that university education was necessary to the well being of the nation. Now, suddenly the nation's bulwark proved to be the amassing of physical force against the physical force of the enemy, and apparently the masters of arts and letters were no longer needed. Even the masters of science were no longer masters — free to resarch the phenomena of the physical world — but servants to the government demands for carrying on what was becoming a mechanized war. We who remained as undergraduates seemed to be cherished by the dons as the remnant of what might be called the *lost generation*. They knew the war must end but they feared that the Magdalen which they loved could never begin again.

"Monday morning (Magdalen College, 23rd February 1915) we had a special commemoration service. While the choir was singing a chant the Estates Bursar went about to all the dons and choir etc. distributing small amounts of money. Each of the choir received two pence while the dons had four pence and the president a shilling. This money was given ages ago at this time of the year, some say, because there is more sickness than usual in this season — perhaps caused by excessive dampness and floods. This money might have been used to buy medicine.

"In the afternoon Brighters came in for tea. I was keen to have him see just how I was doing my work. Prince George, who had been helping me, was asleep in one of my chairs when Mr. B came. Banner and Alington dropped in later.

"My scout brought a note from the *Pree* in which he asked me for 'the names of the ladies and gentlemen I met at your room on Saturday at that charming little tea party that I enjoyed so much. . . .' Further he added, 'We spoke about the special commemoration and the Dole of Fourpenny bits in chapel. As these last are rare I am sending you one in case you would like to have it as a souvenir.'

"We asked Brighters about the commemoration service. He considered the Dole money which he had received that morning had more to do with the spiritual season of Lent than with the climatic season I had been told. He said he also received a certain amount of sugar as Dean and that some fee was paid to Mr. Benecke in the form of a load of hay. He has a keen and dry sense of humor and a wonderful knowledge of Liturgics which makes him interesting and valuable to my work.

"Brighters finally noticed with some amazement the long sheets of kitchen paper covering the walls of my *sitter*. On these I had pasted in comparative columns (typed) the various texts of the Communion Service because Brighters had advised me — 'to see the subject as a whole.' He studied them carefully without comment. Then, waddling over to the window he paused for a few minutes gazing at the tower and rubbing his check as though he were plunged in serious thought. We waited. And finally the words came. 'Langstaff, my advice is on some clear day when there is no wind you attach all these sheets together in one large roll. Then climb the tower and let it unwind so that it hangs down the side of the tower. When you have done this return to your room and study the subject as a whole from this window. You can easily do this,' he added, 'with the help of your American, horn-rimmed glasses.'

"While he was here a letter came from Mr. Lewis Harcourt. I had sent back with the party which came from Nuneham for tea with me one of the copies of the *New York Times* because two had been sent me from America by mistake. It showed a picture of the *Lusitania*. Mr. Harcourt had told me at lunch some time ago that when the *Lusitania* neared the coast of England the passengers brought flags from their staterooms and hung

STATION, CULHAM.
TELEGRAMS, NUNEHAM-COURTENAY.
TELEPHONE Nº 86 ABINGDON.

NUNEHAM PARK,
OXFORD.

21. 2. 15

Dear Mr Langstaff
    Very many thanks
for the papers.
I am told that the
American insistence on
their flag on the Lusitania
was not when it <u>arrived</u>
at Liverpool but when
it left again.
It left however under
the British flag that time.

    Yours very sincly

    L. Harcourt.

Letter from Viscount Harcourt, Secretary of State for The Colonies, referring to the sinking of the Lusitania, written to Brett Langstaff at Oxford.

them over the side of the vessel. This is his note. 'Dear Mr. Langstaff, — Very many thanks for the papers. I am told that the American insistence on their flag on the *Lusitania* was not when it *arrived* at Liverpool but when it left again. It left, however, under the British flag that time. Yours very sincerely, L. Harcourt.' "

The *Lusitania* which Lord Harcourt mentioned in his letter was of course the Cunard liner with the famous Captain Dow. It had been waylaid by an enemy cruiser as it sailed out from New York on August 4, 1914, the day war was declared. At that time I had heard how the *Lusitania's* captain eluded the attacker and escaped in a fog. It was reported that this same Captain Dow had hoisted the American flag on February 10th — when the *Lusitania* was off the Irish coast — and again escaped the enemy vessels. This was an old and legitimate stratagem which brought no comment from the American government. But eight days later Germany gave notice that she would sink all vessels in the waters around Great Britain without warning. Because this was in violation of all international law the date was spoken of in England as *Pirate Day*. It naturally was a matter of concern to Lulu Harcourt and his government as well as to my fellow Americans.

"Just back from Nuneham (27th February). I rang up Mrs. Harcourt at 12.30 — as she had told me always to do — and bicycled out for lunch. Met 'Lulu' coming in from the garden with a basket of pruning tools. Went in most informally to lunch in the small dining room just as though I might be going down stairs a bit late for lunch at home. Stayed a little after to talk with Mrs. Harcourt.

"I can not tell you how much this means. How fortunate I have been in my friends and how little I am able to do in return! But it acts as a spur to my work. What a real ambition it must be to strive to be truly worth knowing!

"You will be glad to hear that I am doing English history. I find to understand the history of the Prayer Book I must know the history of the people who created it. The more I delve into the work the more I can see the practical use I can put it all to in the future. And when a thing is practical in my own estimation — however incorrect that may be — the battle is half won.

"I am reading away and scribbling down on cards whatever I think may be useful for the dissertation. These cards filed in order should make an invaluable storehouse of relevant facts. It is a method Sir William Osler uses and has suggested my using. You see the Reformation period must be gone over thoroughly for out of that arose important causes for the changes in the English text. Then later came the influences which altered the Scottish and American liturgies. I shall send home the chapters of the dissertation as they come along. It will be a regular book when I finish it. Or will this war finish it?"

It was going to be harder as time went on for me to resist the wave of crusading enthusiasm which was sweeping so many of my friends into Lord Kitchener's volunteer army. The day might come — if the fighting continued — that the government would see the wisdom of restraining men engaged in essential services or preparing for them. But for the present the war was looked on as a short interruption in the professional careers of those who had enlisted. Personally I feared that once I had become part of the heroic defensive forces I would find it almost impossible to return to concentrated study at college. It seemed obvious, however, that after the war there was going to be need of men of my vocation to bring the world back to normal. The church would be essential to reconstruction.

"Saturday night (1st March 1915) after I had come back from the Harcourts, Varley Roberts asked me to come up in the organ loft with him. The service he played was one I had often sung in St. John's, Brooklyn. In all I believe he has composed more church music than any other living musician. He and I have come to be great friends. The most beautiful part is that the words of the service mean so much to him. He would stop his accompaniment in the organ loft to remark on the beauty of a psalm while the choir in the stalls below would go on singing acappella without him. It would be at a point where the psalm mentioned something about pits and stumbling, and Varley would say to me. 'Lots of people stumble. It's so easy, you know!' He has been an organist for 53 years.

"On Sunday I accepted Lady Osler's invitation for lunch. One of the Houghton Mifflin firm and a Mr. Harrison were guests. Also an army surgeon and another fellow. Sir William showed us some of his rare treasure books, and he has a fortune of them. One ancient illustrated Syrian botany that had been valued at 200 pounds, etc. Several interesting volumes of Shelley first editions.

"Sir William had been Walt Whitman's physician when he was teaching at Johns Hopkins and the poet was living near Philadelphia. He recalled Whitman's work room piled knee deep with old newspapers. We talked about volunteering to serve in France. It appealed to me as a possible way to make the long vacation of nearly four months count for something in the war effort. Banner is keen to go out during the vac and he would like it if we could go together. I want to have something to do with the good part of this war — such as helping the sick and wounded — and Sir William says he will be able to place me all right. But on the other hand I am getting into my work and the more deeply I go the more I see there is to be done.

"When we came away from the Oslers', Mr. Harrison took a walk with me and stopped in for tea in my room. When he told me he was trying to be an author I sympathized with him. But when he casually mentioned he had written a book called *Queed* I realised he was one of our most popular novelists. Needless to say I was taken aback, a long way back. He told me the history of his life, the early part of which he spent in Brooklyn on the Heights. He is now living in Richmond, Virginia."

When people would refer to us war-time undergraduates as a link with Oxford's past and future I was painfully aware that I was a weak link at best because I had never experienced the undergraduate life under normal conditions. I was more fortunate, however, than the men who were just coming up from school. I had had four years of college life at Harvard and a year before at Columbia not to mention my experience at the theological seminary in New York. I could in some part therefore appreciate the tradition imparted to me by Oxford men returning from the armed services on leave and from dons and college servants in residence. The war seemed to be settling down into a long stretch of watchful waiting, and I could see that I was going to need patience and to counsel the same to my friends who never seemed to realize how much older I was than they.

"The life here, except for my engrossing work and an occasional visit to the Harcourts and the Oslers', is becoming rather dull. Especially when compared with what I hear of the pre-war gaiety. My scout has told me some of the stunts they used to do.

"On one occasion the fellow who occupied my rooms before — Bridges, the poet's son — put up a sign in large letters on the slanting roof over our room reading, DOWN WITH THE DONS. Since it was practically over the Prince of Wales' rooms it was most conspicuous to the crowds of visitors who came every day. Several nights after, Bridges heard somebody on the roof and discovered that a couple of the younger dons were after the sign with a ladder. They were removing the sign. When they had left, Bridges took one of the large sheets of blotting paper from his desk and wrote on it, SOLD AGAIN, and climbing up pasted this in place of the one the dons had taken down.

"Another tale. The inner wall of the cloister is braced with buttresses on which some humorous sculptor has placed almost life sized stone effigies illustrating the Bible — plus his own imagination. One summer vac Lady Warren was planning to have a garden party in the cloister, and about two minutes before the guests arrived each figure was discovered wearing a top hat and pyjamas. Of course such things never happen now. One gloomy person the other day declared that the university could not recover in ten years. But it has been subsidised by the government (if the bill was passed today) and the real work will go on even if the sports drop off and lighter amusements disappear. It will go on but in a very different spirit.

"All the English people are joyful over the prospect of a victory in the Dardanelles and the hope of wheat. Lulu Harcourt tells me wheat is being cornered in Chicago and that the release of abundant stores of grain in the Turkish port will break it. A corner in such a staple product is a miserable thing at best, but I do think in time of stress, such as the present, it is almost criminal. All shilling cakes have gone up a penny and bread about the same. You probably feel this at home too."

The first official hint of this adventure in the Dardanelles came on February 15th after the victory at the Falkland Islands had freed the cruisers and battleships of the British navy. I can still recall Lord Harcourt saying to me at Nuneham, "Tomorrow the world will know that the *Queen Elizabeth* is sailing up the Dardanelles and that her guns outdistance the guns of the Turkish forts." Another of the cabinet ministers spending a weekend at Nuneham had told me that Winston Churchill had talked all night in order to persuade what had originally been a solid opposition to this attack. The bombarding of the outer forts by the *Queen* and other vessels opened on February 19th and the first phase of the campaign was described by Churchill as "successful beyond our hopes."

My proximity with these outstanding figures, scholars and states-men, was not disillusioning but it did impress me with the unpredic-tableness of the human equation as regarding those who were directing the thought and action of the nation. They were men who had access to facts, past and present, but when the final deci-sion was called for, they were just simple human beings using their common sense.

My letter of March 13th noted that "this is the last day of term when we go before the faculty seated at the high table in Hall for the Collector Reports." This, to me, was a deeply impressive scene. The high ceilinged dining hall — which at dinner time with glistening silver and white cloths on the long candle-lighted tables took on a festive air — now at *collecers* appeared dark and fore-boding. The few undergraduates gathered in whispering groups near the entrance doors, and at the far end, where a table on a raised platform extended almost the entire width of the Hall, sat the dons — the dons draped in long black gowns, and the students clad in short sleeveless affairs worn over their jackets as always on official occasions.

Finally I could hear my name being called. I proceeded nervously up toward the high-table and on the way received a comforting glance from a boy who was returning from being questioned. Sir Herbert Warren greeted me as though I were the guest of honour and asked me to be seated on his right. Then, by way of conver-sation, it would seem, he enquired of my tutor — whose place was on the other side of the table, some distance down — "How is Mr. Langstaff getting on?" Canon Brightman was at his height of boredom and apparently had no idea as to how I was doing in my studies. The president was satisfied that there were no complaints from that quarter and endeavoured to prompt some of the other dons to contribute to the conversation regarding me. I did have friends among them but none seemed inclined to say a word.

The awkward silence was broken by Sir Herbert's genial voice enquiring about my health. The answer was absurdly obvious, I was bursting with health. Then came the questions as to how my vacation was to be spent. "Of course you will visit your friend at Lambeth Palace. You must give my warm, personal respects to His Grace and Mrs. Davidson." Without question Sir Herbert was what the vulgar would call a *snob,* but he was careful about his snobbishness. He knew I had been seeing a lot of the Harcourts but they were too liberal for his circle. Lord Bryce had written him concerning me, but Bryce had left a bad impression in his administration of Ireland and had a reputation of having sold Britain to America during his ambassadorship there. Nor could Sir Herbert express the hope that I would go back stage at the *Old Vic* and consort with Sir Philip Ben Greet and his actor friends. But there was Lady Strathcona, he could send his regards to her sons who were at Magdalen and to Pye-Smith whose personality had impressed him.

All this time I was having a chance to study — for the first time nearby — the seemingly carved screen which reached to the ceiling. I noted that the little painted shields of men whose lives had been tied with the history of the college were merely hung against the paneled background. Then gradually I realised the president was dismissing me with a gracious gesture of his outstretched hand. It was rather a fleshy hand and I always took it with a fear that I might squeeze it too hard. As I rose I returned his last word of good will with a smile of relief — and for me *collecers* were over.

"While I was out at Nuneham Park last Sunday," my journal continued on March 16, 1915, "Mr. Harcourt told me that what I should do some day was to offer to help at the hospital in Blenheim Palace and at the same time see the place. This afternoon Humphrey Vernon and I walked about eight miles out to Woodstock as part of our physical training and had lunch at the inn. Then, remembering Mr. Harcourt's suggestion we decided to attack the palace.

"The first arched gate with its gilded porter was no deterrent. We went right past and down the drive. When we came to the second classic entrance which led directly to the palace court I made for the major domo blocking the way. 'I wish to see the nurse-in-charge,' says I. Having received the pass word the great man changed the comfortable jacket he had been wearing for a knee length tunic trimmed with gold lace, placed on his head an equally ornamented top hat. Then, bearing a six foot wand with a large silver ball on one end and bound with silken cords, he led us out into the court. All this was of course a holdover from peace-time days and may have dated back to the time when the hero of the battle of Blenheim first received the palace as a gift from a grateful nation. It is, I think, the most imposing palace front I have ever seen. The colonnaded façade of the house looks out from a considerably high hill over a large lake to where a tremendous column is set in a vista of trees.

"Well, as we made our progress across this vast square I asked if the Duke of Marlborough were at home and received the reply that he was. But we had no desire to see the duke. Up steps, along a corridor and then we waited while the domo took our cards inside. If the domo had been imposing, the nurse-in-charge who now appeared was terrifying. Following Mr. Harcourt's suggestion I ventured that I had been able to be of service to the wounded at Nuneham and I might help here. This was met with an indignant rebuff as though I had lodged a complaint that the soldiers at Blenheim were not being properly treated. Then after a bit of talk she decided to let us have what she called a 'peep in.'

"The state apartment into which we were ushered seemed just as large and costly as money could make it. In it were fifty beds, all filled with wounded. Finally the sister, for so she was addressed, suggested we might like to go down and talk with some of the men who were in the smoking room. On the way she explained that so many people tried to get into the palace under pretence of visiting the soldiers whereas they merely wished to see the house. This she said much to my embarrassment and I took care not to let her see it. Also, she added, some came to spy for the Germans.

"After we had spent some time with the men we came up and thanked the Sister. She then suggested if any of us could sing or play the soldiers would be delighted to hear us. So I promised to bring out a number of fellows during the next term. We parted good friends and walked by another road eight miles back to Magdalen. Vernon and I are hoping these long walks will harden us for whatever we may be called upon to do in service.

"It will take about another year before peace is actually signed — is the general feeling — during which time we will remain mobilized, but doing nothing. One thing is certain that the Germans will not give in too easily because they are on the whole just as determined as our people. The cases the papers talk so much about of Germans giving themselves up because they are fed up with it are only isolated and are to be expected in a large conscript army such as theirs.

"Their spy system must be marvellous! The last story I heard was that when a certain Manchester regiment went into the trenches, they were greeted with shouts of 'Hullo! Manchesters!'

from the German lines, who then proceeded to sing *Tipperary* and
the regimental marching song, the trenches being only about 80
yards apart. I don't think the rumor of sending the Indians off to
Egypt can be true, because the Sikhs seem still to be coming from
India to France.

"Whatever else I do during the vac I must go over to Bath and
see the aunt-to-be and her family in Landsdown Crescent. Mrs. Pye-
Smith has asked me down to Farnham for the weekend coming,
when I shall see Phil. Mrs. Pye has become quite *the mother of the
regiment.* And there are others, but all is uncertain depending on the
course of the war."

The course of the war at this period seemed to center in the
Dardanelles where an attack in force had been ordered. We heard of
brave naval engagements with heavy losses from mine and submarine, but what I did not know until later was that the military —
who should have supported this attack — had found it necessary to
return in their transports to Egypt for redistribution.

In the meantime I was on my way to Bath to undergo family
inspection by relatives of the girl my uncle in Canada was about to
marry. With the thought of seeing the ancient city before I was seen
by the family I took a friend along with me and put up at one of
the commodious resort hotels. Together we examined the remains of
the old Roman baths, recalling the days of Beau Nash and the
descriptions from Charles Dickens' novels. Also we indulged in the
various baths for which the city is famous. Then, on the afternoon
before I was expected by the bride, Josephine Chadwick, and her
aunt, Mrs. Shepherd, at Landsdown Crescent, I happened on the
show rooms of Mallatt, the antique dealer. They were filled with
family treasures which were being offered for sale because people
were beginning to feel the pinch of war time demands. I bought
four Sheffield silver telescope candle sticks.

The next portion of my journal was written at 16 Landsdown
Crescent. "Here I am at last at my aunt-in-law-to-be's aunt's residence. They are charming people and are being most hospitable to
me. Their house is in one of those crescent shaped rows peculiar to
Bath. It is on the side of one of the hills which surround the ancient
city and would seem to be a splendid reminder of Georgian culture.
The walls of their beautifully furnished rooms are lined with portraits of what is apparently a very military family. Among them

General Monk and, I believe, Cromwell is also one of their ances-
tors. The bride-to-be is the centre of attention. She is well built and
pleasing to look upon. She is obviously practical, has good taste and
is full of fun. I do wish I were going to be home for the wedding.
Please write me what I can do in the way of a present.

"I go from here to spend a couple of weeks or more with the
Banners at Bournemouth."

My next portion of the journal was written from the Banners'
on April 2, 1915 in which I noted, "Arthur Howard is an officer in
one of the London Rifle Regiments and Phil Pye-Smith is an officer
in the 11th King's Liverpool. Please send me a goodly number of
socks for their men. I can assure you they would be appreciated
because they have been asked for especially. I shall stop at Arthur's
to pick up my topper and tails on my way to spend several days
with Dr. Longstaff. In the meantime I am included in the meticulous
care which Mrs. Banner rather wastes on her only son since he
dislikes it heartily. Also I am stimulated by Delmar's intellectual
and artistic conversation. I can't see why he cares for me so much,
but we have lots of fun together."

Not until I returned to Magdalen (14th April 1915) do I seem
to have written home. Even then it was not to relate the happenings
in the stimulating homes of my new friends in London, but —
because it was my mother's birthday — it was largely centered on
her activities with the Daughters of the British Empire in America.
Perhaps because my father was a busy physician and my brother
was away at Harvard or later engaged in starting his law business,
my mother had made me as a junior and generally silent partner in
all her charitable endeavors. I could recall sitting in our drawing
room at 19 Seventh Avenue when a small group of English ladies
were first planning the organization of the *Daughters*. Now my
mother was starting the first of a chain of homes for old British men
and women in the United States and I was keen to have the enter-
prise recognized in England.

"I spent two days longer in London than I had thought for,
visiting Arthur Howard and his engaging sister, while I waited for
Miss Talbot to return from the country. I showed her the reports of
the work of the Daughters of the Empire and suggested the possibility of its being granted Royal Patronage. Miss T explained that
the Victoria League first asked — after it had been going for three
years — and was refused the royal patronage because it was too

young and the finances were not secured. A couple of years later, however, their application was put through successfully. The Queen takes great care to look into such things personally so that it means something when it is granted. I said to Miss T that when the American press looked at the situation it was evident that it considered the public was more interested in an organization recognized directly by Her Majesty than in one which worked through an ambassador. Does Mother want the Queen's patronage for the I.O.D.B.E.? Would it not make less danger of a split when she resigns the presidency? Why not secure this and then let somebody else be active president? I know Mother wishes to resign as soon as the organization is securely established."

I could appreciate the difficulty under which a group of British born women — most of whose husbands were loyal American citizens earning their livings in America — must be operating in a country which was strictly neutral. For the present — according to the Britishers with whom I talked — America's stand as a sympathetic neutral was of more value to them than if she were an ally. The enemy was far from being defeated. Furthermore, epidemics resulting from war conditions could be a decisive factor in who would be the final victor.

"I may still go to France," I wrote on April 20th, "but I keep before me first the important work for which I came over here. If my study needs me here, here I shall stay. It is sporting of you not to stop my going if it seems wise. You see I am doing what is really a three years course in two years, and the School of Theology is supposed to be the hardest in the Oxford list. In a couple of weeks — after I have talked with Mr. Brightman and Sir William — I will know for sure. Mrs. Harcourt says that there is trouble in the American hospitals with the French who want to be helped but do not wish to be interfered with. This hospital of Harvard men of which my friend, Mr. Robert Bacon, is at the head should be the best of the American outfits. I could hardly go with Sir W personally, for of course I could not wear the British uniform. But he said that he could and would find a place for me in an American hospital. He seemed to have little use for the French medical outfits and would not hear of my going to Serbia.

"There must be *typhoid Susies* here such as you write about, carrying the disease unknowingly in America, for in spite of all precautions Sir William fears we are on the verge of several epidemics at once. The spotted fever, or cerebral spinal meningitis, is spreading from the camps to the civilian population about the district of Aldershot and elsewhere. Sir W sent down a new vaccine to Phil Pye-Smith, but nobody seems to understand the disease. They don't even know people have it until they are nearly dead. I will let you know just what I do in the matter of going out as soon as ever I decide one way or the other.

"One hears so much about Belgian tragedies over here that it gets tiresome, considering what others are suffering. Dr. Longstaff with whom I have just been staying had had his house full of Belgians for four months and finally wearied of them. Others likewise. The refugees are giving a dreary impression, while we know that there are many of their compatriots still holding out in their homeland."

5

SUMMER TERM, 1915

"ABOUT 29 fellows have come back to Magdalen for the start of the Summer Term," I was writing in the spring of 1915. "Things might be lonely if there were not lots of reading to be done. Every day the country seems to be unfolding its beauty imperceptibly. The grey trees are tinted with green buds and the hedges are white with blackthorn. Banner and I went out yesterday and gathered branches of it, two of which I have put just outside of my windows, their woody ends standing in waterfilled honey pots and their twigs fastened to the casements, so that the bees come and buzz round as though it were a real growing bush.

"One very delightful thing about this term is that the College has numerous punts and canoes moored in the Cher by our Addison's Walk, and all one has to do is to go down the bank, untie the boat and push off into the stream. You probably remember the attractive way it winds about under the trees. It goes for 22 miles up into the country. Then there is the larger stream known as the Isis into which the Cherwell flows. It is a favorite custom to go off in one of these punts and read.

"Prince George — I shall speak of him as George hereafter, since that is the way I write and speak to him now. It will avoid the pomposity of the title. He came back to Magdalen laden with chocolates which had been presented to his father and mother during their visit in the southern part of France where they have just been for the Duke's health."

The following day (April 25th) I noted, "George and I have just been out in canoes. It was a bit rainy but heaps of fun. That is about all the exercise one gets here now, for walking through the city is rather stupid and there are no regular sports except tennis on clear days.

"I have a letter from Mrs. — I meant Lady — Bryce saying that there is nothing in the way of reunions etc. to bring Lord Bryce to Oxford and there is so much in the way of war that they will not be able to come to Oxford this year. He is Chairman of the Committee for the Investigation of Belgian Atrocities. What a job!"

The day I was writing this last letter I heard much later at Nuneham was the start of the attack by the military in Gallipoli. It had taken them a month to go to Egypt, reassemble and return to join the navy in the attempt to capture Constantinople. Whether it was lack of communication or just the policy of withholding immediate war news from the public the point of this precarious expedition was rather dulled by the time we heard of it. The result was that the public was spared an interval of suspense and my work did not suffer from the distraction it might have caused me.

"All this vac," I wrote, "I have plotted away at a general outline for my dissertation, and this is the result. It will be in the form of an opera — for after all that word means work.

"The theme or motive will be the sacred words of the institution as they are found in the Gospels of SS. Matthew and Mark: Jesus took bread, and blessed it, and break it, and gave it to the disciples, and said, Take, eat; this is my body. And he took the cup, and gave thanks, and gave it to them, saying, Drink ye all of it; for this is my blood of the new testament, which is shed for the remission of sins.

"First will come a prologue. In this will be told the history. It will start with the order of service as used by Christian Jews in their synagogues, to which they added, on the day following the Sabbath, Christ's institution as interpreted by the apostles. I plan to trace its development as the early fathers tell of it; through the era when the Roman and Gallican liturgies combined in England; through the Roman usurpation of the English church and the final break in the reign of Henry VIII; through the successive changes under Edward VI to its crystallization after the Restoration. This will be a dissertation of liturgical development showing the effects of the Liturgy on the history of Great Britain and America.

"I have already in my card index each prayer traced back, as far as possible, to its origin. My hope is that beginning from the sources I can show how the prayers accumulated until they finally formed the Liturgy in its present arrangement and contents. Once this introduction, or prologue, is done then I can proceed with the main

HINDLEAP,
FOREST ROW,
SUSSEX.

VISCOUNT (JAMES) BRYCE (author and statesman) written to Brett Langstaff 1913, regarding Magdalen and the Oxford colleges.

divisions which I am thinking of as acts in an opera.

"The first act: The Tudor period. With Cranmer as the hero and Queen Elizabeth as heroine. The second act: Edward VI. First scene; The Protector. Second scene; Warwick. This, as is proper in drama, will be the great act and will contain the climax in the actual publication of the Liturgy. The third act: The Restoration. The Liturgies treated in chronological order of Charles II, the Scots, and the American. The epilogue will deal with the changes about to be made in England.

"Enclosed you will find the Battel Bill which I have been trying to prepare you for in my recent letters. You will remember the bill last term was 40/4/4 so that this term's is better. Don't think that 37 is 57, as I did for some time. The heavy item on this bill is the coal which I understand is usually twice the former amount because there is more need for fires in our open grates during the winter. You will also perceive — I am not sure with approval — that I have managed to save on the bath charges. Now in the summer term it is the custom to go out in the early morning and bathe in the part of the river that is ours. This should obviate the tubs, although here at Magdalen they are pretty grand. The item for care of bicycle is the bicycle which Arthur Howard gave me to use while he is away in service."

My economy in regard to the amenities of life was in part geared to the growing spirit cutting down on unnecessary comforts in the households I visited. "I fear the family life and homes of people over here are showing signs of neglect because of the voluntary interest and generosity needed to meet the immediate demand of the war.

"I am going to the Oslers' tonight for supper. Don't know — but — yes, I shall dress. I called on the great Dr. Sanday and his sister last Sunday ..." It was a privilege for me to come to know William Sanday who was probably the most widely known Oxford scholar in my day. Especially to have tea with him in Peter Martyr's ancient residence in Christ Church cloister. It made the church history I was reading come to life in a vivid way. The fact that at Oxford history was never allowed to become a thing of the past was perhaps why studying it there was so satisfactory. The continuance of old customs had a lot to do with this. Oxford was never burdened with its past — it assimilated it and made it serve its present.

On the 2nd of May I wrote from Magdalen, "It is days since I have written home, so here's to all at once. Yesterday was the celebration of the *First of May*. Many of us sat up all the night before in order to be up at sunrise. I clicked this little machine most of the night.

"The people began to gather in the morning about four o'clock, and by five there were some two hundred on the top of the great tower and as many thousands on the bridge and in the street below. The hourly chime pealed and at the fifth stroke the choir started a Latin hymn. An English hymn of the 17th century, in the Ambrosian style, 'Te Deum Patrem colimus,' Almighty Father, just and good. It was all very short, about five stanzas of four lines and then came a great clanging of chimes which actually made the tower rock. They tell me that it swings from side to side at least four inches, and truly where I was privileged to stand with the choir on the roof of the tower you could distinctly feel it swaying back and forth. This was followed by the Communion Service in the Chapel below.

"Then came Dr. Varley Roberts' breakfast in the 'new rooms' at the foot of the tower. Dr. R had met George T and myself walking along the street several days before and asked us to be his guests. I had to pull G T out of bed so that we arrived a bit late. There was a long table with Dr. R at one end and Mr. Benecke, the grandson of Mendelssohn and the successor of Cardinal Wolsey as our Magdalen bursar, at the other end. Then there were the choir boys and some five other honored guests. The eats were excellent and afterwards, when the boys had left, we stood about and had an inspiring talk. I felt it was a distinct honor which will make the famous *May Morning* mean a lot to me hereafter.

"I spoke of the privileges we enjoy of having punts and canoes moored on the river which we can take out whenever we wish. We all take advantage of it. One can punt right up to the cricket grounds where tea is served every afternoon. This tea is included in the J.C.R. bill and tends to bring the college together in a healthy way. I had a few sets at tennis and seem to be in good form.

"We also use the river for reading. That is, we take a punt and a book and fasten ourselves under some overhanging bough with the long pole stuck in the bottom of the river, and there we study. Unfortunately I have had a lot of work with cards for my file which have to be spread out all over the place, and this has kept me from studying in a punt. My dissertation is growing clearer. I can't tell you what an incentive it is for making one actually work of one's own accord when there is no one pushing. As I look back on my American college experience, there were not many students who went ahead on their own initiative. I hope soon to be able to send home my *prologue*. The getting ready in a job such as this is half the game, and I am nearly ready to start writing."

The difference, to which my letter referred, between two methods of advanced education was not easy to adjust to. The American method, as I had experienced it, was, through lectures and prescribed reading, to implant in your mind important facts related to your subject. Then, through these and tests, to discover whether you had memorized and comprehended them correctly. The English method would seem to be to inspire you to ask questions related to your subject, and then through tutorial conferences and occasional lectures to indicate to you how you might find the answers to your own questions. Canon Brightman made this clear to me at our first conference.

May 6, 1915 — "Dr. Longstaff wrote, as I had asked him to do, telling me he was coming up to Oxford and would stop in for tea. I had everything ready for him in my room in case he had to hurry back for a train. But since time and weather permitted I took him up the Cher in a punt to the cricket pavilion. There we had tea with the undergraduates. Delmar Banner was also there with his people. I was glad they could meet a Langstaff, even if it were spelled wrong. We came back the same way and I carried his bag down to the station for him, just a little one. He has given some 15,000 butterflies to the museum and I think he had been asked to come up and look at a collection of specimens sent from a part of Africa which he had written about. He has explored many of the far away places of the world and converses delightfully about them."

If times were normal I would have found many world travelers coming to Oxford to report their findings and so add to the advancement of knowledge in one field or another. Now travel abroad was precarious. Even as my letter was starting its way across the Atlantic to New York, on the 7th of May, one of the great tragedies of the sea was taking place. The Cunard liner *Lusitania,* of which Lord Harcourt had written me regarding the use of the American flag, was sunk by a German submarine. This was a violation of international law and an offense to the ideals of civilization which turned many citizens of the United States against Germany. All that could be said as to the motive for the attack was that 'because Great Britain refused to allow the U.S.A. to supply the German army with foodstuffs, Germany officially assassinated more than 100 American citizens.'

Four days later I wrote from Magdalen, "My reply to your letter was delayed in the hope that I would have better news about Jim Young. You have probably read the names of J. N. Young and Mrs. Young in the list of first class passengers on board the *Lusitania.* There seems little doubt but that this indicates my James Nelson Young and his mother. Everything points that way, and yet I am praying that it may simply be a coincidence. You can help me find out whether it was Jim by letting me know the name of the church that Mr. Coupland left in Baltimore. You may remember Jim's brother-in-law was called to that parish.

"While I was at Columbia Jim had his locker next to mine. And then later when we were both together at Harvard I asked him to sit at my table in Memorial Hall. There he met several fellows who were his friends through college. We saw a great deal of each other and we formed a real friendship. The last word I had from him was on a card enclosed in a volume of Le Gallienne's *Omar Khayyam* — 'Christmas greeting to Brett from one who thinks of him very often!' and signed James N. Young.

"You know what a splendid man he was to meet. All the gentle courtesy of manliness. His constant care was never to offend anybody. He knew few fellows but it was simply because he preferred to know the friends he had very well. Although he was morally clean for honor's sake I hardly feel that he saw clearly through the glass the Great Master to whom he owed so much of his attractiveness. The one constant witness of his loyalty was his devotion to his dear old mother. She was the timid, refined type which is characteristic among ladies of the old school in the South. My comfort is that they were both together when the terrible end came."

The blunder of the German high command in sinking the *Lusitania,* for me, made my home in New York seem much further away. The sympathy of the English people was naturally touched by those who were drowned and perhaps they found an outlet for this emotion in a friendly gesture toward an American student such as I was. We were not yet allies but in this we had suffered together. Certainly I was conscious of a more friendly feeling.

"Today," (14th May 1915) "when I was coming back from my lec'ers Levett asked me to go with him in his car as far as Warwick. It was a beautiful day and I went and, after lunch, came back in the train. Levett is a new character on my stage. His parents are nice people and one of his great grandfathers had the distinction of being archbishop of both York and Canterbury. He himself is an attractive fellow and comes to Magdalen from Eton.

"Mrs. Clement Webb, the wife of one of the dons, has kindly asked me to lunch with them on Sunday next. It is especially good of them since I do not know them at all, not even having met them. The same with the Archdeacon of Ely, George Hodges, who has asked me to come to Ely and put up with him and see the cathedral and nearby Cambridge. I find this last comes through a lady to whom my new aunt Josephine introduced me in Bath. She told the archdeacon that I would probably like to see the country and forthwith came the invitation. Mr. Cookson, the dean, asked me the other night how I managed to arrive in a country as a stranger and immediately have people from miles about beg me to come and stay with them. It is a bit unusual, but mighty nice for me."

In another five days I was writing, "My work is shaping itself more and more every day so that now I feel I know where I stand. It has reached that encouraging stage where I can see light at the other end of the tunnel. I have written my first chapter and in it I have taken the liturgy of the Jewish service way back in the time of Ezra when the synagogues began and followed it down to the life of Our Lord, showed how Jesus made use of it and how it naturally came to be the outline for the first part of the Christian liturgy, and brought it down through the age of the great liturgies, down to the combination of the Roman and Gallican in England, and finally through the Reformation to the liturgy in our own American prayer book. There should be great force in the centuries of tradition and especially in the fact that it was the liturgy which Our Lord himself used.

"Now I am at work on the Sarum Missal which as you know was the basis for the first prayer book. But I am getting there!"

In my deep research into the sacrament of the Lord's Supper it was hard to find any reconciliation between the peace of God and the wars of mankind. I still had the opportunity of philosophical guidance in my continued contact with George Santayana. Added to this were revealing arguments in the long night sessions with undergraduates. Some of my fellow students were outright pacifists and other were sympathizers with the German people whom they felt had been forced into hostilities with their friends in England. But now the conflict had dug itself deep in the hearts of people. It was too late for reasoning or for diplomatic solution. Whatever might be worked out later for the establishment of international peace, for the present, all must wait for the superior force of arms to decide.

"I have just been to a lecture, or rather what was not a lecture because of the bank holiday (May 24th). It is so interesting to come to know a man like Scott Holland — it was he who was to have given the lec'er. Miss Talbot's introduction has been the means of giving me an unusual personal relationship with him, so instead of a lecture we had a conference. His great size and rapid speech cause people to compare him with Phillips Brooks. I met Sir Herbert Warren on the way and we had a talk on the pamphlet he had sent me of one of his lectures on poetry. Also I met Dr. Sanday in Tom Quad. He was so grieved to hear of Phil Pye-Smith's going out to the front. Said he was not the kind of man who would enjoy fighting, but that he had the spirit that was needed.

"Poor Mrs. Pye-Smith, just widowed, and now her only son at the war. But she insisted he should not stay at home to please her. Lady Strathcona too. Harry, the second son, gone and the other two in the service. It is the bravery they tell us about in the novels of our civil war.

"I went to pay a dinner call at Mr. Ferguson's early in the afternoon and found Mr. Foxton-F, the brother, was there. I stayed for tea, dinner and a concert for the boys of the school after. The Warden was telling me about the condition of the Church of England today. I rejoice to think how much more the influence of laymen and the freedom of clergy is esteemed by our American church.

"The 'Gloomy Dean' of St. Paul's London told us in St. Mary's in the morning that the Church of England was suited for the island for which the organization had been made but that it was not suited for the work of the empire. The laws of this country leave the people freer than our laws leave us, but tradition! tradition! is the burden which makes the individual as slow as the nation.

"I lunched with the Banners yesterday at the *East Gate*. They have planned a course for Delmar in the Foreign Office. A clerk. And they feel this insignificant ambition is greater than the service of the Church in which he will probably enlist. Personally I feel he should concentrate on art. The parents made as much fuss over him as a couple of grown-up chickens with a duckling.

"Whitsunday my silver candle sticks from Bath were placed on the extra organ for the great choral Communion Service in our Chapel. This little organ is put in the centre of the choir so that Varley Roberts can more conveniently conduct the difficult music. Dr. Roberts had taken me in to try over the organ before the Service, and when he found himself in need of additional light I suggested my telescope sticks.

"About going to the front, which I so much want to do. I have talked with Sir William and he agrees with me that it will not be possible for me to get my work done here at college and go out in the hospital work he was planning for me. He said I might do something in a hospital every day here in England and at the same time have opportunity for my study. That will probably be the final solution. You must remember that at present there are long waiting lists for hospital service in France and if I secured a position it would be through influence and that would mean cutting out some Britisher. Of course I might go out on a Belgian relief expedition as Ridge Lytle has, but that would be more for the purpose of 'getting colour,' I fear, than for the ideal of serving England in a time of need. The Harcourts favor my sticking at my work. Lulu Harcourt may be made Viceroy of India. Asquith and some of his cabinet were weekending at Nuneham last Sunday."

The Liberal leaders who were often at the spacious country residence of the Secretary for the Colonies seemed to find a relief in talking to a young American student from Oxford. Their conversation told me much that I would not otherwise have known — indeed showed me in certain important cases how little information they had. However, it soon became obvious that the war I had hoped could not last more than a few months was now assuming greater proportions. It had converted Italy from its stand of armed neutrality to becoming an active belligerent. Italy had not at this time formally declared war, but I learned that on May 22nd the order for general mobilization was published. Three days before my last writing the first offensive against Austrian troops in the Tyrol had started. King Victor Emanuel had left Rome for the military headquarters. But now for about a week unexpected flood waters of the Isonzo river were holding up the Italian advance. Because this was not generally known, one heard much of the "half hearted" participation of the new ally.

My letter from Magdalen on May 27, spoke of "enclosing the pamphlet which Sir Herbert sent me on *Poetry and War*. In replying I sent him the poems of our Civil War which were published in the *New York Times Fiftieth Anniversary Supplement* with the suggestion that Walt Whitman's *Captain, My Captain* might appeal to him as a post war lament. He had not mentioned this poem in his pamphlet. His great forte is Tennyson, and it was something he wrote on this subject that won him the place of *Professor of Poetry* at Oxford. He is regarded more for his critical understanding of poetry than for his creative ability. However, his poem on the tower service on the First of May, which I have described, is good. Read it.

"So Italy is in — and my friend William Roscoe Thayer was right after all about her not being able to stay out. But I don't think anybody here is especially elated. It is hardly an assurance that the war will be ended any sooner, and when it is ended it is sure to add to the complication of peace settlements. All I can see is that it puts another column in the papers.

"What is worrying people here is that the new coalition cabinet will in all probability mean conscription. I know that Lulu Harcourt for one will not agree to such a means of raising troops if anything else in the world can be done. So if it comes you can conclude that things are getting more serious than ever. In the meantime my work is pushing along. I am starting in on the Canon Missae."

It seems incredible to us now that England could have mustered the army she did without the aid of conscription. This which in the spring of 1915 seemed incompatible with democracy was, however, soon to be counted an inherent part of it. Nor, as I was to look back on it, did this form of military service seem anything but equitable. In the growing conception of total war everything and every body in civil life needed for the safety of the country was to fall under conscription. But this was still to come.

"I am enclosing a card from Phil Pye-Smith referring to the socks you are sending for his men at the front," I wrote on May 28th from Magdalen. "I trust the *Lusitania* did not carry any of them. Also I am enclosing some of the wonderful spring blossoms which are making the country so beautiful now. They will be

6. Via Santo Stefano Rotondo,
Roma, June 13. 1951

Dear Langstaff

It is indeed a pleasure to hear from you after so many years and to be vividly reminded of our pleasant circle in Oxford in 1919. I am in touch ignorance about everyone: Raymond Mortimer is the only one, and he not of Magdalen but Balliol, whom I have seen recently, and read a pleasant book of his about literary people. Whatever became of Peter Warren, "your" correspondence and Gray?

As to me, M. Maritain's visit and attention occurred some years ago when he was ambassador to the Pope; he found me in Poterette solitude was always my true background — and I have many old interests and pleasures was left, together with some new ones. Especially I have recently become deeply interested in the new American poets. I have long known Ezra Pound, and have even been often here during the war, but never was reconciled to his ways in speech or in writing. But Robert Lowell from the first attached me for various paradoxes that I found realised in him; and his suggested personality, now that I have seen him, has not frightened me away, but the last few years have also made the political interesting to me, although curious —

Best memories and wishes from your old friend

G Santayana

PROFESSOR GEORGE SANTAYANA (philosopher and poet) written shortly before his death to Brett Langstaff 1951, referring to Maritain, Ezra Pound and Robert Lowell, and recalling the reading-party described in this book.

withered, but there is myrtle, hawthorn and the may-blossom. There
should be some of the yellow laburnum, but it hangs too high.

"Scofield Thayer asked me to come to his rooms in Cloisters and
hear Prof. Santayana speak to the *Nineties Club* last night. Of all
the clubs with which I was associated at Harvard there was not
one that had so vicious a purpose as this society which thrives now
that the undergraduate body is deprived of most of its normal
minded men. The Society conceives of the world as having come
again to the same condition as it found itself in the 1890s, and
following the lead of the obscure men who followed Oscar Wilde
they are busy marking time and making every effort to live only
a sensuous life with no purpose in the future. Santayana's address
was most discouraging to the idea of such a club. He said, among
other things, that when men of Wilde's day went into the Roman
Catholic Church, as many of the leaders did, they indulged in the
sensuous pleasures of incense and candles and colored robes, but
never got further than the media. Today in Oxford they all circle
around one man who is clever and sophisticated. Most of them
at Balliol and Christ Church. Only Thayer at Magdalen. Their
amusing side is odd costumes of long white cloaks, great rings on
their fingers, rare flowers in their rooms, etc., etc. Wait till we have
conscription!"

Scofield and I were born in the same year and spent four years
at Harvard together, but we were poles apart. It is fair to state that
his devotion to the "ultra-modern" in arts and letters as he had
expressed them in the pages of the *Harvard Monthly* seemed to
me genuine. Nevertheless, to my mind he was a product of a Fabian
influence to which I felt our American way of life was opposed. And
why he invited me to this meeting of the Nineties Club in his dining-
room in Cloisters, I don't know. The dark blue curtains were drawn
to shut out any light from the long windows. The crowd of undergraduates — for the most part seated on the floor — and the little
Spanish savant in a chair beside a blazing fire in the open grate
seemed to invite the spirit of the Wilde who once inhabited our
college as an undergraduate. Certainly he would have approved the
vase of three or four dozen tall lilies on a center table stifling
the air with their heavy odor.

In fairness to Scofield Thayer it may be said that when he returned
to America he became part owner and active director of a magazine
called *The Dial* through which he personally encouraged young

artists and writers and was effective in spreading the appreciation of modern art forms. He must have impressed Santayana at Oxford because it would seem that some aspects of a character in Santayana's novel, *The Last Puritan,* are drawn from his memories of Thayer.

Evidently I had missed seeing Sir Philip Ben Greet during my vacation because on June 6, 1915, I wrote, "Just had a letter from Mr. Ben Greet. Says his sister Clare has been ill. He asks me to let him know when he can meet me in London. He will not return to America till after the war." Then I went on to observe, "This knowing people has made me a mystery to the college. It is not that I know any more people here than at home, but somehow everybody has an idea that because the Harcourts and Oslers and Howards have been good to me — and I am only an ordinary American student — I must be some relation of President Wilson's, or of some *titled* American. It is curious to me that where there are so many titles the people never get used to them nor cease to be awed by them."

I never worried about what people thought of my home connections. What did concern me was the person or group of persons with whom I chanced to be thrown. And because this interest was genuine I think people tolerated me. The fact that I felt at ease with men and women who were leaders in different groups of society was doubtless because my mother had made a point of taking me along with her in so many of her public activities. My next letter indicates continued concern in these matters.

"Mother's letter received. I appreciate its length the more because I know how busy she is. The house she has chosen as a home for old British people is indeed charming from the picture. I am happy to think that the idea she has striven to carry out was not hindered by the war stress. I shall take the picture down to Mrs. Harcourt when I go to lunch tomorrow. She was on the original council of the Queen's Needlework Guild.

"As to Queen Mary's Needlework's Guild, I fear things need straightening out so much here that people could not think of attempting to relieve the confusion which may arise from its intrusion into the area served by the Needlework Guild of America. Why not work along with it and affiliate the I.O.D.B.E. with it, with the idea of taking over whatever organization it may create, after the war? Mother never makes any comment of my idea of securing royal patronage for her society.

"My work is developing satisfactorily," the letter continues. "There seems every hope that this experiment I am making in research, for it is that with me, will turn out for the good. There are social interludes such as my recent tea with Dr. Ottley at the 'House.' Tea with Canon Ottley is strictly an affair of men and letters. The spacious study on the ground floor with its large windows looking out over the lawn to the cathedral is filled with furniture and books, and with papers which seem to have fallen like snow on every ledge and into every crevice which can hold them. The same with pictures, until there is no space left uncovered. Somewhere in all this clutter which doubtless has a careful order of its own, nestled a tea pot and cups for two.

"Since the beginning of the year in this room I have been listening to Canon Ottley's popular course on Hooker delivered by him to me alone over the body of a large grey cat which sleeps on his desk. I missed his first lecture scheduled for the Chapter House and found the beautifully vaulted hall empty when I turned up for the second. So I wrote him. I have kept his amusing reply saying, 'Dear Mr. Langstaff, I think you must have made a mistake about the place of my lectures. Both on Tues and today I attended at the Chapter-House for about 8 or 10 minutes, and as nobody appeared, I returned to my house. Perhaps you do not know that lectures begin at 11 by the cathedral clock: 11.5 by Tom Clock. Will you call at my house at 11 on Saturday, & I will arrange to give the lecture as advertised. Believe me to be, yours very truly. R. L. Ottley.'

"Ottley is a quiet mannered scholarly priest of our church who has been most considerate in offering to be of service to me in my work. We went into the garden at the back of the cathedral and saw the old arches of the monastery, or rather nunnery, which first occupied the site in seven hundred something. Christ Church is not blessed with a deer park and gardens as we are at Magdalen. They do have an extensive 'meadow,' however, which borders on the Isis where the rowing barges are moored.

"There are a couple of 'spikers' here at Magdalen who go to St. Mary's where Mr. Ben Greet said the services were so beautifully Catholic. These high-churchers seem to think they have something others have not, but they never seem willing to admit they have not anything *necessary* that other church members have not. I

went to the early 'Mass' this morning with them. Thank goodness
I know more about their liturgy than they do. I feel sure the
secret of their success is an emphasis on this Sacrament of Holy
Communion and not on their extra ritual and vestments. But
since the liturgy has from the beginning been intended to preserve
the unity of the church it should be kept free from party conten-
tions. I can not tell you what boundless joy my study of it is
giving me.

"At 9:30 I heard E. W. Watson, D.D., at St. Mary's, our university church, talk on Tertullian. All the doctors were there in their
gorgeous robes.

"Then I biked down to Nuneham Park for lunch. Mr. and Mrs.
Harcourt, the three daughters and Billy, the son. Mrs. Alexander,
the sister in charge of the hospital, and only four officers as
patients. And Mr. Reginald McKenna, of whom you have probably
read many criticisms and his wife. And Mr. H's secretary and his
sister. We had a game of tennis after lunch, and then after tea
on the great terrace overlooking the Thames, I was sent home in
a motor, bike and all.

"Mr. McK told me that he had had evidence given by the public
of over 200,000 cases of German spies in London alone and that
not one of those cases was found to have been a spy. He gave
this as an example of the ignorance of the public in the way war
was run. He says that on the first day war was declared the twenty
odd leading spies who were in England were put immediately into
prison. These men could have been shot but were not. Since that
time no spy has come into the country who had not been discovered
a few days after landing. In answer to my question whether that
meant the German system was poor, he said yes the system was
not good but also the Germans, not thinking England would come
into the war, did not prepare for spies in England. Many who
had been in the country had probably been withdrawn to France.
You see no bridges have been destroyed nor incendiary fires, etc.,
which could be traced to spies since the war started.

"I spoke of William Jennings Bryan having dined with me at
Harvard. Mr. McKenna did not agree with me that there were no
men like Bryan in English politics. Bryan, he said, was a speaker
and not a politician. He seemed to have no faith in Mr. B's
religious aspirations, which I think rather indicates that there are
no men like Bryan with whom McKenna has come in contact.

Lloyd George, he said, was merely a speaker who would be forgotten as soon as he went out of office. As to the change in attitude of the public in favor of Mr. George, he said that the newspapers had gone over to George's side and that had turned the conversation of people in favor of the man, but he could not believe that newspapers had really much effect on the convictions of the people. I agree with him thoroughly in this last. He had not even heard of the Barnes case, however.

"While I was playing a set of tennis with some of the rest McKenna went into the house and wrote 18 letters. He later told me that there were only two real editors of newspapers in London today. The others were all hired servants and tools of the proprietors. Surely this is not so at home! I ended my day by going up to the Oslers in Norham Gardens for supper."

Checking on what the Chancellor of the Exchequer told me regarding the espionage situation for which he was largely responsible, I found that thanks to the Official Secrets Act of 1911 "the ramifications of the German Secret Service in England" were pretty well uncovered from that year until the war began in 1914. The record stated that "immediately before the outbreak of war 20 known spies were arrested and upwards of 200 kept under special observation," so I did quote him correctly. The French were criticising McKenna's "tempered optimism" and the British public evidently agreed with them, especially because of the questioned loyalty of the Privy Council member, Sir Edgar Speyer. It was hardly a month after my talk with McKenna when the Prime Minister was forced to testify to Speyer not being a spy.

The investigation into persons in high places seemed to reach a crisis after the sinking of the *Lusitania*. Subsequently the Germans must have reorganized their espionage system because the English began throwing more restrictions on resident aliens like myself. Meantime life at Oxford continued on within the limits.

From Magdalen College on June 15 I wrote that I "just had tea with Canon Scott-Holland in the garden behind his lodgings on Tom Quad at the House. I found him with two proper old ladies sitting under a tree. We got from submarines on to whales and after I had given him a *New York Times* story of how air ships were being used for finding whales, he told us the following.

"He and Burne-Jones were dining with somebody-famous-whose-name-I-can't-remember and the host described an incident in a fishing village somewhere in the north at a time when the whales had come into a fjord nearby. The bishop of the place stood on a barrel and told the people that there was their winter provender and that they should go and kill. So the people drove the female whales on the shore for the women to kill and the men killed what was left in the water. And after a bit they had killed so many that the water became like blood. Thereupon the bishop rose up again to give thanks and commend them for what they had done.

"By this time Burne-Jones had about all he could stand of the story and he burst forth, 'Cursed be the religion of that bishop!' You can imagine how the painter of the delicate ladies would be appalled by such a story.

"On returning to my rooms I found a telegram from the Cunard company saying that J. N. Young and Mrs. Young whom I had thought drowned with the *Lusitania* 'registered from Hamilton, Ontario.' This makes me question whether they are my friends, as I thought at first. The message goes on to say 'could you identify bodies if found?' No. I am sure Jim would not wish me to go out and look over the hundreds of unfortunate victims whose bodies have been picked up. Even if it were Jim and his dear old mother, what could I do?"

Under the same date I noted, "The fellow whose letters I have quoted several times in my letters is gone. Got five wounds in the leg. He was probably left too long on the field. And blood poisoning took him off. Also Harry Howard, Lady Strathcona's second son whom I spoke of as having gone out, was picked off by a sniper. He was the sort of man men admire, and is well remembered here at Magdalen. One sympathizes with his mother. She had only recently lost her father and mother, and with her eldest son at the front since the beginning of the war, and the youngest, Arthur, about to go out. There will probably not be a man above seventeen who will not have received some wounds even if he survives this war. But people are set. There is something dreadful in the grimness with which the problem — the English seem to take it as a serious problem — has settled down on the nation.

"Don't let America come into this war. It would solve nothing at this time anyway. But do let her pay close attention and learn. Learn what a truly bad state the world is in and how far we are from the ideal which our pride made us think we had reached."

As Sir William Osler had advised, I spent most of my spare

time working at local military hospitals until on June 21st I wrote, "I was sick. Coming home from singing to wounded soldiers in a hospital I took a real cold, and then with the farewell parties which mean so much to the men who are going out to the war I finished up in bed on Saturday. George Teck had asked me to go up with him to London where we were to take lunch with his father and go to the play after. Then I planned to do a lot of other things. This was all out. And now I am recovering."

To add to complications, some time before this I had learned that Bishop Boyd Carpenter was scheduled to preach in Oxford. Because I had come to know him on the occasion of his giving a course of lectures at Harvard and had promised to let him know should I come to England, I ventured to suggest at this time that he and his wife have tea with me at Magdalen. Mrs. Boyd Carpenter — or Lady as we called her in America because he had been knighted — accompanied him everywhere.

"You remember," I wrote home, "he was my guest at dinner one time at Harvard. Now at Oxford, however, he had promised two old ladies before I asked him, and since they lived a distance out in the country he would not be able to get back in time. Thereupon the Vice Chancellor, with whom the bishop was staying during his visit here, invited me to lunch with them on Sunday.

"Lady Boyd Carpenter and the bishop and the Vice Chancellor and a man named Langley were there. One delightful story the V C told was of the time when Lloyd George was visiting Christ Church. It was soon after he had declared the acres preserved for hunting should be planted with mangel wurtzels. The undergraduates, who do a lot of hunting, decided to give him a serenade, and seeing a light in the part of the house where it was thought the Liberal leader was to sleep they made a great din of coach horns and shouts about pheasants. But the truth was that an old missionary bishop who had come up to preach at the cathedral was fast asleep in that room with the light and did not wake through all their serenading.

"While this was going on Lloyd George was talking with the V C and the Bishop of Winchester in another part of the house and was finally sent to sleep in the room over the arch where visiting kings had once slept. The next morning when the porter sent in the daily report of the happening of the night the serenade was of course recorded and the V C handed it to Lloyd George at breakfast and told him it was meant for him.

"After Bishop Boyd Carpenter had gone to rest the V C took me by the arm and walked me about the garden. Lady Warren's coy suggestion later in the afternoon that the V C, who has no wife, needed somebody to look after his garden is true, but it is a delightful bit of green in spite of that. He was most cordial and showed me early American prayer books and talked with me about my work. We parted the closest of friends with many promises that I would come and see him often next term. All the men whom I had invited to meet the bishop in my rooms paid a call on Lady Warren in our President's garden and then came and had strawberries and tea with me. This ended the summer term."

6

THE LONG VACATION, 1915

THE Long Vacation constituted an important part of the academic year at Oxford. It was the beginning of the warm sunny days when one appreciated the leafy shade of great trees, when one could relax listlessly on the soft green turf with an open book, when in the lingering twilight the twittering notes of birds invited the mind to abandon the search for reality. For the scholar it was the beginning of a season of contemplation when he could take the multitude of facts and ideas culled from lectures and forced reading and weave them into a pattern of self expression. Take them to some far away place with two or three friends and perhaps a tutor — to the Isle of Skye or some chalet on an Alp in Switzerland — and there setting his own pace make these findings of the past part of himself.

At this time, in the normal course of things, Oxford would attract many former students returning nostalgically for reunion parties or scholars coming up for the award of degrees in recognition of service to humanity in the world outside. Among these latter would often be foreigners of distinction. All this was curtailed by the war in the June of 1915. Yet there was a foreign scholar who had come to live with us at Magdalen during the past few months with the purpose, as I understood it, of completing his studies in international law. This Georges Kaeckenbeeck gave me the privilege of a friendship which was to continue throughout our lives.

Kaeckenbeeck had been invalided out of the Belgian army early on in the invasion and had finally been sent to Oxford to recuperate and complete a university course which had been interrupted in his native country. He came speaking little, if any, English, and it was doubtless for that reason Sir Herbert Warren steered him in our direction — to me because I was myself a 'Foreign Student' although I spoke French haltingly and to Delmar Banner, my friend and neighbour in Cloisters, who was fluent and practiced in the language. How this Belgian student mastered the English language of his instructors at Oxford in time to take his degree in Civil Law was a mystery to all.

It was the mind of Georges K which fascinated me. It seemed to grasp ideas with the cold, quick precision of a steel trap. It followed a code of courtesy and infinite consideration which stood apart from any sentiment or emotion. It allowed for our faith in a personal God. It would have been polite to the Deity if He had ever entered his world, but so far He never had. In a country of strong Catholic and Protestant differences G K's mind seemed to have been created or shaped impervious to either. The clear thinking of George Santayana had something of these qualities, and next to Santayana this Belgian student impressed me as having the most incisive mind with which I had come in contact.

The fact that Kaeckenbeeck's career was to carry him on to become the genius of the League of Nations who solved single-handed their Upper Silesian problem and later into the legal functioning of the United Nations was hid from us undergraduates. But many years later visiting him at Dusseldorf when he was presiding over the economic conferences which led toward the consolidation of Europe, or in New York where he had been sent as ambassador extraordinary by the Belgian government, or in his charming home overlooking Lake Geneva to which he retired with a cousin of Delmar Banner's whom he had married, one discovered a winsome and affectionate personality which found expression in playing his violin.

From Magdalen College, 26th June 1915, I wrote, "Term ended last Saturday, but there are still several fellows up. I had breakfast with Treseder Griffin this morning because the J.C.R. is closed down. He has just taken a 'first with distinction' in a school which has never before given a first. He was 'frightfully bucked' with it, and had a letter from one of his dons which gave him unlimited praise. There is another scholastic genius at Magdalen, Georges Kaeckenbeeck, a Belgian, who came up for his B.C.L. degree. This is supposed to be the hardest exam in the kingdom and has the same blue and white hood as my B.Litt. Final exams cause as much excitement here as a great football match might at home. But it is a regrettable thing to see a university without any organized athletics, as we are at present. It shows the valuable part sports play and how necessary they are to healthy college life.

"I had Mother's letter from Canada and I was happy all over to see what true appreciation her home town people of St. Catherine's were showing. But why this sudden realization of all she has done with the Daughters of the Empire? I was also glad to have the *New York Times* account of the opening of the Victoria Home. I have sent the Durham sanctuary knocker for its front door."

Up to this time I had not determined where I should spend the four summer months during which I must compose the first draft of my dissertation. The delightful distraction of visiting friends was out of question. It required the solitary for concentrated work. Even to remain in my rooms at Magdalen risked the probability of friends dropping in or inviting me out. The usual reading parties which had formerly taken care of this problem were not being organized for obvious reasons.

Two days later I was writing, "Lady Osler took me down to Ewelme with a couple of her nephews and a girl cousin of the Howards yesterday. This Ewelme is an ancient alms house where Sir William, as Regius Professor of Medicine, has apartments overlooking an enchanting cloister. We had a delicious picnic lunch there. Great strawberries, for this is their season as you know, and plenty of heavy cream — almost a scarcity in this part of the country any more.

"A quantity of valuable documents have been preserved here which Sir William has had elaborately mounted. They are now secure in a great safe. A receipt for gun powder before it was used in warfare. The transfer of an extensive wardrobe of ecclesiastical vestments in which each article is noted. The original seals of people connected with the house in years past. And a thousand other interesting things. We went on from there to call at the Parkins'. George Parkin was, and I think is, in charge of the Rhodes Scholars. A fine old man. Pleasant cottage on the river. It was an all day trip and we all had a grand time."

Sir George Parkin was evidently indebted to Lady Osler for her tireless interest in American undergraduates at Oxford. She was the sort of wellgroomed intelligent hostess I had become accustomed to in Boston, an ideal professor's wife. She never spoke to me of her Paul Revere ancestry but she was of that family. There was a dependable thoroughness in everything she did without any suggestion of imposing her will on the person she was helping. She made one conscious of a powerful amount of physical energy well under control, and whereas there could be no doubt that she was a woman of decided opinions they were withheld by a reserve which might be mistaken for coldness or indifference. When one came from a visit to Norham Gardens one could not forget what Sir William had said but one never recalled Lady O differing with him. One thing they were both outspoken about was that my long vac should be spent at Ewelme.

It was July 2nd when I wrote, "My residence for the next four months has been determined by the generous invitation of Sir William and Lady Osler to be their guest in the lodgings at Ewelme. Thus I shall enter an alms house a little later in the summer. So while Mother is starting an alms house for old British people on Staten Island this poor American student will become an inmate of one here in England.

"This English home for old people was started by Alice, Duchess of Suffolk six centuries ago. Before Magdalen was founded, before our little continent was discovered, Alice provided for the keep of thirteen old men. A large and wonderfully wrought church and an adjacent cloister built of brick and now-blackened oak has been their sanctuary for six hundred uninterrupted years. Each man has a garden of his own. And a school at the back in pleasant contrast still provides for descendants of the old men of the cloister and other children of the village.

"The rooms overlooking the cloister and next to the church were reserved for the Master of the Alms House. This honored person received two hundred pounds for his service, and when the Regius Professor of Medicine complained to King James the First that his salary did not afford him a living, the good king made him in addition Master of this alms house or *hospital,* as it was called in 1436, which is not too far from Oxford. Sir Henry Acland and Sir John Burdon-Sanderson equipped the Master's rooms for modern living, and their successor, Sir William Osler, spent a good part of his summers there, so that the place is very comfortable. Now, following the procession of historic figures of over 14 generations comes the son of Dr. John Elliot Langstaff, whose present financial condition makes him a fit candidate for any alms house. Please send money!"

There were several days of waiting at Magdalen before Lady Osler could have the apartment at Ewelme ready for my occupancy and during that time I had plenty to do assembling my work and plenty of distraction in saying goodbye to friends.

"Except for a paddle up to 'rollers' this morning, I have been working all day, and Sunday the 4th of July at that. Just at present I am translating the Mozarabic Liturgy and the Latin it is written in seems to know no rules at all.

"We have just had a terrific rain-thunder-hail-and-lightning storm which made it like night for about half an hour and sent great smashes of lightning plump on the great tower so that you could almost imagine it smoked. Now suddenly the sky is blue and the birds are singing.

"I went to tea and tennis with Mr. Kempshead, one of our college dons, last Friday. He had been a tutor at a German university and said that it was extraordinary how much immorality the lack of athletics was accountable for in German schools. But this immorality, he feels, is one of the fundamentals of the German character. He also remarked that since in England the distinction between people who were in business and those who were not, has ceased, the distinction between different kinds of businesses takes place."

Mr. Kempshead's remark about the persistence of distinction seemed to me worth thinking through. Although it was difficult for me to recall the day when business was looked down on, there was with us in America a distinctly professional class. I had no way of foretelling the day when professions would be so stream-lined for efficiency's sake that they would be on a level with business. When music even, because of modern methods of record-ing and broadcasting, would become one of our biggest businesses. Yet if mechanics and business methods were to bring great music to the people, who were we to complain who during the war were being deprived of the normal number of concerts and especially of music by enemy composers. Now and then a great artist could be heard in the Sheldonian, and the Gilbert and Sullivan operas had their annual week in Oxford. The great church music we still had.

"Last night," my chronicle noted, "I dropped in on Varley Roberts to get his opinion of Sir Walter Parrat who was giving an organ recital in the New College chapel for the Red Cross, and then went on to the concert. 'Wonderful executant,' Dr. Roberts called him, and so he was. The choir in back of the church sang several selections from the Missa Papae Marcelli, things I had just been working with. At present I am deep in translating the Mozarabic Missal, as I may have told you. The Latin is so poor that it is necessary to do a good deal of guessing, and that is a thing I am not good at.

"Yesterday, the Fourth, I had two little flags, Canadian and American, which I brought away with me from home, stuck in my window. The result was it attracted a lady visitor. She came quietly up my steep stone stairway and discovered me in my red study robe and goggle glasses. When she poked her head in my door I invited her to come in. Then, hearing my voice, she fled. In my attempt to make her understand that I didn't care if she came in I pursued her. When I say she fled, I really think she went down those high steps *bini ac bini.*"

My little Gothic window looking out toward the tower would have been a lot more private if it were not that the Prince of Wales' windows were on the same side of the cloister. Opposite us there was an opening in the cloister wall and a paved platform extended into the lawn as though inviting any group of tourists to stand there and gaze with awe in hopes of catching a glimpse of the prince. This was becoming more of a nuisance as summer approached, but now a greater interruption was forced upon me.

"The college insists in redecorating my room in spite of my protest that in such a time of stress the college should not go to the expense. They give me a choice of design, however. So I shall have a pomegranate-grape-leaf-tapestry wall paper and have the woodwork painted some dark color to match. But during this operation I must vacate my rooms.

"First I plan to go to the student conference at Swanick in Derbyshire with Delmar Banner. This should not be expensive and the experience of having been there will be of value in my work at home. After my visit there from July 15 to 29 I shall return to Magdalen to pick up my box and bike, and sending them down by a carrier's wagon, I shall paddle down the river in a canoe I have rented for $0.50 per week to Nuneham Park. After lunch there I shall continue to the William Greets' house at Shillingford where I shall hope to meet his brother Ben at tea. From there I shall go by foot three miles to Ewelme."

The alms house was ready to receive me and on the 8th I noted, "Lady Osler said the other day when she came to have tea in my rooms that there is no more lovely place in England I could spend the summer than Ewelme. As far as I can see it makes little difference to the Oslers how long I remain there. The decoration of my college rooms will take over a month, and if I can get good dinners at Ewelme and manage about the other meals for myself, I think I shall stay a good while.

"I've been talking with a Mr. U —, come here from the U.S.A. with an appeal for justice in the matter of international trade. It seems that England is sending ten times the amount of rice to neutral countries than is her normal export, and likewise of castor oil, etc. The British government winks at this and complains that the U.S.A. is doing the same thing. (The U — s are sightseeing the college). Although this question of export may be technically right for both governments, it doesn't seem fair, especially with a threatening food shortage in England."

I was to find the economic situation straitening from now on. Less than a month before my last letter there appeared in *The Times* a communication from "A Banker" which started public misgiving as to the government's ability to handle the increasing war costs. At Nuneham I listened to comments regarding recent speeches by Asquith and Bonar Law on national economy. Then, on July 6th had come a motion in the House of Lords "that in view of the necessary expenditure on the war it is the opinion of this House incumbent on His Majesty's Government to take immediate steps to reduce the civil expenditure of the country." This meant what was to be called "Retrenchment."

From Magdalen still I was writing on July 10th, "Most exciting day in progress. Five men to breakfast this morning — each ordering and paying for their own eats but eating them in my rooms. And now Tres Griffin and his father for lunch. Goodness but my table looks wonderfully! A huge five ton tankard in the centre and my telescope candle sticks and the flat silver of the college on the bare mahogany!

"The tankard is drained and father and son have gone. The father, H. A. Treseder, is a very successful coal merchant in Wales and has small opinion of the men at the head of the government today. Says he has thousands of young men pass under him and he has always told them that to have your word taken for your bond means success in business. Deficit spending meant more trouble ahead.

"And now Reginald Windram — St. Paul's, Concord, boy come to Magdalen — has telephoned from London to ask me to play tennis with him and will come to tea. But he will have to eat what is left over, I can get nothing more.

"This morning was degree day when Tres Griffin, William Walker and Edward Chapman received their rewards. Two 'firsts' and a 'second.' Sir William Osler — who is curator of the Bodleian library, delegate of the University Press and one of the Radcliffe trustees — met me at the door of the Divinity Hall where the ceremonies were to take place and introduced me to Mr. Bannister, an eminent authority on the musical side of my subject. Professor E. K. Rand, who was head of the American School in Rome where Mr. Bannister is connected with the British School, wrote from Harvard some time ago saying he would like to introduce me to this scholar. At the time Mr. B was not in Oxford. After he had asked me to come and see him, Sir William took me by the arm and marched me into the hall where the degrees were to be conferred.

"This small hall of Divinity is used now because of the number of men up. We were late and the full assemblage of the university dignitaries were seated about and lots of visitors with them. But Sir William in his gorgeous red gown insisted on holding on to my arm and going right up to the end of the hall talking about this man I had just met. I finally broke away and returned in confusion with — what I thought — everybody staring at my old grey jacket and trousers. Heaps of Latin talk followed, and much bowing and taking off of mortar-boards and going out with one kind of hood and returning with another. Finally with two Magdalen undergrads, Conrad Snow and Gov Hoffman (also Americans) whom I had joined at the door, we escaped.

"I wonder if you sometimes fear that all this will rather unsettle me for my work than prepare me for it. I can assure you that the former will not be the case, for every day I am learning the simplicity of great things and the greatness of simple things. I take little space for telling you about my research here, and yet that takes up practically all my time."

On July the 11th I was recording, "Each day seems more wonderful than the one just passed. This morning at eight the Communion administered by our Estates Bursar — the clergy here can be found doing all sorts of things other than running a parish. Then, breaker with Hodgson and the morning service after. Then, work till the time when I went to lodge to post a letter and found a message had come from Lady Osler asking me to lunch and had not been delivered. Then a hustle to dress for lunch.

"Miss Wright from Montreal, a cousin of Arthur Howard's, was there. And also Sir W's brother and his wife. They had all been to tea with me the week before. It seems I can probably make arrangements with a Belgian refugee and wife for my dinners at Ewelme. They are all very keen about my going down there, and so is everybody else who hears of it. Mr. Cookson said that this was the last straw, that I should have a palace put at my disposal, for he thinks Ewelme is the most beautiful place in England. Sir W was in his best form. When I went away he presented me with

13, NORHAM GARDENS,
OXFORD.

3rd May, 1919.

Dear St. Augustine,

I am delighted to see the

prospectus of your book, for which

I predict a great success. Thanks

in advance for the copy.

Greetings to your father

when you write.

Sincerely yours,

W Osler

SIR WILLIAM OSLER (professor of medicine at Johns Hopkins and Oxford) typical notes written to Brett Langstaff addressing him as "Origen" and "St. Augustine." (See page 182) three books that he has written and inscribed my name and his own 'W. O.' Half the time he calls me St. Augustine and the other half Origen. Alas, I am neither saint nor scholar!

"After lunch I rode away on Arthur Howard's bike and at my rooms dressed in my 'yachting clothes' — unfortunately the canvas shoes I wore on my trip to Panama have split in playing tennis. But white trousers and black jacket. Then to my canoe, of which I wrote before, and sticking in it a little mast on which I hoisted a small red sail, I was off down stream. Sail and paddle, as wind and wave required, winding through the beautiful Oxford country-side, with river-bank flora at its best, through two locks which quite terrified me — and finally moored at the Harcourts' boat house. A romantic little structure on an island among the trees. Then by foot up through Nuneham's famous gardens, over the terraces and into the front hall. I went in, washed up in the lavatory and then came out and rang the front door bell for the butler. Then in to tea.

"Mr. and Mrs. Harcourt were very cordial. What a well setup pair they are! Physically, mentally, spiritually. England and America at their best. Then there was Sister Alexander and one of the officer-patients with whom I had played tennis before. But there are only a few patients left because the hospitals are not crowded at present. There were the two Misses Burden among the guests, Lord Allendale and certain other Lords whose rank is conveniently covered by this courtesy title. The remarkable thing about *the eats* was that the strawberries were the deep dark red Waterloo berries — the best I have ever tasted.

"I had brought along the picture sections of the last two copies of the *New York Times* and when I gave them to Lulu Harcourt he asked in a meaning way if there were any more pictures of the sinking of the *Audacious.* This American publicising of events which the English government sees fit to keep from its people is sometimes bothersome. I started back soon after tea and had the good luck of sailing before the wind most of the way. I sang like a lark and the little red sail made me feel like an Arabian night.

"Arrived safe in Magdalen, I have had some grapenuts and after this letter I am off to bed with the books Sir William Osler gave me."

That matter of the *Audacious* to which Lord Harcourt referred was kept from the British public for a long time. It was a sort of newspaper scoop which resulted in publishing an illustration of the sinking vessel. The fact was that the Battleship *Audacious* was sunk by a mine off the west coast of Ireland. Her complement was rescued, I understood, by the White Star liner *Olympic*. But what I did not know, nor the American reporters either, that the *Olympic* was at this time carrying troops to Gallipoli. I did learn at Nuneham, however, that the fighting was still heavy on the Belgian front with the Canadians doing heroic deeds.

My letter of July 19 enclosed "a Twenty Pfennig Deutsches Reich stamp surcharged by the German invaders, 'Belgium 25 Centimes' and postmarked 'Verviers, Belgium.' The Belgian student, Georges Kaeckenbeeck, who is our guest here at Magdalen, received it on a letter from his parents. By the way, the sister of the Belgian king, The Duchess de Vendome, will lunch in College this week. Lady Osler says she is doing good work in grouping the refugees from her country in a sort of colony. They can't stand the English cooking!

"'Last night I called on the Oslers to make final arrangements about going down to Ewelme. Lady O says there is nothing for me to do. She will see that things are ready for me when I come back from the conference at Swanick. It is certainly royal treatment to have this historic establishment given over to me for the summer.

"It is always delightful to hear Sir William talk of my grandfather 'owning all of Yonge Street.' He seems to recall 'the doctor' best of all, the uncle with whom father started his practice." Sir William was born at Bond Head in 1849 and spent some time with his uncle who was vicar of York Mills on Yonge Street. Both he and my father attended Toronto University.

The Swanick Conference to which I was going with some fifteen or twenty other Oxford men was the annual gathering of students from various parts of the United Kingdom together with many foreign students in England at that time. Its purpose was the mutual edification and help in carrying forth the work of Christ in the world. The contact it might afford me with men from other nations still remaining neutral as well as those who came from distant parts of the British Empire I felt would have special significance in this year of 1915. It was difficult for youth such as I to comprehend the international complications which had led to the present conflict. Yet the brunt of the fighting must be born by men of our age. If the Christian ideal of love and forgiveness were not to be compromised, what were we to do?

It was not until I was settled at Ewelme that I was able to report on July 30th. "The conference cost me a bit over three pounds and was well worth while. They had a large house to shelter the prominent speakers and women and numerous tents for the students. Two Oxford tents. Also a few sizeable tents for the lectures. The Bishops of Oxford, Lichfield and Bombay were there, along with several distinguished nonconformists. We were soaked with rain and religion, but it was a chance to see how the war was affecting the younger people for whom it is largely being fought. An attempted meeting of pacifists was rather rudely broken up with my help. The East Indians took the opportunity of expressing themselves frankly in an open meeting on their adverse attitude toward the British Imperial policy. The war was the dominant note in every lecture and discussion. When it became too much for me I persuaded Banner to run away with me to have a looksee at the fabled mansion of nearby Haddon Hall.

"When we arrived back at Magdalen I found my lunch laid for me (This does not mean I had eggs for lunch). And between the beginning of that lunch and its end I had another lunch with Lady Osler and Miss Wright. Lady O told of having brought the sister of King Albert of the Belgians to lunch with Sir Herbert at Magdalen several days ago. I understand our good president nearly stood on his head with excitement. But it rained and the final climax of the garden couldn't be did! The Oslers also invited all the nice Belgians to meet Her Highness in the Great Hall of Christ Church. The 'Belgiums' mistook Lady O for the duchess and were funny and businesslike.

"After lunches I packed and set out to find Norman Nash with whom I had tea some time ago. He had been strolling around the college, seen my name on the staircase and left his card for me. Meredith will remember Norman B. Nash, probably of his Harvard Class of 1908, who went in for Law and then changed for the Ministry. His father was the great scholar of our church in his day. I found Norman with heaps of introduction letters and with the intention of spending his Sheldon Fellowship at Cambridge under Burkitt. Then, having asked him about things in America and receiving the answers I had expected, I biked down to Ewelme.

"A beautiful twelve miles past Nuneham Park and up into the foothills of the Chiltern range. The village of Ewelme straggling

along a tree-arched road for about a mile. And over a mosaic of
sparkling pebbles by the side of the road murmurs a small stream.
I know of no more fascinating entrance drive to any estate than
this village road which could hardly be thought of as public. So
near London, yet five miles from a railway.

"An old school building rises abruptly from the side of the
road, and over the terrace wall next to it can always be seen some
of the old men of the alms house peering like gargoyles as though
to protect the children from evil spirits. But if you pass the iron-
bound door which for 479 years has held the children of the village
prisoners for a few precious hours of every school day and go
through the gate in the brick wall you will find yourself in a
thriving garden where the rose and the potato vie with each other
in beauty and usefulness. And if you look closely you will see
that there are thirteeen distinct plots where since early in the 15th
century thirteen ancients have raised what best suited the tastes
of each.

"To the left runs a path to Sister Annette's cottage, and on the
right is a door into the cloister. I have told you of this cloister
with its red brick and blackened oak, the chimney pots peeping
above a high peaked roof, and a row of bright geraniums on the
top of a low wall which separates the brick-paved court from the
shade of the covered passageway around it."

I went at once to pay my respects to the vicar, and he gave me
some of the history of this lovely spot which was to become part
of me during the months of vacation ahead. On the site of a former
church whose existence was mentioned in the 13th century, he
assured me, this 'new' church — and the cloister in which I was
now to live — were erected by William de la Pole, Earl (afterwards
Duke) of Suffolk, and Alice, his wife, in 1431. (The year he
returned from fighting Jeanne D'Arc and the French.) The church
could hardly have been completed when the father of the duchess
— he was the son of the poet Geoffrey Chaucer of the *Canterbury
Tales* — was laid in a tomb in the chapel.

Except for the elaborate tomb which the second Duke of Suffolk,
John, had constructed to extol the memory of Alice, his mother,
and a richly carved chapel roof, the church seemed to have preserved its ancient simplicity. This Duke John, I knew from my
history reading, married Elizabeth, daughter of Richard Duke of
York, and thereby became brother-in-law to two reigning princes,

Edward IV, King of England, and Charles the Bold, Duke of Burgundy. Even a civil war which destroyed so much of the ecclesiastical glass and carving in England spared this little church of Ewelme. This the vicar said was out of consideration for a native of the village who stood high among Cromwell's officers.

"The Reverend Mr. Dodd — the Rector of Ewelme — is an accumulator of etchings and engravings," I wrote from Ewelme, Oxford, 3rd August 1915. "I already have him interested in helping me to extraillustrate Andrew Lang's *Oxford*. On Sunday, after service, I had lunch with him in a rectory with a concealed room. He explains this room as a hideout for political refugees, but I think maybe some rector may have used it at times to get away from his parishioners. The Manor people in the village have also asked me to tea, and in return for these courtesies I have asked them all to drink tea with me in my new apartment.

"The tea in my lodgings was this afternoon. Miss Quinn and Miss Jervis from the Manor, Lady Vere Hughes, Lord Buckingham's sister, the rector and Norman Nash who came down unexpectedly. With Lady Osler's old pictured tea cups and my candlesticks and the quaint surroundings, we had a memorable tea party. The Bishop of Oxford — Gore, whom I had come to know at Swanick — was also here showing Lord Somebody the place, but he had with him also a multitude of the Lord's children, about ten, so that I could not ask him in. I have written the kindly bishop to say that when he comes this way again, to stop in for tea. He is one of the promoters of the prayer book revision and a worthy scholar. Although he looks rather disappointing — for the great man he is — he has a delightful sense of humour." Charles Gore brother of the 4th Earl of Arran, was sixty-two at the time and at the height of his influence whereby the Oxford Movement had changed from the former Tractarian lines to a Modernist trend.

The day folowing "I rushed into Oxford [it takes about an hour's hard riding] to deposit my money. On the $35. I made a bit in the exchange because the rate has gone up. The five pounds in the draft went at face value.

"My dinners with the Belgians are delicious and the opportunity for speaking French is good in view of the fact that they refuse to understand English. This afternoon the Reverend Mr. Bidlake called with a message from the Manor asking me to tea. He was one time curate here. Lady Vere Hughes and I played partners at croquet, and the ladies who inhabit this historic residence were most hospitable in asking me to come any afternoon. Part of the Manor House was part of the ancient palace in which Alice, Duchess of Suffolk, lived almost five hundred years ago.

"When the carrier delivered my books from Oxford late this afternoon he surprised me by saying good night. It seems the country folk in Oxfordshire have a way of saying 'good night' at any time after the noon hour. Now in this secluded spot, thanks to the granddaughter of the *Canterbury Tales* and my good friends the Oslers, I have an ideal atmosphere for studying my church history."

At Ewelme I was to have the companionship of the spirits of many predecessors of the present rector. They had not only studied English church history but also had helped to make it. There was John Prideux, Rector of Ewelme in 1620 and later Bishop of Worcester; Robert Sanderson, Rector in 1642 and later Bishop of Lincoln; John Potter, Rector in 1707 and later Bishop of Oxford and Archbishop of Canterbury; John Randolph, Rector in 1783 and later Bishop of Bangor and London; William Rowley, Rector in 1809 and later Bishop of London and Archbishop of Canterbury; William van Mildert, Rector in 1813 and later Bishop of Llandaff and Durham; Charles Lloyd, Rector in 1822 and later Bishop of Oxford; R. Dickson Hampden, Rector in 1836 and later Bishop of Hereford; William Jacobson, Rector in 1848 and later Bishop of Chester.

In 1871 the appointment of Rector of Ewelme was one of Gladstone's famous dilemmas in the House of Commons, and much later when Lloyd George was Prime Minister another embarrassment arose when I was offered the *living* of Ewelme. But now in 1915 my friend Mr. Dodd was the Rector. All these men had been familiar with my ancient cloister and in the adjoining church had celebrated the Liturgy I was studying. To these distinguished clerics I could add in years to come my friend Norman Nash who, after serving as head of St. Paul's School, Concord, was to become Bishop of Massachusetts.

"Professor Comfort of Cornell came out and had tea with me the day before yesterday," my journal noted on August 10th. "When Sir Herbert Warren first introduced me to him at college he said, 'Of course you know Professor Comfort's name?,' and

Dear L.

[handwritten letter:]

Prof Comfortis anxious to see Ewelme so on Monday (weather permitting) or Tuesday (whether or no) he & I are biking down. I hope we may find you at home, but pray don't change your program at all. He has been told of the rarity of the place, & wants to see it.

N.B.N

Sat. night.

NORMAN BURDETT NASH (Bishop of Massachusetts) written Brett Langstaff 1915 of intention to bring Professor Comfort to visit Ewelme (see index).

since the good man was right there I had to asssent, whereas I really did not at all. Now I am happy to say I do know the man, even if later I may forget his name.

"Yesterday I went into Oxford to see the Oslers and thank them for all they have done. Sir W was lecturing on Greek Medicine and I missed them. But I did see the Clement Webbs in their house overhanging the stream, Canon Brightman (my tutor), Walker and some other men — and my college room. The latter is coming on well. A marvelous sunset on the way back to Ewelme!

"The Countess of Macclesfield has asked me to take tea with her at Shirburn Castle this afternoon. I am rather anxious to see her residence because it is one of the few castles in England which still has its moat filled with water. I think they are cousins of the Tecks."

The Macclesfield I had come to know in my historical research had fled to France after the capitulation of Charles I at Oxford in 1646 and returned to England at the Restoration, was created earl in '79, forced to flee again and finally returned with William

III. He needed the deep moat and all that went with it. But the present family whose hospitality I enjoyed evidently never had need nor inclination for pulling up the drawbridge over which I passed to their front door. There were chickens walking over it at the same time.

Castles and drawbridges — howbeit of an earlier date — had always to my mind belonged on a Shakespearian stage and I was all in the mood when I received a suggestion from Sir Philip Ben Greet to join him for the plays at Stratford. His company of Ben Greet Players had long been a household word in the United States where his open air performances had done much to raise the standard of the American stage. It was there I first met him. I had acted small parts for him and he had trained a small group of theological students for me.

The theatre in England was hard hit because of war conditions. No companies touring the counties and little more than music shows to amuse men on leave in London. Many of the actors had joined the Artists Rifles whose uniform I would later find myself wearing before the war was over. There were groups of stage folk sent to the fighting areas for the entertainment of the soldiers, and Shakespeare's plays were being produced by Sir Frank Benson at Stratford-on-Avon. Thanks to Sir Philip's hospitality this seemed to be an opportunity to see the native town of William Shakespeare in a delightfully personal way.

My next writing came from the Swan's Nest Hotel, Stratford-on-Avon, 21st August 1915, saying, "Let me jot down a few of the things as they have happened during the past week. I sent my kit by carrier to Wallingford, and followed on my bike. The bicycle I left there at a machinist to be professionally cleaned, thus doing my duty to another man's bike and saving storage while away.

"Then came a long tiresome train journey with many waitings on noisy stations until I reached Stratford. There, I sent my kit to the hotel and myself walked through the town and across the bridge to where the Swan's Nest is beside the Avon.

"Mr. Ben Greet's invitation has brought me to this famous spot and I found the great Shakespearian interpreter under a tree on the bank of the River Avon. (There has been no rain since I came out and the air is mild.) We had eats — cold meat, salad, etc. Talked of the dear 'Duchess of Brooklyn,' as Mr. Greet calls Mother. And then to the theatre.

"*Richard II* with Mr. Frank Benson as Richard. It is the best thing he does and he certainly did a difficult part skillfully. His setting so completely fitted in with the ancient house at Ewelme, for it was the son of Richard II's Chancellor Michael de la Pole who built my alms house. Mr. Benson spotted us sitting in the gallery and sent for Mr. Greet to come and see him after the play On the stage behind the scenes after everybody had gone, there we were: Frank Benson, Ben Greet and my insignificant self in the Shakespeare Theatre. Mr. Greet was one of the first to produce Shakespeare in Stratford in years past.

"Frank Benson talked of his son who had been seriously wounded and sent home — had been told to hold a trench at all costs and then when the shells from their own lines had destroyed their earthworks and exploded their bombs, they had to defend the trench with stones and anything they could lay their hands on. The enemy was only 'this distance,' said Mr. Benson, walking a few paces away. His son was the only officer left alive. Mr. Benson told Mr. Greet he would come over quietly to the Swan's Nest later on.

"The next day after breakfast we went sightseeing, dear Mr. Ben Shakespeare with his familiar shock of white hair attracting the attention of many who knew him, and myself. We went to the church and saw what you are too familiar with for me to give you any news about. The great nave and choir with its stained glass windows, the tomb with its well rubbed epitaph, and all the other beauties of the church. Then we continued around outside where the chancel window looks toward the tree-arched river — here is Mr. Greet's favorite resting place.

"We were looking in the windows of the Shakespeare Head Press, when out popped a lady and asked us to come back and see an ancient house in the rear. There in the garden we met Mr. Bullen, a famous printer. He showed us a cluster of rustic gables rising above a mass of bright flowers. Some noted person had lived in the house before Shakespeare's time.

"The old publisher remembered the days when Ben Greet used to produce the plays in the Stratford theatre and was thrilled at his return after so many years. Among his reminiscences was this. He said someone had set up a book shop which he called by a name which confused many people with Mr. Bullen's old establishment, and brought undeserved discredit on it. Mr. Bullen went

Jan. 14. 18.
9 Southwick St.
W.2.

Dear Mr. Langstaff,

Thank you for your kind letter.
Yes, I will with pleasure. Had pleasure in
meeting you in Stratford-on-Avon. You are
engaged in a great Crusade, more constructive
than the War (among the causes of which
may be numbered the neglect of such work
as you are doing).
Let me wish you all success in your
labours.

Yours very truly
Frank R Benson

SIR FRANK BENSON (actor and Shakespearean producer) written Brett Langstaff 1918, in which he refers to the slum clearance by the Magdalen Mission of which Langstaff was then Head.

to Mr. Longman, who was then at the head of the publishing world, and asked his advice. 'Well,' said Mr. L, 'I don't know what you may do. This fellow is a bad sort and you can't stop him. What I should do would be to write him just as strong a letter as I possibly could and *then tear it up!'*

"In the afternoon of the second day we went to see the matinee performance of *As You Like It*. The love story cut me deep! Goodness, how the author must have loved to write such a play! The acting could not have been done better in most of the parts, Mr. Greet said, and added that he himself had produced *As You Like It* more times than anyone living. He is so looked up to! It is like walking around London with the king, impossible of course since the king never has the chance to walk around London.

"Then came supper. And supper over, the Second Part of Henry IV. A marvelous, fat, jovial Falstaff. Mrs. Benson took the part of Doll. She shrieked and carried on so that it was hard and even unpleasant to think of her in connection with the charming Mrs. Benson we had met and talked with on the street earlier in the day. I remember in telling us about their son's bravery she had also said, 'It makes our work seem very useless and empty,' and Mr. Greet had replied, 'At least we have something to say. It's the musical comedy people who have it hardest in these days of war.' But the play went off with great effect.

"The next day, after we had seen the birth place, the school, Anne's cottage and all the rest — on which, by the way, Mr. Greet's comments were delightful — we went to the theatre for *Hamlet*.

"But just before this I rushed up to the house where the mother of the founder of Harvard College had lived. There I signed in the Harvard Book with many other familiar names of Harvard men. On the tables are some of the Harvard magazines, and there is also a place for Harvard men to write on college stationery. I shall send them my HARVARD OF TODAY to add to their collection of books which, they tell me, I must direct to Marie Corelli who is the originator and guardian of the house.

"Then came *Hamlet* at six o'clock, so that there might be time for the entire play as Shakespeare wrote it. Indeed, although I have seen most of the actors of my day present the play and read it many times, I don't think I have really understood it before. The words and the scenes which it is necessary to leave out for modern audiences spoil the clear meaning of the drama. It was as though some skilful artist had restored what had always been for me a fragmentary work. And having seen the play thus in its entirety I shall hereafter be able to appreciate shorter versions.

"Costumes were much the same as usual, except the traditional red wig of the King was changed for a black one, and other touches which made him rather oriental, and the mother was younger than traditional. With these Mr. Greet was not in full accord. Between the two halves of the play he and I went around the gardens to the back and talked with *Polonius*. He said that the reason Mr. Benson had *floated*, or 'dried up' in his first speech, with which he was more familiar than any, was because there was one line that he had always cut, and he was worried with fear he would leave it out. (It took me back to my memory troubles when playing *Aguecheek* for Professor Baker's production of *Twelfth Night* at Harvard.) But Mr. Greet agreed that it was a difficult thing to

198 BRATTLE STREET
CAMBRIDGE, MASS.

Sept.23,1913

Dear Mr. Langstaff,

    Now that I have just heard the Pageant clock striking the half hour,I realize that I have not answered your kind letter of the early summer. I take much pleasure in this gift, which I happen to know was suggested by you. For that and for the spirit in which you chose the inscription,let me thank you very heartily.

    With all good wishes for your success, I am

    Yours sincerely,

Geo.P.Baker.

PROFESSOR GEORGE PIERCE BAKER (teacher of drama at Harvard and later at Yale) wrote script for the *Hollis Hall Pageant* which Brett Langstaff produced at Harvard 1913.

remember to put in lines which one was accustomed to leave out, for he had done *Hamlet* in full himself. After we had talked with Mr. Benson — supper at the Swan's Nest and then to bed. Tomorrow morning at 9.30 I am off for Ewelme.

"Home in good time," I wrote from Ewelme, "to get things ready for the Harcourt family whom I had invited to take tea with me and inspect the treasured monuments of Ewelme. I found waiting for me a letter from Andrew Nugee who has been serving with the 9th Service Battalion Rifle Brigade. He says he has lost an eye and will therefore probably be back at Magdalen next year since the government can have no further use for him. Another from Prince George to say that he was coming over from Windsor to see me but at present he is working from one to six in a munitions factory. A third from Norman Nash to let me know he was coming down again.

"Now to tell of the *eats* I had for the Harcourt party. I had arranged with my Belgians to make me a couple of their most delicious cakes. This was to be the one specialty, for they create unbelievable confections. For the rest I planned the regular thin bread and butter and jam which I have every day. Then to grace the party my candlesticks from Bath.

"Well, the guests arrived. First Norman, who had been spending the weekend near Stratford with friends. And then Mrs. Harcourt in a becoming cool pink dress. She had spoken with the sexton about having the chancel unlocked and I think felt hesitant at disturbing me at all; but they have been so hospitable to me that I wanted to give them a good time, and one they would remember. There came with Mrs. Harcourt her mother, Mrs. Burns — that would be J. P. Morgan's sister, Mr. Jack's aunt, wouldn't it? Also in the party was Mrs. H's brother and his brother-in-law, and a girl to whom I was never introduced and a Russian who spoke nothing but Russian — which means nothing at all — but instead he had great decorations on his front which did the speaking for him. Thus with Norman and myself there were eight in all.

"I showed them the treasures of Ewelme from the alabaster tomb to the rare manuscripts in the muniment room. Mrs. Burns I marched off by herself because I recalled Ben Greet's amusing account of a struggle with Mrs. B in front of the Grand Opera House in Paris as to who had hailed a certain fiacre first. She has a rather imperious manner. But Mrs. B was very gracious with all and she seemed thoroughly to enjoy hearing all my stories.

"I must break in here to tell you that while I was coming down in the train from Stratford, I met a man with whom I talked in the railway carriage about the plays we had just seen. On parting he presented me with a book he had bought in Stratford. The very book which I had looked at while there and had wished to buy but feared to because of the cost. Curious, a perfect stranger, but before I left I asked him his name which was Dumello. That makes him the noted theological publisher who had recently brought out a teenth edition of the *Complete One Volume Commentary of the Bible.* Perhaps it will be well to know a theological publisher when my dissertation is done."

Not long after my return from Stratford I had the rare privilege of an intimate association with the English geographer and historical writer, Clements Robert Markham, K. C. B. As Santayana had delved into the realms of the intellect, as Osler had examined the processes of the human body, so — it seemed to me — Markham had explored the surface of the globe. All three were master explorers. And when I came to know Sir Clements he was engaged in setting down a record of polar expeditions with which he had been concerned personally. It was to be completed posthumously and published as *Lands of Silence* and recognized as an important history of Arctic and Antarctic exploration.

"Let me tell you the story of Sir Clements Markham," I began on August 23rd. "Miss Quinn introduced me to him after my return from Stratford. He and Lady Markham have taken the Maxwells' house across the road from me. I asked them all to tea Sunday afternoon. He is a dear old white haired gentleman of about eighty-four years, I should say, and was in California when General Fremont came out to take possession of the country for the U. S. A. It was he who first took the Peruvian bark from its native land to India and thus made possible the widespread use of quinine. He was president of the Royal Geographical Society for twenty years, and it was to him that Mr. Longstaff gave 30,000 pounds for the Antarctic Expedition which effected the discovery of the South Pole. He has been to Harvard and seems to know most of the old professors there. He asked me to supper the same evening, and we had another long talk.

"Well, this Sir Clements married a Miss Chichester whose father's father had married the heir of some vast county seat designed to preserve the name of Brett. I gave him the information I had concerning our own part of the Brett family, and this greatly interested him, so much so that he wrote it all down. He seemed to think there would be no difficulty in finding out where my grandmother joined up with the other Bretts. As for Lord Esher, that he counted a comparatively recent creation.

"Work on my dissertation often takes me late into the night. Several times recently I have been disturbed by a shadowy white object which appears through the leaded glass of my window over-looking the cloister, glares at me with glowing eyes, and then, when I cautiously approach it, silently melts into the darkness. There is a rather interesting clergyman staying with Mr. Dodd now with whom I had supper Saturday night. He is a believer in psychical research and was little comfort to me in the matter of my ghostly apparition. Even Sir Clements Markham responded by telling me a terrifying story which he had first hand. It was this. In a certain old residence they were making a passage through a thick wall and while the bricks were being removed they found wedged a skull below which there was a large cavity in the wall with a heap of bones, glass and leather at the bottom. The leather was declared by the British Museum to be about 16th century work. Now, the night of the day this discovery was made, the lady of the house was awakened by her husband's screams that a ghost was choking him. The lady went immediately, gathered up the bones and all, and buried them. This was supposed to be the explanation of numerous queer things which had happened near where the bones were found. I have since discovered that my 'ghost' was a white owl with which the Oslers were familiar."

The repose of the soul of the founder of the alms house, Sir William did take seriously, and since this was the original purpose of the foundation Sir William arranged to have prayers said to this end. The church at Ewelme was indeed a remarkable building. Set not quite square with the cloister, and yet so close that one passed up the stone steps from the cloister into the west portal of the church without coming out from cover — a convenience for the old people who went daily to pray for the soul of the duchess. The original stone font at the church door with its elaborate carved-wood cover, aisles paved with bronze tablets, an ancient choir-screen of oak and painted iron were just visible in the tempered light from the original windows. The lady chapel to the right of the chancel was partially screened off by the famous tomb of the Duchess of Suffolk — her alabaster figure wearing on its arm the badge of the Order of the Garter (the first to be conferred on a woman) and on the ceiling of the fretted canopy above her the unmolested painting of the Virgin Mary.

The circle of friends widened as I wrote on the 25th that I had "just come from having tea with the Eagle-Botts who are my nearest neighbours. They heard me laugh and asked me on the strength of that! In the family is a youngster who is building a miniature railway through their garden with the aid of his sisters. In this garden an ample stream springs full-born from a chalky bank and flows under the garden wall and on beside the village road, crystal clear.

"The Belgian couple who have been giving me my dinners are going away, and that will throw me back on my little housekeeper. I will not be able to astonish my guests any longer with delicious Belgian confections. But it suits my work to stay a bit longer in these delightful surroundings. Perhaps I shall go visiting in London before I return to my rooms at Magdalen.

"I am indeed glad to hear that a box is coming to me for the Relief Work," the journal continued on the 16th. "It will just answer a letter from my friend, Mrs. Pye-Smith, asking help for Phil's regiment. I have written her telling of the good luck and I will look for the box daily.

"Day before yesterday I had tea with Sister Annette in her lovely little cottage. She is a good friend in great need and often helps me when I would otherwise be lost. Miss Babcock, her name, and she is the trained nurse whose special care is the health of the thirteen old men of the Alms House. At one time she had charge of a ward in a London hospital, and now she is resting up a bit."

Another three days, and I was still writing from Ewelme. "Last night while I was dining with Sir Clements and Lady Markham I said to him, When are you coming over to see the rest of our muniments? And he said, I'll come tomorrow. Come to tea, says I. I'll do it and come at 2.30. So he came and brought with him his nephew, a Mr. Steuart. We went all through the ancient documents, meticulously mounted in a series of large volumes and preserved in huge safes. This priceless collection of manuscripts, kept securely now in the environment in which most of them were written, has been made under Sir William Osler's personal supervision and probably at his own expense. It is a monument to his literary appreciation and to his sense of fitness. I find a book in Sir William's library here on the Revd. Dr. Markham who was Dean of Christ Church and later Archbishop of York, written by his grandson, Sir Clements Markham.

"Before my guests left Windram came down by motor from Magdalen to see what I was doing. He told me that on his way to Oxford by train with his mother he had occasion shortly before arriving to go into the lavatory. Well, when the train began to slow down for the station he could not open the door — and he is such a punctilious person! His mother went to warn him and finding him so incarcerated summoned all the king's horses, but the door would not give. The train stopped and had to wait until a panel was broken open enough to allow Windram to crawl out. By the time he reached me he could laugh at his utter embarrassment and was once again the sophisticated well groomed youth. Before he motored back to Oxford he took me for a good spin about the country. I seem to be set in the midst of the most beautiful hills in the south of England.

"Sir William Osler stopped in on me while I was on my way yesterday afternoon to see him — and it's a great distance to come and go." It was now the 1st of September and I had just received an exciting notice from Louis Livingston Seaman, head of the British War Relief Society in New York, that he was "sending me a crate of hospital supplies." I needed advice badly. The secretary who wrote the letter made the mistake of thinking that I was operating a military hospital because the Ewelme alms house is often referred to as a *hospital* in the ancient sense of the word.

"However, the case of medical and surgical things could not come to a better place for distribution for I am surrounded by people who know where such equipment is most needed. Certain items such as mosquito netting, which the box contains, I shall give to Lady Osler for the British hospital in Malta where it will find immediate use. I shall offer the Harcourts some other things. And some I shall reserve for our own hospital nearby at Swincome House. This will give me a good lot of letters to send back to the War Relief society in New York, for they seem anxious to have thank-you letters to publish for further appeals. I need not say that this is a wonderful gift for the cause and a privilege that I should be allowed to distribute it."

Because the flow of American tourists was cut off and those who came on business were welcome in England only as it benefited the Allies, the comparatively few Americans — resident or temporally resident such as myself — were happy to be made use of by those working in the interest of England overseas. Also the few new student arrivals from the U. S. A. were hailed gladly by us already in England. Thus I wrote from Ewelme, "My old Harvard room-mate, Gilbert Elliott, has arrived from New York safely. He says from what I have written him he can not tell anything about my plans, but then that is one of my difficulties. Circumstances alter! But for the present and for a good deal of the near future I intend to continue accepting the hospitality of Sir William Osler. Lady Osler has been as good to me as my own mother is to many people who deserve it as little. They came out and took tea with me yesterday.

"This afternoon I was summoned to the Manor for tea and there met a Mrs. Pochin, the grandmother of the Countess of Macclesfield of whom I have spoken before. Mrs. P, who has a county seat not far away, invited me to lunch. It is strange to have people come and apologize for not calling. These strict conventions among county families are being waived as war demands increase. I go now to have dinner with my friends the Markhams and I must dress of course."

There was something about the amenities of a formal dinner that kept conversation on a high level and concerned with important topics. After the men had risen to permit the ladies to leave the room at the conclusion of dinner, there was probably gossip among the latter over the coffee and liqueurs in the drawingroom. And certainly what followed in the diningroom when the host had changed his seat to the other end of the table and the long cigars had been lighted was not always fit for feminine ears. But conversation during dinner — necessarily accompanied by a proper manipulation of knives and forks and spoons — was an art.

On this occasion I learned from Sir Clements Markham that fifteen years after he had been in South America arranging to have the cinchona plant shipped to India, he joined an Arctic expedition which took him to Greenland in 1875. It was while he was president of the Royal Geographical Society — and largely due to his personal effort in 1901 — that Robert Scott was sent to the Antarctic. His observations on controversial subjects came with first hand authority, especially on the current contention as to who discovered the North Pole and as to the fate of the Scott expedition to the South Pole.

The day following my dinner with the Markhams (4th September 1915) I noted, "Sir Clements has just been paying a morning call. He has of course been closely connected with the Arctic explorations and has a fund of interesting reminiscences. He says Dr. Cook was a good man and that his book is certainly of value, but neither he nor Admiral Peary reached the North Pole. They would not have known had they come to it because they depended on compasses and did not make their observations according to the sun. This was why Cook came out 100 miles from where he intended. Nor did Sir C consider there was much use of an expedition to the North Pole since there was nothing to be learned at that point.

"Sir Ernest Shackelton was discounted in Sir Clements' conversation as a fraud. The kind of man who can talk and makes people think that he knows more than he does. Scott had made Sir E and in return Sir E talked people into giving him enough money to make an expedition his own. And then, after writing Scott that he would not go on the track which they had prepared formerly and which Scott planned to use later to reach the Pole by — as soon as he received his captaincy — Sir E deliberately broke his word and went over the same ground. It was only by the most inexcusable miscalculations that Shackelton failed to reach the Pole. His plan now to cross from one side of the polar region to the other is merely sensational. Sir Clements Markham was utterly disgusted with him.

"He said there could be no doubt that Colonel Roosevelt had discovered the river he claimed, but that the newspapers made so much more of it than the colonel himself because he was such a prominent figure. He seemed satisfied that Theodore Roosevelt had not attempted to make more of his 'Lost River' than it was worth. (How's that for whitewashing and mud slinging!)" I had had the privilege of visiting Sir Ernest Shackelton alone in his hotel room and he was my hero, even more than Lord Kitchener who was in New York at the same time.

"I have perhaps told you," the letter went on, "that I am copying an ancient wooden chandelier, one of the three which have always hung in St. Friedswide's Chapel in Christ Church

Cathedral, Oxford. Sir William Osler considers it the earliest lighting in the cathedral. He held a long step ladder while I climbed up and measured enough detail to be able to construct a replica. The original is dark oak with geometric designs painted in gold and bright colours. I think if it turns out as successfully as it promises at this present moment, I will make two. Leave one in the Muniment Room here and have another for my own room at college. By the way, my college rooms are now redecorated and they look attractive." Sir William and Revere had been keen on cabinet work and I had been caught up in their enthusiasm although I had never done any wood carving before. Just how old the three triangular shaped chandeliers with three tapered arms extending from their sides were, the professors in Tom Quad never decided. Years later when electric fixtures were installed in the cathedral the wooden relics were taken down and lost. The replica — and I had time only to do one — now hangs in the Kedge in Morristown, New Jersey.

On September 9th I sent a long letter home from Ewelme. "Thanks to Dr. Seaman's generous gift I have been able to help those who have beeen so helpful to me. But what I would like for a certain regiment are the socks which the *New York Times* states are 'piled on Mrs. Langstaff's table.'

"I took lunch with Lady Osler today. Just went there for it. She advised me to have the crate of medical supplies sent to 13 Norham Gardens and then we could distribute them from there. She has a large sewing class of Queen Mary's Needlework Guild in the School of Forestry Building in Oxford. I have written thanking Dr. Seaman and the secretary of the British American War Relief Assoc., but the box is not here yet.

"Mrs. Harcourt is planning to close her hospital in November for cleaning purposes and for a bit of a rest to the household. She has given herself without stint to the care of the officers convalescing at Nuneham. Yesterday while lunching there, one of the Australian officers said that he would have to go to Oxford to keep an appointment with Dr. Hill, the dentist, the next day. Whereupon I told him I had just been to Dr. Hill's office and found that he would not be back from his vacation till the 27th. It took only a few more words for me to see that it was a bogus excuse the man had given to Mrs. Harcourt for his going to Oxford. Mrs. Harcourt merely remarked that she had thought this was the time Dr. Hill took his vacation. But in spite of the fact that they lie in this way and are sometimes very rude, Mrs. H treats them as guests. Although I know she must get tired she never is anything but cheerful.

"I should like to call your attention to the list for the 11th King's Comfort Fund. You may remember my telling you how I went to stay with Phil Pye-Smith when I first went to London. He is an officer in the battalion and his mother is secretary for this fund. Do let me have a nice box for them."

There were the personal happenings regardless of war which my letter continued to record. "The Manor people asked me to dinner last night, and I dressed and went. They are gentle conservative ladies, and I found them in rather a dither over a runaway match of two of their guests. It seems the Lady Vere Hughes, whose late husband was the son of the author of *Tom Brown's School Days,* had suddenly taken off with the handsome young curate whom I have mentioned before.

"Lady Boyd-Carpenter died the other day. When I lunched with them at the Vice Chancellor's recently she was so active and so much the prop to the frail elderly bishop that I wonder now what he will do without her. I shall never forget her concern for the bishop when he was about to preach to a crowded chapel at Harvard. She was out of breath with panic and caught hold of me who was serving as an usher at the chapel door. 'You must put hassocks in the pulpit,' she panted. 'The sides of the pulpit are so high they will only see the top of my husband's head.' I protested that in our 'unitarian' chapel there were no hassocks because the congregation was not encouraged to kneel. We hastened around back and collected bibles with which we literally floored the pulpit. Never was a sermon preached on firmer scriptural basis. The overflow congregation — attracted by a series of lectures on Dante which Boyd-Carpenter was then giving in one of our largest halls where the sound of his voice had the effect on his audience of a symphony concert — was duly impressed. I am especially sorry for her death at this time because I had been expected for a visit with them in the Little Cloisters beside the Abbey in London.

"A letter from Gilbert Elliott informs me he has found himself a fashionable flat in Paris where he plans to study music. He suggests I come and stop with him, but it can't be done. Time, money, risk, and most of all my own work prevent my considering it."

Among my letters was one from my friend Prince George
which I received about this time. He wrote from Frogmore
Cottage, Windsor, to say, "My dear Brett, Thank you very much
for your two letters which I ought to have answered before. I
suppose you know poor Pawle, the Master, is missing & supposed
to be killed. I will write to Fortescue & see if he wants to take
the beagles over again or not. If he does not I will come over
to Oxford & have a consultation with you & Joe. I am glad you
found your grandfather, I don't expect he minded seeing a kill.
I am keeping my beagle accounts very nicely & working from
1 to 6 in a munitions factory in Slough. I will let you know when
I propose to come to Oxford. Yours ever, George of Teck. P.S. The
Lord hath delivered Herbert's nephew into our hands. (How's
your father?)" Prince George — later to be known as the Marquess
of Cambridge — referred to Sir Herbert's nephew, Peter Warren,
who was coming up to Magdalen from Westminster next term. It
seemed as though Teck and I and that utterly sporting member
of our group, George Fortescue, were to have the responsibility
of the Magdalen-New College beagle hounds for the rest of our
time at Oxford.

"Yesterday I had a letter from Windsor," I noted on the
13th, "to say that Prince George was coming to Oxford to see
me about the beagles, and not finding me there he would come
to the nearest station to Ewelme which is Watlington. If he came
at the hour he mentioned he could not get away the same night,
so I took it he was coming for the weekend. Whereupon I arranged
my spare room for him, ordered a chicken and had the house
cleaned and garnished. It was also necessary to ask Miss Maxwell
to let me off from a dinner engagement that night. But of course
Miss M insisted I bring my visitor along. When she heard it was
the eldest son of the Duke of Teck, she was all excitement. The
news got about until the whole village was in expectation, and
the idea of a prince in the Alms House was astounding to say
the least. But it all ended in George's having to go out to Abingdon
to see about the beagles and not having time to make connections
which are at the best very bad for this place.

"I went to Miss Maxwell's for dinner. They have a distinguished
set of brothers. One the head of the Cowley Fathers, another a
general on French's staff, another a general — I think in the South

2d Oct 1915

FROGMORE COTTAGE,
WINDSOR.

My dear Brett

Thank you very much for your letter & that card. I ought to have written to you before. I have not been out tho you have these shooting parties for the Beagles?

I saw Cyr- Smith then he was home. He's return. seemed very well I lunched with him and to I hend about about your visit to Farnham. Can you collect any I hope to see you on

Fairly week, then? Yours ever, Geo. of Teck

H.S.H. PRINCE GEORGE OF TECK (later Marquess of Cambridge) written to Brett Langstaff 1915 (for reference to Malvern Student Conference, beagle hounds, military camp at Farnham, Pye-Smith, see index).

African War — and two others who are majors in the present army. I had had a fall from Arthur Howard's bike and they bandaged me up — that was in the afternoon.

"The next day, Sunday, I went to the Holy Communion at eight and read the Lessons at eleven. Then I had Sister Annette to help me eat the chicken which I had secured for Teck. The Manor ladies sent for me for tea, and I came back with a basket full of all sorts of fruit and flowers. The Lessons again in the evening and supper with Mr. Dodd, the rector. He showed me all over the rectory, which was largely built by Randolph, afterward Bishop of London, just following the American revolution.

"Now it is Monday. The excitement of today is that I have had my hand on the very large case of supplies which Dr. Seaman has sent from New York. The freight is rather high, but the good part is to be able to send it to the Oslers for distribution. I have also had notice of four dozen bottles of tonic coming from the same place. Mrs. Burns suggested I give the Sister-in-charge at Ewelme something for her dispensary. This I shall do, and the rest to be distributed from 13 Norham Gardens, although Sir William is in France at the moment. I have written to Lady Strathcona asking if she might have a hospital to which I could contribute. They have been so kind to me.

"I rather want to get back to college. I don't know why it is but after I have been in a place for a while I get to know the people about so well that it soon becomes a distraction. There is hardly anybody within biking distance from whom I have not received a general invitation, and the food I buy to eat at home just stays uneaten. It is certainly entertaining, but it begins to interfere with my work, and so I think I will back to Oxford. Also I have made quite a stay — over six weeks already."

Finally a letter recorded, "My chandelier is nearly finished! The symbolic designs against a background of natural oak are rich in blue, red and green, and bright with touches of gold leaf following the pattern of the original in Oxford cathedral. I find myself involved in correspondence with Dr. Sanday, Scott Holland and Tommy Strong, the vice chancellor, because a typical Oxford controversy has arisen over the earliest lighting in churches.

"The question now is whether the cables by which the wooden chandeliers are at present suspended in the cathedral are the originals. Reginald Windram is researching about in London for the right answer. Here is his letter written from The Berkeley Hotel, Piccadilly.

" 'Dear Langstaff, I have been looking for your cord but with very little success. The more I think of it the more appropriate a chain seems. You could have a small hand-forged one; in all probability you could find an antique one. It seems to me a cord belongs to a later period...' (And so it goes on but he adds what may interest you more.)

" 'As you probably saw by the newspapers we had a very brisk air raid the other night. I had exceptional opportunities to watch it, being so high and having access to the roof.

" 'I was awakened by a terrific salvo and when I got out on the roof, suddenly, almost directly overhead, I caught a momentary glimpse of a slim silvery shape very small at great height. It was like catching sight for the first time of some particular mouse that has been doing a lot of damage. THERE YOU ARE VERMIN!, I thought.

" 'Then the searchlights steadied on it and the cannonade became terrific. I was right in the midst of the affair too. Every now and then the gun shots were alternated by the sharp stammer of bombs dropped in series; it was a very sinister sound. But the best part was that you could judge the shooting by the bursting shells. Most of it was pretty rotten; miles out of the way, literally; they didn't seem to have an idea how high up the Zeppelin was.

" 'I must say that the Zeppelin was one of the most beautiful things I have ever seen, so sleek and shimmering and gliding so serenely among the stars; while the shells were bursting below it like fireflies at the great height. All of London that I could see was spouting flame.

" 'It really was very exciting wondering if anyone would hit it, and dreadfully disappointing that it got away—though I must say I admired their pluck to turn and cross London in the very teeth of the firing. At first when it was coming toward me I must confess I was rather nervous.'

"From what I hear the damage done by this Zeppelin was considerable although nothing about it is allowed in the papers. Three factories and a bridge over the tracks out of the Liverpool station which delayed the trains five hours. Probably more. Somebody saw a Zeppelin falling and there are rumors that one was caught. I think probably this was true, but there is no substantial evidence. The recruiting is doubtless a bit better just where the raid occurred, but the English people are not easily frightened, as you know."

My friend's description of the first air raid on London seemed to check with others I heard later. There had been a raid on the outlying districts on the seventh of September, but it was on the following night that a concentrated attack was aimed at the very heart of London. Theatres and music halls were open, streets full of the usual crowds, when suddenly the sound of bursting bombs followed by the rapid firing of anti-aircraft caught the attention of the seven million inhabitants of the world's largest city. The crowds in the streets, I was told, were spellbound at the unique display of fireworks. A bomb did fall in a square surrounded by hospitals and a certain slum area was damaged. Also a bomb exploded near an omnibus killing nine and injuring eleven. The fires which Windram could have seen from the roof of his hotel to the north and south were soon extinguished by the London Fire Brigade. No military targets were hit in spite of the exaggerated reports circulated by the Germans to the contrary. There was to be another raid on October 13th, and then a pause of three months because of the stormy autumn weather. It seemed obvious to me that it was not enough for Britannia to rule the waves, but to rule the air waves as well!

My next letter was written from Magdalen College, 24th September 1915. "It does seem an age since I wrote. I hardly know where I stopped telling. But I left Ewelme about a week ago and I have been able to get a good bit done on my dissertation since I returned. Just think, the first two hundred pages of the work will be in Latin, solid — and you know what a classical scholar I am not!

"The electrician has just fixed a light in my chandelier and now it hangs from the ceiling of my cloister room in Magdalen. To say it is a success is putting it mildly. An oak triangle with blunt corners, very heavy but hollow in the centre with a circle cut in the middle. (Symbolic of Trinity and Unity of course, and the Light of the World.) At right angles from the sides are three arms which are carved to taper to the ends. Candles stand on the ends of these arms and on the blunt corners of the triangle. The whole decorated with geometrical designs and suspended with three chains from the centre of the ceiling.

"In the circular hollow of the chandelier I have dropped a bowl, white enameled inside, which contains the electric light and reflects it on the ceiling. A deep white border on the walls has the effect of bringing the high ceiling down to the dark tapestry paper and makes an excellent counter reflector. You will think this a great waste of time perhaps, but I have been able to do it in between work. I find it recreative to have something to do with my hands when my head is so immersed in liturgical Latin.

"I have just had a letter from Canon Scott-Holland which rather depreciates the age of the original chandeliers in the cathedral, but that doesn't mean they are not the first lighting. I took Norman Nash to have tea with him the other day. I have also had a letter from Lady Strathcona in answer to the offer I was able to make for her hospital in Bath of certain four dozen bottles of tonic which are coming from the British War Relief Association. She again kindly asks me to let them know when I can come and stop with them in London. I don't think they have gone down to the country for any length of time this summer.

"Also I have been having a course of correspondence with Mrs. Beavan, our cousin in Worcester. She will see me on Monday afternoon, and my invitation to visit them lasts till the end of the week. I rather grudge the time for I am turning the corner with my dissertation and I want to be at it, but I have so long heard of the Beavan cousins that I look forward with interest to seeing them all at Hardwicke Manor. Term does not begin until the 14th of October, but that makes little difference with my work.

"My 'friend' Reginald McKenna has put on the national budget taxes in good heavy style so that prices are become about twice what they were before. Just how this will affect my living here at college I do not know yet, but I must say that with all this war condition, the college is far less expensive because the round of entertaining among the undergraduates is necessarily cut down.

"This afternoon the Banners are motoring to Oxford, and tomorrow I have invited Sir William Osler to meet Mrs. Tiffin, the grandmother of Delmar, who knew the then Dr. Osler in Montreal and has asked to meet him again. Sir William's acceptance for himself and Lady O reads, 'Dear Origen, Yes — thanks — both — 4.30 today. Yours, W. O.' Origines Adamantius was a Christian teacher and writer of Alexandria in the second century, and that means me."

Sunday

13, NORHAM GARDENS,
OXFORD.

Dear Origen

Yes — thanks —

both — 4 30 Friday.

Yours

A. D.

There were young scholars at Oxford to whom this appelation might have been applied, but I was a mere plodder. Among such brilliant undergraduates whom I was privileged to have as friends was T. B. Simpson, whom we called *Tibi*. There is a passage in his unpublished MEMORIES OF MAGDALEN DONS which years later has afforded me some consolation in recalling my difficulties when entering the "royal enclosure" of Magdalen. Here it is.

"The tutor to whose guidance and tender care I was consigned on my arrival at Magdalen was A. D. Godley, author of 'Lyra Frivola' and other works of genuine wit and even brilliance. Knowing his reputation as a scholar and poet I had formed a pretty clear idea of what the man would look like — keen, clean shaven I was sure, intellectual, humorous. I never suffered a ruder shock than on entering his room for the first time. Before me stood a long, lanky, gone-at-the-knees, out-at-the-elbow, broken-down-looking man, without a spark of life in his expression. I had a fellow-victim in Cable, and the two talked disjointedly of Harrow, where they had both been educated.

"Eventually Godley went over to a corner of the room and returned with two dusty paper-bound booklets which he handed to us, saying as he did so, in tones of profound gloom, 'This pamphlet is entitled *Guide to Candidates for Honour Moderations* but is more frequently known as the *Unattainable Ideal.*' This, though funny, was rather a damper to youths who had come filled with the first enthusiasm of a new experience to learn wisdom at the feet of a justly celebrated scholar."

To this A. D. Godley my own journal referred. (Magdalen College, October 6th) "Miss Selena Quinn — one of the Manor ladies who were so hospitable to me while I was at Ewelme — let me know she was coming in to accept the invitation I had given them for tea whenever they came to town. She brought with her a niece whom I had met there. And since they were old friends of one of our dons, Mr. Godley, a relative of our friend Cyril Maude, and the organizer of the famous volunteer corps known by his name, I took the opportunity of inviting him. Windram, the American I've mentioned, also came.

"*Godley's Army* is composed of the Oxford dons chiefly and was written up in an article mother sent me with pictures, I think in the *Tribune*. The sight of Walter Raleigh, Gilbert Murray and other known scholars marching through the streets of Oxford or forming fours and presenting arms in the Parks is not to be forgotten. One of the characters who attracted great attention was the Poet Laureate, Mr. G said that this Robert Bridges, whose son was the former occupant of my rooms, was causing him a lot of trouble. It seems he had contracted a cold while drilling. And at last, Mr. Godley said, while keeping his name on the list because of the keen spirit of that 'over aged' gentleman, he felt obligated to ameliorate the poet's military enthusiasm by ordering him to rest at home. The result was that many now write Mr. Godley congratulations on having successfully 'killed' the nation's distinguished bard.

"Godley's Own has just finished one of the great battles of the war against the *Devil's Own,* which is a volunteer corps formed of recruits from the Inner Temple. There were 18 'K. Cs' in one company, and I judge from Mr. Godley's report at tea that his victory is to be attributed to the difficulty experienced in keeping the Counselors quiet. But there was the usual dispute of 'Who won?', as comes at the end of every mock battle. This Mr. Godley is of course one of the most respected of Oxford's scholars, and he is also a master of the art of humorous verse."

This mobilizing of loyal subjects in a civilian volunteer defence organization — of which our Oxford corps may well have been among the earliest — was to have significance in time to come as the National Volunteer Reserve. It was not only made up of the "over aged" but also often of men suffering from some complaint or defect which debarred them from the army because the medical standards were set high. Also they may have been men whose employers would not release or men engaged in work of national importance who insisted on "doing their bit" in the military. The recognition by the War Office did not come until Easter of 1916. Then their champion, Sir Francis Lloyd, was able to address them, "Soldiers! For you are soldiers now!" Among such groups of volunteers were the Artists' Rifles garnered from the fields of arts and letters. In October 1914 only 700 strong but by the time I was to be training in their ranks they were part of the regular army and added 14,000 recruits.

7

MICHAELMAS, 1915

THE privilege of being admitted into the intimacy of a family with whom I was connected through my grandfather, Bridgewater Meredith, gave me some idea as to how the war was affecting many similar families throughout the provinces. As the Chadwicks in Bath had been an army family, the Beavans in Worcester were a church family presided over by a motherly widow whose husband had served on one of the cathedral staffs. Their ample house surrounded by protecting trees was, as I remember, on the east bank of the Severn. Within, it was furnished in the comfortable Victorian manner and well regulated.

Worcester itself — a little over fifty miles from Oxford — had been the victim of wars ever since the Romans had captured it from the early Britains, but for centuries it had been dominated by the cathedral in which years later I was to preach to a large congregation. In the Beavans's parish church nearby they were preparing for a harvest festival on the coming Sunday, and I persuaded them to let me decorate the interior with pod-laden hop vines which were plentiful in the neighbourhood. This really bothered the temperance-minded vicar. Nevertheless, he waived his scruples for the time because his chief concern was the war, as it was the concern of every member of his congregation. It was from homes such as the Beavans's that most of the undergraduates at Oxford came, and I was to understand them better on my return to Magdalen from having experienced this typical family life even for a few days.

From Magdalen College (9th October 1915) I wrote my parents in New York, "There is not time to tell you in detail about my two days visit with Mrs. James Beavan in Worcester. Mrs. B said that I was like her younger brother, and so they treated me. I much appreciate being made part of such a delightful family and thus adding to my visiting places their comfortable residence overlooking the river.

"Several of the men and dons — because of a wrong notice posted last term — thought college was to start yesterday and came up for it, so that on my return I found a number of them already here. Windram, who remains uncompromisingly *St. Paul's Concord;* M. G. Chrussachi, nephew of the Greek prime minister, whose star is Constantinople but who does not wish to see his country in the war; Dick Graham, who has a 'Quaker bug' of 'not fighting' but makes everybody feel like punching his head for the things he does and says; another is mentally over-strained and still another who is a careless goodhearted Van Winkle.

"I might add that since the common college baths are not yet available, I have just had a bath in that private tub which for the last three years has been employed in cleansing the royal body of H.R.H. the P. of W."

Just how much the censor would permit me to write regarding the private bathroom installed for the king's eldest son when he came into residence at Magdalen, I was not sure. Even at this late date when his abdication has removed the protective barriers I am not without the feeling of *lèse majesté.* I can not forget, however, that cold, converted, torture chamber where I stood shivering while the infernal geyser trickled hot water at such a slow rate that it was merely warm by the time the tub was ankle deep.

What a contrast was this dribbling affair to the oversized tubs gushing with hot water in the undergraduates baths around by the "kitchen stair!" There, scouts stood ready to serve the men who came in bath robes from their far away rooms to find their baths drawn and luxurious fresh towels waiting. Much might be said as to the privations which British royalty inflict on themselves out of consideration for their position. Self-indulgence may have been characteristic of certain monarchs in history, but for the ruling family of George V the opposite seemed to be the rule. Nor did they see fit to parade this virtue before the public.

I was not starry-eyed socially about the royal family, but I did feel that the Queen's interest, if not patronage, in my mother's philanthropic work in America was in order. Thus I wrote on October 12th, "Mother's letter came with the *Daughters of the*

Empire reports. I will see that the matter is laid before the Queen. Grand your being able to add a motor ambulance to the many other supplies you have sent to the British army and navy. Motor ambulances are expensive. I will enquire as to motor manufacturers here and let you know.

"Perhaps I have not been eating all I should, but I've not been starving as you fear. One likes to feel by a bit of economy the men at the front will be better provided with food. It may be false economy in the end. Perhaps I have been doing more work than I generally do, which I fear is very little. But at any rate I am as healthy as a Greek god and certainly much happier. And the dissertation becoming more and more a real thing!

"I am writing Phil about the box you are sending him. He's a splendid little fellow, and I wish I could bring him home to dinner some night and introduce him to you. I enclose a card from him. Arthur Howard has just gone out to the front. It is difficult for him to see without his glasses, so that it worries me to think of him in action.

"I should be able to say something more about the war, but except that the people have determined to win with so grim an obstinacy that there can be no doubt as to the final result, I have little to report. The 'drive' of which you speak has caused little excitement here. It was rather the relief one feels after having worked hard for a thing, to see it in part accomplished."

Exactly what the "drive" was to which my letter from home referred I was not sure. American newspapers had their own way of telling the story. I did know that the offensive which began on September 25th in the Champagne Pouilleuse district had been a tremendous battle. Now at the beginning of October there was another drive starting. The immediate objective seemed to be the Brazancourt-Challerange-Apremont railway. Our maps showed this as the most southerly of the railways connecting the army of von Einem with that of the German Crown Prince in the northern sector of the Argonne and the region north of Verdun. I was told that it started on October first when the airship *Alsace* crossed the Aisne and bombed a key point of the railway. On the 10th French aviators released a hundred large bombs on the objective itself. And on the day after I had written my last letter nineteen French aeroplanes dropped 140 bombs on the railway station at Brazancourt.

On October 19 I could write, "Here is the final letter from the Queen. I must say that the great courtesy with which my letters were received is a lesson to me. It also shows that Her Majesty appreciates the work of the Daughters of the Empire in the U.S.A. Mr. Wallington makes it clear that Queen Mary understands the situation and the difficulties in connection with her Needlework Guild in America and the Needlework Guild already established there. Even here the Red Cross and Queen Mary's Guild tend to overlap. But all for the cause.

"We are off to run the beagles this afternoon. I have managed to involve myself with Prince George in the job of keeping our beagle hounds together until the men return from the fighting. Thus with the understanding that I keep track of the accounts, Teck is to be Acting Master of Hounds, and together we will carry on the responsibility of the only organized sport in the university. A letter from George's 'noble cousin David,' enclosing twenty-five pounds, and another from George's mother, the duchess, with an additional subscription, are a necessary help. The cost comes not alone in the upkeep but also in placating the farmers over whose ploughed fields the beagles must run."

The following day I wrote from Magdalen, "Last night I went to my tutor, ('Brighters' as we called him now), and stopped with him till twelve. This morning I woke up just too late for the Communion Service in chapel but I went to hear a man from the Navy Mission preach at St. Mary's later. Then I started off for Nuneham.

"On the way I met a man named Davison who has been taken up by Sir William Osler, for Sir W told me that he considered him one of the most promising medical students he had had in a long while. An attractive man personally. He is coming to take me to his Presbyterian church here in Oxford tonight. At Nuneham I found it was the last day of the hospital there, and when I left they were having a sort of 'jolly-up' to celebrate the closing. Mrs. Harcourt said she felt sad at breaking up. She will go and stay with Mrs. Burns, her mother, until Christmas, when they will all return to Nuneham.

"Besides the host and hostess at Nuneham there were Miss Asquith, the prime minister's daughter, the man she is going to marry, a Mr. Bonham Carter who is her father's secretary, Mr. Spender, the editor of the *Westminster,* Major Gatewood who wrote *The Only Way*, etc. and who has the further distinction of having just brought out a play which does *not* deal with the war. And then of course there were Billie and his three sisters and all the officer-patients and the not-to-be forgotten governess.

"One rather amusing thing happened to Mr. Harcourt lately. He found a bomb concealed behind the balustrade of the terrace, and not wishing to handle it alone he called the gardener to bring a pail of water. When they had carefully put it in the water and were conveying it away to a safe place, they were pursued by one of the patients in great distress. It seems he had brought the bomb back from the front as a souvenir and had for a long time been trying to get it dry enough to remove the plug which had swollen from a former ducking.

"Mr. Harcourt told me the *Globe* newspaper had its office raided last night. You will know all about it by the time this reaches you. It is not all certain what trouble it will cause, and I think he is expecting some strong defence and protest. Some suppose tomorrow will see another *Globe* published in another office.

"I have just returned from the Presbyterian service with Mr. Davison. It was conducted by the famous Dr. Sclater of Edinburgh University. Then coffee after in the minister's house. His name is Lusk, a young man of much promise. He has offered to tell me about the Presbyterian communion service — a subject which much interests me in connection with my present research. Lytle was also there and many other Americans.

"One amusing thing I left out of yesterday's beagling account was that I was constantly being mistaken for Teck by the farmer. He finally protested, 'Now you are not Prince George of Teck? It's the other gentleman, isn't it?' This he said to Teck when we were all gathered for tea in his house, indicating me as the 'other gentleman.' We try to avoid this matter of rank in undergraduate life. If the Prince of Wales should come out to run with the beagles — which is his favorite sport — it would not be done to say anything about it. I must say the pictures of the P. of W. do not do him justice."

What had once been the hope of university authorities, that undergraduates who had been enlisted in the armed services would shortly return and pick up their studies from where they had left off, was now abandoned completely. On October 22nd I wrote, "I found Scott-Holland in his garden at tea the other day. He had recently come from a meeting of Convocation. In this meeting Mr. Walker had proposed that all men who by going to war had thus sacrificed their chance of taking degrees should be given them anyway, i.e. all men who had gone through 'Pass Mods' — which is a preliminary exam that a man could easily work off in a couple of terms or a half year — should be granted the full 'B.A.' degree. This would normally require three years to take. The contention was that anybody who could get through 'P. Mods' could with time get through the 'B. A.' schools.

"One of the proper old ladies whom one often finds sipping tea with the canon made the remark that such degrees would be discredited and become known as 'War B.A.s.' To which Scott-Holland replied that it was just what he had said in Convocation, that it hardly seemed fitting that Oxford should be held responsible for so many *'War Babies!'* The old lady and her friend turned a hair and I spilled my tea.

"Mr. Turner, one of our dons, later told me he had strongly objected because it was like treating wounded soldiers to beer at a pub. It was not a case of doing them any good, but simply showing our good feeling toward them. When he had expressed himself in Convocation — comparing an Oxford B.A. to a drink of beer — his colleagues were shocked. Of course there will be the difficulty of other people not knowing whether a man with a degree is up to standard. There will be a couple of thousand men perhaps with B.A. degrees who have not had a college education."

In comprehending this cooperative gesture of the university toward the men in service I had fair evidence of how thorough the intellectual grounding of an English public school was. Once the university authorities were satisfied this schooling had made its imprint on a man it was only a matter of time for maturing in disciplined surroundings when they could feel such a student might reasonably be granted a pass degree. The army in war time afforded an opportunity comparable with the university for maturing under discipline. On the other hand, in our American schools I knew much of the intellectual grounding was left for the colleges. Nevertheless, there was a danger in tampering with the public's confidence in academic degrees.

It was with such thoughts that I wrote from Magdalen on the 26th, "A Rhodes Scholar has come back from his Red Cross work in Belgium and told me it was worth three years of Oxford. I fear this rather indicates how little he is getting out of Oxford, more than any great advantage he derived from military service. Govy Hoffman's brother, Stoddard, has just come over from New York to do the same kind of work.

"As for my own work, it is really coming along quite satisfactorily. I am doing everything to secure the degree at the soonest possible moment.

"Teck and I have succceeded in keeping each other interested in the beagles with the result that I find it makes me take the exercise I need so badly. My spiked shoes, which I had bought while at Harvard for use on the track, have come in handy for this cross country running after the hounds. We pay a shilling as capping fee each time, and that with contributions from the Prince of Wales and others makes enough to cover the costs of the hunt. Which costs come largely in feeding the hounds and carrying them to and from the meets, and of course the salary of Joe, the keeper. After the run we all as a rule have tea, paying another bob to the farmer, or occasionally a 'free-ers' where we are invited by the local vicar or squire. Several of us bicycle out and the rest go in a brake. It is healthful exercise so that twice a week running with the beagles seems to be enough to serve for the whole time of working at my desk.

"I went down to a meeting of the High Church society last night and heard an address from a Mr. Williams who used to be called 'Nippy' when he was here at Magdalen because, I suppose, he struck people that way. His idea — like that of Bishop Gore — was that their party should emphasize the progressiveness of the hierarchical church in contrast to the retrogressiveness of the Protestant party. Whereupon he declared that the church was founded by Abraham and was merely given definition by the Holy Spirit at Pentecost. Thus it had continued to go ahead until the Reformation when the Protestant element made their stand for a return to the church as it had been, not at the time of Christ, but at the time of the early Jews. He said further, following out this idea, he felt that nothing in the way of ceremony, church furniture, etc. should be tolerated which could give an idea to the people that the church wished to return to the Middle Ages or any other earlier state of development. Let it be the Protestants who must bear the popular disgust of any retroactive movement.

"The chairman, Canon Carew Wood, had announced this as the beginning of another 'Oxford Movement,' and Darwell Stone, who has covered acres with his literary tracks, rose to the rescue. He summed up what 'Nippy' had said and added that although the Protestants were retroactive and not progressive, they were not correctly retroactive for they never wished to return to forms or customs which had really been practised in the past."

Days later my journal noted, "I ran smack into the profound scholar, Darwell Stone, in a manner that discomfitted me muchly. It was like this. Several of us were asked by one of our dons to go and help at a hospital in Heddington. It was to dig down a heap of sod which had been thrown up behind a new wing to the hospital. It started to rain, and when the other men thought of backing out from going, I declared I would go alone. To prevent this — while I was in the process of changing my clothes — George grabbed my trousers and dashed out to throw them in the Cher. Trouserless I pursued him and finally managed not only to rescue my own flannel bags, as we call them, but also to 'debag' him. Half clad but waving both bags triumphantly as I was coming through the narrow passageway into the cloister, I confronted the academically robed Dr. Stone. So much for the 'new Oxford Movement!' Subsequently, we all went and dug at the hospital.

"Brighters has just stopped in to borrow an umbrella, for it is suddenly pouring with rain and the lawn between Cloisters and New Builders is a long stretch in such a shower. I took the opportunity for getting him to help me with my dissertation and he remained a long time talking about his new book. It is sure to be the standard treatise on the English Prayer Book for years to come."

The English Rite by Canon F. E. Brightman did on publication prove itself, as I predicted, the authoritative source book, a sort of scholar's bible of the *Book of Common Prayer*. In the first days of my tutelage at Magdalen the author of this weighty classic had pushed the proof sheets at me saying, 'I don't know why they want to print it but that's everything I know about the subject,' advising me to read them and so save him the trouble of having to lecture me on the Liturgy. The truth was that Brightman had read to sources, and there was nothing more that could be said. And how amused I had been on one of my visits to Lambeth Palace when I had mentioned the forthcoming publication to Randall

My dear Langstaff

I have been rather an invalid today & I am not sure I could listen profitably to your dissertation tonight.

Yours ever

F.E.B

(Brightman)

CANON F. E. BRIGHTMAN (author and liturgical authority) typical note written as tutor at Magdalen College 1916 to Brett Langstaff.

Davidson, and the archbishop had replied, 'When I have a few hours leisure I hope to read that book.'

At Magdalen on November 3rd I noted, "Prince George has just given me to understand that in all probability his 'noble cousin,' David, will run the beagles with us next Saturday. If the Prince of Wales comes, he has asked that the meet shall be at one thirty, because to come back here, have a bath and catch the six o'clock train for London means leaving Fyfield, which is about ten miles distant, rather early. And further, since George depends on my being with him on this occasion, I will have to recall my acceptance of Mr. Benecke's invitation for lunch.

"I went up to Wytham Park this afternoon to see if Mr. Ford and Mr. Burns would come and have tea with me again — you remember my telling you of their visit with Mrs. Harcourt while

I was at Ewelme. The place is the seat of Lord Abingdon and the
Abbey was built with old bits taken from Cumnor Hall which
stood near by. The story is that here Amy Robsart was thrown
down stairs. The grounds of the park are beautiful and the house
is snuggled down in a valley, but neither compare with Nuneham.

"I have just secured six new books from the history library
bearing on my subject, and I am going through them. There seems
a tremendous amount to do, but the dissertation is coming along.

"The Greek of whom I have spoken as an undergraduate here
is finding himself in rather an awkward position but he is just as
you might expect a member of that two-faced nation would be.
I told him that I had read the English were not going to have
raisins in their plum puddings this Christmas, and he quickly
replied that Greece would find an excellent market for their raisins
in Germany. Personally I feel they are probably doing a trade with
the Teutons which makes them feel loath to declare war on them.
Italy also seems nearly as bad. All that region whose imperial
pride once dazzled the world seems to have lost its classic sense
of idealism."

My Greek at Magdalen was a nephew, I was told later, of the
rich banker, M. Skouloudis, who represented Greece at the London
Conference. The uncle would seem to have been a more apt tool
of the king's than his predecessor. He not only stood for noninter-
vention in the hostilities between Serbia and Bulgaria, but also he
presented difficulties regarding the presence of Allied troops on
Greek soil. Thus he was not popular in England, nor his nephew
at Madgalen.

"The Prince of Wales, or 'Pragger' as he is referred to among
undergraduates, did come," I wrote from Magdalen on November
6th, "and here I have preserved it all in detail for you at home.
Not adding to it as did the old woman at the pub on a previous
occasion who found the three pennies which the Prince had given
her in change so valuable that she became popular by giving them
to dozens of her friends.

"Teck came yesterday with certain news that his 'noble cousin'
would be with us on Saturday, and I wrote asking Mr. Benecke
to grant me the further courtesy of excusing me from his luncheon.
The Prince was bringing two men with him and they were to have
lunch in Teck's room. I tidied things up and saw George off to
meet the party. Then went to my own room for lunch.

Feb. 16/1925

Magdalen College
Oxford

My dear Langstaff,

It was very good of you to let me have a copy of your book on the Children's Library, which is a most interesting record in itself as well as containing much that one is glad to know about the different times when you were in Somers Town. I hope that your present life is also full of interest, though one may well trust that some elements of excitement are absent from it. The College goes on fairly quietly, so far as the undergraduates (who count most after all) are concerned. The senior of us are left employed by the University Commission, which has reached the stage of drafting new Statutes for or in combination with us: and we have to make up our minds what is the best compromise between what we should like and what is possible! All good wishes.

Yours very sincerely,
P. V. M. Benecke

PAUL VICTOR MENDELSSOHN BENECKE (Bursar of Magdalen College) written to Brett Langstaff regarding the College and its Mission in London 1925.

"Windram asked me to go out in a motor with him and suggested my getting two other men. This I did, Peter Warren, the president's nephew, and an American, Hugh Terris. In this way we arrived at Fyfield a bit earlier than the rest. Farmer Lay, who was entertaining us, took us in for a little early refreshment, and while we were there the royal party arrived. The good farmer thereupon sent me to bring them in. This I did. And with the Pragger first, Teck next and your humbleness following, we came into the farm house. The farmer met us at the door and greeting the Pragger whom he had seen in times of former meets, turned to me and said, 'Of course I know you,' and then to Teck who was escorting his royal cousin, 'But who are you?' Whereupon the confusion caused Teck to introduce me to the farmer, and, since the Prince of Wales was right there, to His Royal Highness also. I speak of this especially not because Teck and I have not known each other enough to dispense with formalities, but because it is almost a custom among Englishmen not to introduce at all. So it was that no one but myself and the farmer, I believe, was presented on this occasion to the Prince. I was glad because it gave me an opportunity of speaking to him later.

"When we had taken off some of our clothes, and I had changed to my running shoes, we started. I must say, however, the Pragger wore a muffler and heavy cap all the time we were out. There was a long stretch of walking, with the farmer and his sons on horses to scout out the hares, and a number of village people in the rear. But when the hounds did strike the scent, the Pragger was at the front in a jiffy and there he remained all the time. With my running shoes and all the force I could put into it, I could not possibly keep up with him, nor could anybody else.

"After some time the hare threw the hounds off the trail and we were compelled to stand about waiting while the hounds frantically tried to pick up the scent again. Then, taking several breaths, I mustered up courage to say to the Pragger, 'You don't run as though you were out of training.' To this he answered that he had not run during the entire time he had been away from Magdalen. This led to a conversation which was resumed at intervals for the whole time of our run.

"The Prince said, among other things, that his father, the king, was practically recovered from his accident. (You remember he was thrown from his horse.) The Pragger had just had word of the death of one of his closest friends, Pawle, our former Master of the beagles who had been reported as missing for some time. It seems the men had deserted their officers and left them to the mercy of the enemy. The Pragger was much pleased at the spirit of the upper classes who had volunteered in such numbers, but he seemed to think the lower classes had failed to come up to scratch. This talk of enthusiasm was in response to my lead to tell of the enthusiasm in America for the allied cause and so I hoped to bring to H.R.H.'s attention the activities of the Daughters of the Empire in the U.S.A. But at this crucial moment when I had only had time to introduce the subject of the Daughters, the hounds caught the scent again and with a great yelping and booing started off. We after them. I was feeling rather frustrated because it would be hard to bring the subject up in conversation again.

"But long after, when the hounds had lost the scent a second time, the Prince ran up to me and said, 'I am very interested in what you were saying about your mother and the women in America when we were interrupted.' This of course gave me a much greater chance to tell him the story of the Daughters of the Empire and how Mother had recently crossed the continent in Sir William MacKenzie's private car with certain executives of the Canadian Order spreading the organization. Especially when I told him how many women of British birth there were in the U.S.A., he was surprised. I will not repeat all I told him, but you can imagine, for there was plenty of time, and my listener was interested.

"As we were turning on to another topic, the Pragger caught sight of the hare crouched in a clump of dry grass immediately in front of him. Another step and he would have trod on it. At the time we had wandered a long way off from the rest of the men. He whispered to me to go and tell George, which I did while he stood perfectly quiet. The others finally brought the hounds around to the right position and the chase started again. But we never did catch up with the hare, however, nor did we make a *kill* all the afternoon.

"We came back to the farmer's with a healthy weariness and a great desire for food. This last was spread lavishly over a huge table in the diningroom. A royal feast for a royal guest. The Prince of Wales spoke of many things which I can not set down here, but let me sum it up in saying that with a naive genuineness his

approach secured in me a love and affection that will never lessen
no matter how future events may tend to isolate him from ordinary
people like myself. To be a king and preserve 'the common touch'
— there will be the test.

"When the crowd was waiting for the Pragger to get into his car
after tea, I sought refuge because of my modesty or perhaps cow-
ardice, which is often mistaken for modesty, in the furthest rear.
I was more than delighted when His Royal Highness made a point
of fishing me out and shaking hands with me, saying at the same
time that he would do his best to come out again. We followed his
motor to Oxford where he took the train for Buckingham Palace.

"I remember you always thought the Prince of Wales a nice
looking boy, but I am sure that if you could have seen him as I
saw him last Saturday, you would be tremendously attracted by
him. He has one of the most winning smiles I have ever seen,
splendid colour, short but well proportioned and with this a
delightfully intimate way about him which makes you feel good
friends in an afternoon. Running with him through the fields,
crawling through hedges after or before him, splashing into mud
and stream, often with nobody in sight — it all gave me a better
chance of getting to know him than if I had gone to hundreds of
levees and things at the palace. This makes me sorry that I did
not have the opportunity of being in college during the past two
years that he was in residence, for apart from his title, for which I
have due regard, there are few men I have met whom I should
more like to have as a friend."

I would have been distressed to have seen ahead the chain of
events which led to the abdication of my new friend from the
exalted position he was to inherit as king-emperor of the most
powerful and most populous nation in world history. The Pragger,
as Magdalen knew him, or the Duke of Windsor, as he was later
to become, was in time to write his own story, a story without
friends. He abdicated not only a titular crown but also a circle of
friends who loved him enough to be ready to lay down their lives
for him. Personally, I was always to remember him as I first saw
him. Not as 'The Salesman of the Empire' nor 'The uncrowned
King of England,' but as a fine example of English youth, devoted
to sport and bent on serving God and his country. It was his best,
and as such few excelled him.

"I spoke of taking Peter Warren with us in the motor," my

letter continued. "His uncle, Sir Herbert Warren, asked me to look out for him. He is certainly a delightful person, tall and remarkably good looking — fair hair, blue eyes and a keen mind — but only seventeen. He often comes and has cocoa with me late at night just before bedtime.

"From America Sam Eliot has written me a surprising letter. A wife seems to have changed his extreme radical views of life. What has become of the long arguments with which he used to keep me awake far into the night at Harvard? I would not have believed it was the grandson of President Eliot if it had not been signed, 'Affectionately, Sam.' "

"Funny mail this morning. (12th November 1915). A letter from a lady asking me to use my influence to have her son put on some staff where he would be out of danger; another from a man who wishes me to do carpenter work in some way connected with the war — the reputation I get from work on my wooden chandelier — and a third from Dr. Sanday.

"The noted New Testament critic writes from Christ Church in printed script, 'My dear Langstaff, I have been wondering whether the lectures that I expect to be giving the next week or two would be of any use for your thesis. I don't remember exactly what it is but I believe it is liturgical. I shall begin tomorrow by speaking about Origins, about which you will probably know — through Dr. Maret — more than I can tell you. But I shall go on to speak of Babylonian and Egyptian psalms and hymns and prayers; and this I thought might perhaps be helpful. I shall not expect you to go out of your way, but I just mention the fact for what it is worth. Yours sincerely, W. Sanday.'

"I was going to dig the hospital garden this afternoon, but the other men backed out, and so — since I can't do it alone — I walked around *Adders* instead for exercise with Banner and meeting Jimmy Street went around a second time with him. Then my box of tonic which the British War Relief Ass'n sent me, arrived. I found that the dock charges for the time I had been negotiating with the Hon. Board of Customs came to 3/1, while the duty which I managed to get excused was only 7/6, and thus I was to some extent twitted. It is a comparatively small box this time, and I have left it together with a bundle of illustrations from the *New York Times* in the lodge for the ambulance to call for.

"While I was in the lodge, Mr. Dodd, of whom I have written as the Rector of Ewelme, came in. I took him to my rooms. We had hardly settled ourselves when slowly up my stone stairway came an old gentleman who paused at the door. He waited to make sure that I knew a Mrs. Phelp who had asked him to call on me. I had never known the name Phelp, but so appealing was the distinguished face of my visitor, flushed with the effort of mounting the high rises of my stairway, I could not avoid going all out for 'my dear old friend', Mrs. Phelp. Only then did he deign to enter my sitter and reveal himself as the noted Rev. H. W. Moss, long headmaster of Shrewsbury School. His stories of great men who had been under him as pupils so enthralled us that we did little more than say, Yes or No, or Ah and Oh. After several cups of tea Dr. Moss rose exclaiming he had enjoyed the conversation immensely and with a few more exclamations from Mr. Dodd and myself he made his way down the stairs. He was a delightful experience."

Three days later I wrote, "Yesterday after the service I heard the Bishop of Liverpool give a sermon at St. Mary's filled with telling incidents of the war. It showed how much the stress of the times had brought out the characters of men whose sensitive natures would never have been exposed to such experiences in the normal course. I do hope people at home will also learn from this war the importance of expressing their best.

"The Clement Webbs asked me to lunch with them and a Miss Stony who is to be Brighter's only other pupil. Victor Murray and another fellow were there. Mr. Webb has just brought out a great book on religious philosophy. Their attractively furnished house, I may have told you before, is built directly over a little waterfall and was one time the grist mill for the college.

"After lunch I went up to see Dr. Moss, for he had asked me to call on Sunday afternoon. In my account of the way he had come to see me you remember I told you how I pretended, in order to save embarrassment, to know the Mrs. Phelp whom he said asked him to call on me. The next day he wrote to say that is was not Mrs. Phelp but a Mrs. Beavan, friend of his wife's, — so I was twitted again. He gave me a full account of his old school, Shrewsbury. Established by Edward VI, dropping to a low ebb together with other schools in England under the Georges and finally revived by Dr. Butler, Dr. Kennedy and himself, which last three covered a space of 120 years headmastering.

Letter from Lady Osler (née Grace Revere) written to Brett Langstaff
referring to his presentation to The Lord Mayor the boyhood home of
Charles Dickens and suggesting his becoming Rector of Ewelme.

"He has numerous stories of embryo greats such as this one. Dr. Kennedy was walking one April Fool's Day, when one of the boys stepped up to him and said, 'Pardon, Sir, but did you drop your handkerchief?' Whereupon the unsuspecting doctor turned about in his pompous way, and pretending that he did not see the handkerchief referred to, was informed that it was the First of April. At this he seemed to become greatly enraged and told the boy to come up to the First Form and bring his Horace with him. By way of punishment he was to write the Fortieth Ode of the First Book fifty times. At the appointed time the boy sorrowfully came up, and while he was waiting for the doctor, he looked to see how long the Fortieth Ode was. This disclosed the fact that the First Book contained only 38 odes, and the lad realized that the First of April had come but had not passed.

"My host declared that he would not be able to tell from my conversation that I came from America. Protesting that the same reason for people in various parts of the empire speaking English with different intonations held good for people in the U.S.A. not all talking as English people do, I asked him, 'From what part of England would you have said I came?' 'That,' he replied, 'is the first indication I have had that you came from anywhere in particular, for if you had come from the southern part of England you would have said *should*.' He went on to say that next to the railways, the school teachers served to mix dialects. Especially in England, the *cockney* was being carried from London where the teachers were being trained, to all the country districts. He took me into the hall for tea with his wife and two daughters. They were very charming. Mrs. Moss knew Cousin Blanch Beavan through the *Mothers Workers*. Their house is beautifully situated on the top of a hill overlooking Oxford.

"This second part of the call lengthened out till I missed getting back in time for Peter Warren's tea. However, I met his mother and told her about my mother. Mrs. Warren is on a hospital strike because a wealthy lady whose bounty supplied the hospital is said to have turned the matron out unjustly. This is not an infrequent occurrence, as you can imagine, where hospitals are under private control. We had the usual good anthem in chapel, and later in the evening we formed a Bible study group.

"This morning I received a note from Mrs. Pochin asking me to take tea with her. The exercise of biking out the six miles did me good. Miss Gibbs was there. I think I met her father, Lord Alden-ham, at Nuneham. Also Mrs. Pochin's grandson and a friend of his who had just come from flying at the front. We had a splendid time. They were all three quite young. When Miss Gibbs left she asked me to come to lunch with them the following Sunday, while the grandson who lives in the Priory at Stadhampton made sacred by memories of Milton, made me promise to come to tea on Friday. These little expeditions do not really take up so much time and they afford me the exercise and recreation I suppose I need.

"Thanks for the present to Pye-Smith. I have an expression of appreciation from Mrs. P-S. Wish you could come over and meet some of the people of whom I write, but this is hardly a time for visiting England. Every household is anxious for some of its members in service — but the war will be over some day. Why not think of endowing beds in a hospital for Nurse Cavell's memory?"

I was convinced that more than anything since the sinking of the *Lusitania* the execution of the nurse to whom my letter referred should turn American public opinion against the German high command. I had the facts from the Oslers. Edith Cavell had been trained at London Hospital and in 1900 was invited by Dr. Depage to head his nurses institute in Brussels with the purpose of modernizing the system in Belgium. When the Germans invaded Belgium she remained at her post. The service of Nurse Cavell and her staff were given freely to friend and foe, but — as everybody was to know — in her trial she admitted helping the Allied soldiers to escape. For this she had been arrested and placed in solitary confinement without benefit of legal advice until the day of her trial. The trial lasted five days and she was shot to death within nine hours after her conviction. At the time it seemed cruel that clemency should not have been allowed a woman. Those were the days when in England *woman's suffrage* was still an open question, but years later with the equalization of the sexes one was to wonder why the world was so outraged.

There were more serious matters troubling the British govern-ment as I learned from conversations at Nuneham. The day I was writing my last letter I heard Winston Churchill was resigning from the cabinet. The Dardanelles campaign, of which he was the champion from the first, must now be admitted a tragic example of miscalculation. Another three days and Lord Ribblesdale was

announcing the 'withdrawal report.' This meant that all troops
would be removed from Suvla and Anzac. Small wonder that Mr.
Asquith and his government were left in a fog of speculation. My
letter closed with the observation, "The British cabinet is composed of clever men, but from my talks with some of them they
seem to have to do a lot of guessing."

At Magdalen on the 19th I noted, "Last night when I was
visiting Dr. Varley Roberts I learned of a fire which had burned
the Oslers' diningroom about a week ago. I shall go up this afternoon and apologize for not having come sooner.

"The venerable Varley talked of Prince Christian Victor, who
spent three years here at Magdalen. It seems he was in the habit
of going to chapel with strict regularity during the week and
sometimes sat with the doctor in the organ loft, as I do now. On
one of these occasions — the doctor told the story with such
emotion that tears filled his eyes — he said to Prince Christian,
'You know you do me good by coming so regularly to the services.'
To this the Prince replied, 'I am not any better than other people,
but I can not forget that I am Queen Victoria's grandson, and for
this reason I feel it my duty to come regularly and kneel upright
on the hard benches.' In all respect for the boy's reverence, it
struck me as rather priggish, but he certainly proved himself a
brave man if one can judge by his heroic death in the South
African war. However, I recall seeing in the diary Captain Scott
had written while on his last expedition to the South Pole, 'A man
can not be too good, but he can appear too good.' This is of course
the opposite of the Victorian ideal.

"Yesterday I took a walk with George Gifford, one of my
Harvard classmates who is now a Rhodes Scholar at Balliol.
Banner came along too. Later I dropped in at the Radcliffe Hospital to see Captain Gabites, whom Mrs. Harcourt asked me to
look out for after he was discharged from the hospital at Nuneham. The officers are accommodated in Somerville, the once girls'
college, next to the hospital.

"The afternoon of the day before — if you know what I mean
— I was asked by Ridgely Lytle to meet some ladies at his room
in Merton. As you know, this is our most ancient college and can
boast having had as its Warden the discoverer of the circulation
of the blood. On this occasion, however, it was boasting Americans.
An atrocious lady was there from New York who seemed not a bit

pleased when I replied to her remark, 'We both hail from the same city,' by saying the place from which I come is no longer a city, merely a metropolitan area from which few that hail are hearty. Also a Miss Buckler from Baltimore. She was attractive and it was good to hear her southern intonation. I had an interesting talk with a man named Paradise who is rather well known for his running at Yale. He is now reading at Balliol and like most Americans here favours the English system of instruction rather than our own. I can not altogether agree with this idea. He spoke of the large number of East Indians with which Balliol is burdened. He referred to them as the sort of 'greasy grinds' who take small part in college life. We don't have any at Magdalen, although the government requires that they shall not be discriminated against, I understand.

"The other day I met Rosina Fillipi, a noted producer especially of juvenile actors, and her daughter at tea. A rather curious remark she made when we were talking of the Latin plays at Westminster School where the boys use the same designs for their costumes as they used originally in their first Latin play hundreds of years ago — she said that while not understanding either Latin or Greek she could follow the Greek play with far greater ease. Probably it is unfair to compare the Greek tragedy with the Latin comedy, as she was doing.

"My thesis is coming slow but sure."

It was the 22nd before I again wrote from Magdalen saying, "We had a session of our Bible study group. It is encouraging to see how much religious spirit there is in the fellows who are left here in college, but do you know, I think these men have a hard task to comprehend Christianity because there has dropped out of the grasp of the present day all idea of the natural religion upon which the faith in Christ was built. The tide of natural religion has gone down, and the ice-crust of Christianity must crack if the tide does not soon rise.

"Lady Osler was in bed with a cold, perhaps from the smoke of the fire they have just had, so I went on to the Wrights. There I found Sir William. Mrs. Wrong was also there at the Wrights — the pun is not mine. Her grandfather was a Dr. Blake, Chancellor of something in or near Toronto, I think. At least Sir William said he probably knew my grandfather in the old days. During the course of conversation Sir W said that the idea of reserving medical students so that they should stay in England and go on with their medical education was rather giving way. The fact that so many hundreds were taking medicine seemed to imply that they were doing so to escape being enlisted in the army.

"The fire in the Oslers' house was caused by a beam over an open fireplace gradually smouldering until at three o'clock one morning, it burst into flame and was discovered by Lady O. They were forced to wait 35 minutes with the fire roaring in the dining-room before the engines came. In the meantime Sir William and Revere, who had come home for a week's leave, bustled the books they most wanted to save, out of the library above. There were no serious consequences.

"Lord Aldenham gave me lunch in his charming house at Clifton Hampden on the other side of Nuneham Park. After lunch one of his daughters went out on the lawn and clanged a great bell to call the birds. And sure enough in a few minutes the trees filled with birds. When she scattered food for them on the grass they soon flew down and covered the ground around the sun dial. Mostly starlings, some sparrows and an occasional wag-tail.

"Lord A and his son took me for a walk. The little church next the manor house is delightful with its columns dating from the time of Stephen. The renovating was done carefully by Sir Gilbert Scott and its position with the house on a cliff overlooking the Thames is ideal. We also went to an ancient tollhouse across the bridge which has many evidences of antiquity. In fact it was near this pub that they found the tooth of a mammoth which Lord A has in his library. They have a town house and a manor in another part of England. Certainly they could not have been more hospitable in urging me to telephone and let them know whenever I could come out for lunch.

"I attended three services today, but heard no preaching. The event of yesterday was a Christian Union meeting for the new men who have come up this year. Tea and talk, you know the sort of thing. One man suggested that it was better to talk to one person about the weather than to a group of persons about the *Absolute*. If people would only keep to fundamentals and remember, as Henry Van Dyke once wrote me, 'that after all, personality is the basis of all reality' — but I have just had a letter from my old roommate Gilbert Elliott in Paris to say I am writing in too pious a manner, so I'll not go on."

The matter of hospitals in which I found myself involved was a concern of importance, I was led to believe, not alone for our present but also for the future of the medical profession. The doctor of 1914, as far as Europe was concerned, seemed bent on attempting to cure rather than prevent disease. Sir William Osler would often speak of a new type of hospital, the Lycée Pasteur, at Neuilly, which the American residents in Paris founded and endowed early in the war. Now, a group of American doctors known as The Harvard Unit had volunteered their services and he expected they would be coming through Oxford on their way to France. Sir William saw the importance of helping the wounded soldier back to a normal state of mind as well as body. It presented itself as a modern problem, and was being recognized for its psychological importance. Especially the after-treatment of injuries about the face and in regard to stiff joints was to be the special concern of the American surgeons and dentists who were coming over. They apparently expected guidance and direction from Sir William.

Thus it was I recorded on December 3, 1915, "Here I am waiting for Sir William Osler to bring 35 doctors who are going out to the Harvard Unit's hospital in France. They are lunching in Christ Church and teaing in Norham Gardens, and between the two they are coming to see Magdalen and me. Last Sunday while I was lunching at the Oslers' Colonel Parry, Dr. Cheever and another doctor came down from London. In talking about the Harvard men who had come out on the expedition, I happened to mention the little book I pulled together that summer at Stony Brook, and Dr. Cheever said, 'Oh, you are the editor of HARVARD OF TODAY. Now I place you clearly.' It is good to think of having made a place in connection with the University, even if it be a small one.

"The Oslers' fire, much like our own library fire in Brooklyn, was confined to the one room, but it burned everything in the dining-room so that we have to eat in Sir W's study. Sir William gave me a copy of a book on Sarpi with which I went off into a corner after lunch and read. Sarpi had been given credit for the discovery of the circulation of the blood, but Sir W would have none of it. I think he must be writing of that subject.

"I went last night to sing to the wounded at Heddington with several other boys and girls. The others were really quite good, and a little girl who might just have stepped off the professional stage sang a song called 'Too Too' to perfection. They say they need me for sentiment, and, tell the truth, it does give me a chance to let off steam.

"By the way, it is hardly fair to let you think I am never going to get married. The truth is that negotiations are approaching the stage of ultimatumizing. I can't say that I have reached the height of happiness, but I have no reason to be glum. When anything definite occurs I will let you know. Till then don't you bother about it. This much is certain, I will never marry unless the right girl says, Yes.

"I can't remember where I left off telling in my last letter, but work on the dissertation takes most of the time now as usual. I went beagling yesterday and enjoyed a marvelous 'free-ers' tea afterwards with the other fellows at a farmer's house. It is certainly splendid exercise biking out some ten miles, running hard for a couple of hours or more and then biking home. It is so necessary in this weather.

"What I shall do for Christmas this year I do not know. It can hardly be expected to be a merry time anywhere. Lady Strathcona, Mrs. Pye-Smith, Dr. Longstaff and Teck have offered to put me up whenever I might happen to go up to London, and Sir Clements Markham and Mrs. Burns and several others have asked me to come and see them, so that I shall probably go up to London for part of the vac. Then Banner has asked me to come and stay at Bournemouth for the entire vac, and I shall probably go out there for a week. And since the officers now billeted in Swithers Quad will mean the college must keep open for the vac, I shall probably remain here most of the time working on my thesis. But you must hang the stockings as always and, as the song goes, 'keep the home fires burning.'"

My father, whose medical practice was to keep him active for seventy years, seldom wandered far from his many patients in the metropolitan area. His hours of recreation were entirely taken up with inventing many things, from a rotary engine to a surgical needle-holder, from a surface riding power-boat to a highly successful liquid soap container. But except for his student days in Edinburgh and London and a trip as surgeon on a Mediterranean cruise, he was always home even if he were most of the time out. It was with some surprise I wrote from Magdalen on December 9th, "What is this I hear about father crossing the continent for a consultation in Alaska? Certainly looks as though his practice were becoming more extensive than when he used to go off to the Bronx or into the wilds of New Jersey late at night."

Then my letter went on to note, "Last Sunday I went to pay a party call on the Vice Chancellor, who also holds the position of Dean of Christ Church. He is a delightfully humorous scholar. He said it was his duty to count the books in the college library, and spoke of 'running his nose along the shelves'—admitting at the same time he found them very dusty. The pack of hounds belonging to his college had been left on his hands for the duration of the war, and he protested that personally he could see more incentive for running if you were chased by a dog than in chasing the dogs when they were running away from you. Dean Armitage Robinson, a well known author, and his wife were staying with him. Also Sir Herbert Warren was there and talked at length about his nephew. It was a delightful half hour in the Dean's luxurious lodgings in Tom Quad.

"Mr. Seigel of Meredith's law firm has brought over a picture of the British Home for Aged on Staten Island and suggests giving it to me if I can meet him in London and spend the night with him at the Savoy Hotel. It is vacation time and the picture is important, so I propose to accept his invitation."

8

CHRISTMAS VACATION, 1915

"MAGDALEN College, 13th December 1915," I wrote home. "Another Christmas comes and measures out the long, long time since I have had the privilege of occupying my seat in the family circle. I do hope father will have returned from his professional duties in Alaska, for it would be unfortunate at Christmas with half the family at the opposite ends of the earth. I shall be with you all in spirit so don't forget my stocking by the fire place, and let the candle wax drip freely from every branch of the family tree.

"This is the first day of the vac, and most of the men have either gone or are on the point of leaving. Teck went yesterday to London. He says that all his sisters have been sent into the country with all the other London children of those who can afford to get them out of range of the Zeppelins. Windram and Banner are off today, the former to his mother in London and the latter to Bournemouth. Peter Warren is staying on for a Demyship examination on Thursday. If he is given this, it will probably mean that he will be with us till June, because he is not yet eighteen. He is a noble looking, light-haired fellow with a delightfully affectionate nature. Hough, who plays my accompaniments at hospital concerts; Chrussachi the Greek prime minister's nephew who spends his time trying to prove that he is a-moral, Street and the 'freshers' will be gone shortly. Then I shall be alone and not unhappy. Magdalen is a fascinating place even after the men have gone down.

"But these are my plans. Mr. Seigel (shall I say Meredith's partner-in-law) has asked me to go to the theatre with him when I pick up the pictures of the Victoria Home which mother is sending by him. I'll stop with him at the Savoy Thursday night.

Teck suggested putting me up for the night if I came in to see a play, and so I will go to him either before or after. Then I shall visit Lady Strathcona for perhaps a couple of days, because she has been good enough to ask me so often. Then if the Longstaffs are at their place, *Highlands,* I may spend a night there.

"Whether I can get these all in I do not know, but I shall stay in the city as little as possible and get back to my work here right off. There is an interesting Christmas Eve celebration in our Hall with the choir boys and everybody else left up — candle lighted tree, carols, etc. This I am looking forward to, and per- haps if the Harcourts come back I shall go down there for the day.

"Wherever I am I shall be happy from thinking of you all at home, so do back me up and have a wonderful time at '19, 7th.' The battlements around the cloister are covered with snow and the tower shoots up into the crisp sunshine. Everything is beautiful and lovely and happy — except for the war. My little sitting room rejoices in its treasures, and my heart is glad with thoughts of you at home; and of somebody else who has not had time yet to answer the most important letter I have ever written in my life."

Then, nine days later I was writing from 28 Grosvenor Square, London, "I was unable to accept Mr. Seigel's invitation to stay at the Savoy because certain men came back from the front and looked to find me at Magdalen. But I took lunch with him, and we went to the House of Commons. This was especially interesting to me because it gave me the chance to see Lloyd George, Asquith and others who had been at Nuneham, now participating in their public functions. Mr. Harcourt answered certain questions about traffic regulations in the city. A committee discussion which fol- lowed, centred about Mr. Reginald McKenna with whom I had had many conversations. Here the question was whether securities for the war loans should not be restricted to foreign securities. There were several good speeches on the danger of letting Canadian interests — for example the C.P.R. — fall under American control by offering them as securities. So much emphasis was given to Canadian interests that it was a relief to hear Mr. McKenna say that he would not only take care of the Canadians but also of the people England was borrowing from, i.e. the U.S.A.

"I left Mr. Seigel at the Savoy and with the pictures of the Victoria Home and my luggage went on to Lady Strathcona's for tea. Here I found Arthur back from the front. Young as he is, his tall, almost powerful frame, the steady penetrating gaze of his blue eyes and his utter scorn for pretense of any kind, high or low, makes one feel there is no use of being anything but genuine with him at whatever cost. He is in no sense pious, but he is good to know.

"From Grosvenor Square I went on to '4, Devonshire Place.' I had asked Prince George to go to the theatre with me and he still insisted on 'giving me a bed.' I was to come and dress, and we were then going out to dinner together. He was doing something in connection with sending out notices of casualties and did not come home till late. It gave me the opportunity for a long talk with his father, the Duke.

"His Highness the Duke is tall, remarkably handsome, bald head, a keen listener, and in all well worthy of being Her Majesty's brother. The town house is comparatively small, but, as you know, he is Governor of Windsor Castle. Impressive portraits, especially of his mother Adelaide, the 'Fat' Duchess of Teck, about whom so many amusing stories are told. A painted screen in the diningroom made of pannels from the family coach. I think it was George the Third's. A bowl in the morning room cut from the hide of a rhinoceros shot by the duke in India. So often had His Highness been called upon to represent the King at important funerals that he described himself as being a 'royal undertaker.'

"Finally George came home, and the duchess met me on the way up stairs with apologies for not having received me at first. Up to my bedroom where my clothes were laid out. We dined so late that I had to leave after soup to pick up Pye-Smith who was also to be my guest. We saw *Romance,* a play written in excellent form by Ned Sheldon, one of Meredith's friends at Harvard. It seemed appropriate since the setting was in my home town and was well acted. But to my surprise both of my guests seemed rather shocked at the play!

"The next day I might have gone to Debden Hall for a day's shooting, but the Tecks did not break their fast till a bit after eight. Instead, I walked to Claridges Hotel to see Windram. Found him still in his pyjamas and sat with him and his mother (dressed) during breakfast. On the way back I stopped in at Grosvenor Square whither I shall go for a visit on Saturday.

"Lunch with the Tecks. His Highness (note they created this special title which omits both the serenity of George's title and the royal quality of the King's more immediate family), the Duchess — who is daughter of the Duke of Westminster — George and my humble self. George's two sisters and his younger brother were off in the country. The duke recalled driving out to Sulgrave Manor with mother to arrange for its purchase and preservation as the English home of the Washington family. I showed the duchess a cordial note which had just arrived from Mrs. Randall Davidson and decided to act on her advice and call at once.

"On my way to Lambeth Palace I stopped in to see Bishop Boyd-Carpenter in the Little Cloisters of the Abbey at No. 3. Had a rewarding talk with the master orator about my Oxford work. I wish I could note down and send the inspiration to you. He rejoiced that the Church of England combined the two-party ideal and admitted a point very dear to me, that it was not a compromise but a combination of legitimate extremes. He told me in unforgettable phrases what the Communion Service meant to him and gave me all sorts of ideas on my dissertation.

"Since I was at Westminster, I dropped into Miss Meriel Talbot's office as she suggested. She was suffering from a 'chill' but was enthusiastic about a 'club' they have opened. She is responsible for 'land girls' filling in for men on farms. She asked after mother, and I told her of the home for aged British which the Daughters of the Empire had started in America.

"On my way home I called at a confectioner's to pick up a trick Japanese box, its cover decorated with a landscape of inlay work. The box would open only when you pressed the moon in the picture. This in turn worked a spring and shot out of the side a little drawer. I had brought the box from Oxford with the idea of having it packed with chocolates for my hostess. But the thing was that I had left Mother's pictures of the Victoria Home in the sweet shop for convenience, and they had wrapped them in the same bundle. The result was when I arrived at Devonshire Place with the package under my arm I was shown into a room where the duke and duchess were sitting. It seemed an opportunity to present my gift. But when the duchess opened the wrappings there was not only the box of sweets which she graciously accepted but also the pictures. She naturally asked me about them and finally urged me to let her show them to Her Majesty. There they are now. But honestly, I had not planned it that way.

"That night George and I went to dinner at the Pye-Smiths.

Mrs. P-S was very grateful for the supplies Mother sent. Arthur Howard was also there. And thus, we four together again, perhaps for the' last time. We had great fun ragging each other. It included my having to stand in front of the drawingroom fireplace and sing *The Star Spangled Banner.* After dinner we went to a sort of music show — minus the music. Another night at the Tecks', and in the morning in spite of very sincere hospitable protests, I left.

"Then to Lady Strathcona's. Francis Manners and Maurice Peterson came for dinner. We had a rollicking time after, singing. Edith, Arthur's sister, is good fun. Arthur left the next day at 9:50. Sunday I went with the family to St. Mark's Church, North Audley Street, and heard Mr. Cronshaw preach. He has a happy way of turning his pulpit into an arm chair. Miss Edith Howard and I took tea with the Pye-Smiths. Said goodbye to Phil, for he was returning to France, or perhaps Salonika, the next morning.

"Monday I called on Peter Warren in Bedford Square. Made arrangements for the day, and then went on to Eccleston Square to see my dear old friend (dating from Ewelme days), Sir Clements Markham. I found Sir C and Lady Markham in good form, and after going over an extensive collection of rare coins and seeing a good Coverdale, unfortunately cut at the edges, I promised to come to lunch the next day.

"While I was at lunch with the Howards, Peter Warren rang up to say Mr. Frank Benson's sister-in-law had sent tickets for *Midsummer Night's Dream.* We met at the theatre and, as usual with first performances, it dragged a bit. I sent my card to Mr. Benson and was asked to come back stage after the play. Mr. Benson in the best of spirits asked after Mr. Ben Greet who, he said, was doing excellent work with his Shakespeare productions at popular prices in Victoria Hall. Mr. B said his son had recovered and was going back to the front, and finally promised to look up a little book I had sent him to sign. Too late for tea at Grosvenor Square, but I dressed and went to dinner with the Warrens.

"Mr. Edward Warren is an architect and his house is furnished with exquisite taste. He is a younger brother of Sir Herbert's. Dinner over, Peter and I went off to see a famous comedian, Bert Coot, in an amusing farce called SAMPLES. Lady Strathcona had given me a latch key, but we were not too late."

London was changing for me. It was no longer an objective place — with its museums and libraries, its historic buildings and colourful spectacles — to be looked at. London had become for me a place of people — uncommon people with a common interest, sets of people tied together like merging villages whose winding streets were being by-passed by the superhighway of war — a personalized place, not to be lived in but to be lived with. If I ever looked out at London it was from the windows of friends who had taken me into their homes. So my journal continued to record.

"Tuesday morning I walked to the river to watch the boats struggle with the swift current and the little birds bobbing on the muddy waves. Then on to the Markhams'. What a treasure house! Sir Clements' discoveries in Peru, his connection with the polar explorations in person and as president of the Royal Geographical, and the historic family of which he is a member, has meant a varied collection of priceless relics. He has the most appealing Sir Thomas Lawrence, a painting of Lady Milnor, his great grandmother.

"Then I came back to Grosvenor Square, left a pig skin safety-razor kit as a present for Arthur and sailed off in a taxi for Putney Heath. There I found Dr. Longstaff with his brilliant conversation so enriched by his intelligent globe trotting. He was in good form, and Mrs. L still wild about snails and architecture. Dr. L had been acting as head of the voluntary constables, and when I arrived was up to his neck in hundreds of thousands of registration forms which had to be filed. Under National Registration all the inhabitants of this island have been required to fill out these blanks.

"When I leave *Highlands* my head is whirling with the infinite number of important facts which Dr. L fires out like a machine gun in the course of conversation. While there on Putney Heath I visited the best private-house convalescent hospital I have yet seen. There were 140 beds, and since the beginning of the war over 1,000 patients had been entirely cared for voluntarily by gentlewomen, kitchen and all. I also went with Dr. L and helped file registration blanks. The filing was going on in a spacious reading room given by Dr. L's father who had originally established the library. The librarian, however, soon carried me away and gave me certain invaluable books and papers connected with my liturgical study. I also went through the catalogue of the British Museum there and found *no* publication covering the subject of

my dissertation. This pleases me, it means I may be able to make
a real contribution to the great mass of liturgical literature.

"In addition to Mount Longstaff near the South Pole there is a
mountain in the Canadian Rockies named 'Katherine' after a
niece of Dr. Longstaff, but the recent picture of a Canadian
'Mount Langstaff' in the *New York Times* is a mystery to us.
The Longstaffs always ask to be remembered to my mother whose
visit they never forget.

"Dr. L sent me in his motor to the tube and then by taxi I
arrived again at Grosvenor Square. Lady Strathcona and her
daughter Edith had insisted on my coming back for Christmas. I
found waiting for me a letter from the Duchess of Teck and a
cordial note from the Old Palace at Canterbury, speaking of 'the
Archbishop having influenza and the Ordination in the house.'

"The Queen's message to Mother comes through the enclosed
letter from the Duchess of Teck which reads as follows: 'Dear
Mr. Langstaff, I am sorry I did not see you to say goodbye, but
I have been laid up with a horrid chill and been a miserable
creature! I showed your pictures to the Queen. She thought them
charming, and she appreciates the good work your mother is
doing in behalf of our English. She was very much interested in
seeing the pictures of the Home, and please tell your mother this.
I meant to have come round today to leave the pictures at Grosvenor Square, but I was laid low with a very bad headache and
never got out at all! It was a great pleasure to put you up here
and I only hope you were really comfortable and happy in our
little house. I remain, Yours sincerely, Margaret of Teck.' "

The Grosvenor Square which I was coming to know through
the hospitality of the Howards, and with which years later I
became more familiar through my short administration of the
local parish, still maintained an atmosphere of solid luxury. I
would have been bewildered could I have foreseen an American
eagle spreading over an administration building which was to
cover the entire side of the square where I was to spend my 1915
Christmas and to have discovered in the formerly exclusive park
a large bronze statue of my President, Franklin D. Roosevelt.

Three days after Christmas I wrote from No. 28, "What a
historic atmosphere is created by these Grosvenor Square man-
sions overlooking their own private park. It was in Lord Chester-
field's residence in this square that Dr. Samuel Johnson was kept

indignantly waiting in an anteroom, and here in the square Lord North died three years after our American revolution for which he was in a way responsible. Each house has its own continuing story. Three of them are now embassies including the Japanese and our own with Walter Hines Page in residence. What a setting for a Christmas dinner! And just as the plum pudding was being served what sounded like a heavy thud upstairs was quietly explained to Lady Strathcona by the butler as, 'Just another of those Zeppelins, my Lady.'

"Lady S is a wonderful little woman, simple in her tastes, active to the exclusion of pleasurable indulgences, and so full of good thoughts and kindnesses that it is an education in character to be near her. Her dominating shyness has made her a stranger to most of her neighbours but her keen observation seems to enable her to penetrate most of the masks they wear. Her husband, Dr. Howard, contrastingly tall, a gentlemanly physician of the old school, I feel gives me all the advice he would like to give his own sons.

"Lady Strathcona took me in her motor to Frognal where the Pomeroy Burtons have their 'Old Mansion' of which I have written. I have just come back. Mrs. Burton insisted on telling me the impression I had made on her husband when I had spent an evening with them a year ago. And since he is a man of few compliments and wide association with other men, I note in his words the following more to sum them up for myself perhaps than to attempt to give you information. It seems he found in me an ability of being at home in any society into which I may be thrown. An intellect which prompts the asking of advice and a modesty which makes it easy. There is something which causes people to forget themselves and go beyond the natural limits of friendship with me. I can not forget, however, Mr. Burton's reply to my statement that I was going into the ministry. 'You should be able to do something better than that.' One thing Mrs. B said which seemed to me especially true was that this power was not to be used, but it was well to feel the pulse and know that it was there."

I might have known Sir Pomeroy Burton when he was managing editor of the *Brooklyn Eagle* or later of *The World* under Joseph Pulitzer, but when I did come to know him in London he was managing director of Associated Newspapers, Ltd., the Northcliffe chain of daily newspapers, weeklies and magazines. *The Daily Mail,* in which he had a controlling interest, was not circulated in Grosvenor Square and Mr. Howard was probably correct in attributing to him the injection of American sensational methods into British journalism. Nevertheless, at the time he was one of the top men directing British propaganda in connection with the war.

I gathered from Pomeroy Burton that this winter was being a trying one for the armies in France. Ever since the king's visit to the front when at a burst of cheering from the soldiers his horse had reared, fell backward and rolled over on the king's leg. This was the accident to which the Pragger had referred when we were beagling at Oxford. Mr. Burton shared my admiration for the Prince of Wales and said that recently at a parade of the Indian Army Corps before their departure for Mesopotamia the prince had delivered a message to them from the king. In days to come, he advised me, it might be well for you to remember the king's words in this message, 'Before you leave France I send My dear and gallant son, the Prince of Wales, who has shared with My Armies the dangers and hardships of the campaign, to thank you in My name for your service.' Mr. Burton, I am sure, had no thought of the abdication nor could he have foretold the time when he was to lease his villa with a gold bathtub and swimming pool 250 feet long to a man known as the Duke of Windsor.

In France there had been changes in command. Joffre appointed early in December, Commander-in-chief of all French armies, and sometime later Sir John French relieved of command of British armies in France and succeeded by Sir Douglas Haig. Of this I heard from Teck. And on December 30th I wrote from Grosvenor Square, "The Duke of Teck told me when I saw him at church last Sunday that he was off to France in the morning. He will be military secretary to General Haig. You can be sure he will make good.

"Christmas here has been very tense, but thanks to Lady Strathcona's hospitality I have not had the chance of being gloomy. This afternoon Dr. Howard and Lady S took me to a cinema production called 'Britain Prepared.' I must say, some of it was a bit too realistic, but we were thoroughly impressed and hoped the still lethargic public was also. We were going across

HARVARD UNIVERSITY
CAMBRIDGE

November 30, 1932.

Dear Mr Langstaff:

Do I not remember you well in college
and the territorial clubs which you got out!.
The House plan is better because it throws men
from differents parts of the country irresistably
together. It is kind of you to write to me, and
I wish you every success in your work at St.
Edmund's Church.

Yours very sincerely,

A. Lawrence Lowell -

Rev. John Brett Langstaff
   St. Edmund's Church
      Morris Avenue and 177th Street
         New York City

A. LAWRENCE LOWELL (President of Harvard University) 1932, referring to The Federation of Territorial Clubs which first put in his mind
the division of Harvard College into "Houses" after the Oxford pattern.

the square to call on the Pages at the American embassy, but Lady Strathcona's head was aching from the flickering pictures, so we put it off to another day. Instead, I motored to Buckingham Gate to call on the Bryces. Lord B is making effective use of his literary gift for the Empire's benefit.

"By the way, now there is compulsion for all unmarried men. You will remember what Mr. Harcourt told me of his view on a possible conscription. He and others are now taking a stand against it which threatens a change in government. But I understand Mr. H was only anxious to continue voluntary military service as long as possible, so he is sure to give in before any national calamity. There is little opposition to this compulsion among the people, as far as I can see."

Since I had promised the president of Harvard to keep him in touch with events as I saw them I wrote him on this matter and received the following reply: "Dear Mr. Langstaff, Your letter from Grosvenor Square has just come, and you must certainly be having an extremely interesting time, being in the midst of people of influence at the most momentous period of England's history for a century. As you say, I suppose the bill for compulsory service of unmarried men will pass the Houses of Parliament by large majorities; but will the Trade Unionists make trouble in consequence? Nothing very decisive, I presume, is likely to happen during the winter, but we are in hopes that the spring will bring action that will show Germany to be losing strength. Very truly yours, A. Lawrence Lowell (Mrs. Lowell also wishes to be remembered to you)." Correspondence of this sort with a man who was a leading authority on English government was stimulating. In something more than a month came the great German offensive to be known as the Battle of Verdun.

"The last day of the year," I noted at 28 Grosvenor Square, London. "The coming year will decide the course of the world for the rest of the time we are on it, and also the course of my studies at Oxford. But for us all, and for you at home especially, may it combine all the brightness that sun, moon and stars can give it.

"Yes, I have received a card from Sir Courtenay Bennett. Always remembering with gratitude the cooperation given by the Daughters of the Empire during his consul generalship in New York. This desire on Mother's part to resign from the presidency of the *Daughters* is all right in a way, but if she finds there is nobody who can run the organization better than herself — and I fear this is the case — she must go ahead. England needs Mother and her Daughters in this present crisis. There are times when God makes it possible for us to go a little beyond our own strength. That's what is happening with many women here in England, and Lady Jersey is one of them."

The Countess of Jersey as president of the Victoria League in England was closely affiliated with my mother's work in the U.S.A. and wrote to my mother from 18 Montague Square at this time, "Dear Mrs. Langstaff, Thank you so much for the most interesting Report of the work of your Order which you were kind enough to send me. It was laid before the Executive Committee of the Victoria League last week, and the members of the Committee were delighted to hear of the great activity of the Chapters. I am sure that we at home, in the midst of War and Tumults, are deeply grateful for the help and sympathy of our sisters, the British women in the United States. If you have an opportunity pray convey to them the expression of our gratitude. With kindest remembrances, Believe me, Very sincerely yours, M. E. Jersey."

Thanks to a friendly association with Sir Philip Ben Greet I became involved in the beginning of an important epoch in British drama at this time. In America Ben Greet had toured with his company of players from coast to coast, producing Shakespeare in school auditoriums and college campuses, in abandoned theatres and public parks, almost anywhere and with the aid of meager costumes and little more scenery than nature provided. The play was the thing. And Greet's obsession was to enable students and others who could not afford costly theatre tickets to witness Shakespearian plays well acted. He had come to the U.S.A. originally at the invitation of certain New York managers to raise the American stage from a low level to which it had fallen. This he did by producing the mystery play *Everyman* introducing Edith Wynn Matheson to the American public.

At the start of the war — as my early letters indicated — he had returned home to England to offer his services in the general cause. Coincident with this one of his many friends, Miss Lilian Baylis, — encouraged by Greet, if not prompted by him, but certainly against the advice of other experts — founded her Drama Company in *The Old Vic* on the south bank of the Thames. From this beginning *The Old Vic* was to emerge from a struggling repertory theatre into one of the best known playhouses in the world. One of the young actresses at the *Old Vic* in these beginning days was Sybil Thorndike who years later came with her Casson children and acted for me in a Dickens matinee I put on in a Shaftesbury Avenue theatre. But in the winter of 1915 I was trying to persuade my friends from the West End to cross the Waterloo Bridge to witness Ben Greet's productions, for the *Old Vic* had not yet been accepted. Certainly it was not appreciated as a training ground for many of the great actors of the future, the cradle of what became the Royal Ballet.

On January 2, 1916, my letter from Grosvenor Square noted, "I have just walked down to the Royal Victoria Hall to see Mr. Ben Greet. He is producing Shakespeare and such like under the auspices of a charitable society of which the Princess Christian is president. A means of giving high-class drama to the poor. Mr. Greet says that he has been surprised by the popularity of a mystery play like *The Star of Bethlehem,* and finds it hard to tell what the people really want. He had just come from seeing George Vivian off for America where he has been offered the management of the second company producing the new play, *Treasure Island.* Mr. Greet was very generous in offering me boxes whenever I cared to come and bring a party.

"Yesterday I went with Edith Howard to W. W. Astor's gorgeous residence on Carlton House Terrace and helped file a lot of cards. They keep track of all the men and officers there for those who make inquiries. The house is done in gold and carved marble, grand stairway, glass doors, mirrors, etc. It might be impressive if it were not so like a hotel lobby."

The following day my journal continued, "This afternoon Lady Strathcona, Dr. Howard and myself went to the great hospital on the other side of the river beyond Battersea Park. There were 1,500 beds, which means it has the capacity of three military hospitals. A girls' school of some size had been used as a central building from which you could go through long passages to numerous huts. The term 'hut' seems to imply a long low building with peaked roof and many windows along the sides. It is made of corrugated iron and lined with wood covered with asbestos. The windows hinge at the bottom and open inwards to prevent the air from coming directly on the patients.

"It was like going in a royal party. The officer of the day seemed

SIR PHILIP BEN GREET (actor and producer) written to Brett Langstaff 1915, referring to his pioneering plays at *The Old Vic* in London as "settlement work."

overawed at the benefactress whom he was showing about, and if Lady Strathcona had not sent word that she wished to come in a private way, there would have been no end of ceremony. As she said to me a moment ago, 'They say Americans make such a fuss over titles, but our own people are just as foolish.' I have seldom seen such a retiring person who was at the same time so great a force in the community because of her generous giving. She is running a hospital in Bath entirely at her own expense and really puts herself to labour at her many charities."

My letter of the 7th had more about *The Old Vic* saying, "Did I tell you how I went down to the Royal Victoria Hall to see Mr. Greet in *She Stoops to Conquer?* I took Peter Warren and his sister Dorothy. Mr. G acted beautifully as Tom and during the course of the play sent for me to come back-stage. He greeted me from the other side of a crowd with his 'Well, Brett' and seemed happy to meet my guests. I went back to Bedford Square for tea with the Warrens with the cannon booming away at Zeps.

"I spent this morning seeing Mr. Greet at his 'Old Vic.' He gave me certain pamphlets which show the good work this People's Theatre is accomplishing. Particularly valuable to keep up the morale in such a time. He has given me a box for Monday night and I will make up a party. On leaving, Mr. G insisted I go to Southwark Cathedral. It is located at one end of London Bridge near where the Globe Theatre of Shakespearean fame once stood. Impressive nave and choir forming a vista of stone pillars, but all a bit dingy — as perhaps a cathedral has to be. I walked back through mud that would rival the trenches in France.

"Yesterday Lady Strathcona and I called on our ambassador's wife, Mrs. Page. Everybody speaks nicely of her homely, simple ways as so befitting a republic. She is certainly far different from the former ambassadoress, Mrs. Whitelaw Reid, upon whom we called a short time ago at Dudley House in Park Lane. We intended to go on to Sir James McGrigor, but we stopped in at the Kitsons' to see Lady S's grandbaby and stayed too long."

From Grosvenor Square on the 10th I wrote, "Tomorrow I planned to go to Bournemouth to stay ten days and return with Banner on the 21st when term begins. But Delmar wires me just now that I must have a passport. This document is with my letters in Oxford. I am now left the alternatives either to go to Mr. Page to arrange for some sort of passport or return to Oxford for my present one. Once back with my work on the table where I left it I shall never get away, for my vac has been long and full of distraction and now I am itching to be finishing my dissertation. Mrs. Walter Burns, Mr. J. P. Morgan's sister of whom I have spoken before, sent a message this morning to say she would like to see me at 1 o'clock tomorrow. She is coming up from some nearby park of hers only for a few hours because the town house, a tremendous place in Brook Street, is being painted.

"I have just returned from lunching with Maurice Peterson at the St. James's Club, 67 Piccadilly, large and comfortable. Peterson's father is the Principal of McGill University. P himself is doing regular Foreign Office work in the dept of the Board of Trade. I have come to know him through the Howards. It seems Mr. Howard's brother who left Iowa University to take charge of the McGill Hospital in France, is going back because he finds that he is not indispensable. He is a splendid man, but it is a blessing in a way to think there are enough doctors to care for the wounded. Aunt Josephine wrote me about her doctor husband coming on from Canada, but I should say from this my uncle Gari had better stay home and take care of his sanitarium in Thornhill.

"Yesterday, Sunday, besides the regular occupations of service at 8.30 and 11. in St. Mark's North Audley Street and a trip with the two dogs, Jock and Coccles, across Hyde Park to see Frances Kitson, whose husband is in the navy, I called on the Harcourts in Berkeley Square and then went on to tea with Mrs. Pye-Smith. Spent hours there and came away with Phil's photograph in uniform.

"I don't think I told you Edith Howard had given me Arthur's photo in his uniform with a bronze frame bearing the insignia of the Scots Guards. Also Lady Strathcona made me a Christmas present of a handsome pair of gold enamel sleeve links with the arms of Canada and Mr. Howard two volumes of Percy's *Reliques* which he prizes."

The final letter from 28 Grosvenor Square was written on January 11, 1916. "Last night I took — we went in the Howards' motor — Mrs. Melladew, Edith Howard and Captain Hayward, an Australian who went up with me to Magdalen, to the 'Old Vic.' Nobody seemed to know of the wonderful work that is being done for the people of Southwark, and they all teased me a lot about my 'Old Vic,' because there was a time when it had a miserable reputation as a low music hall.

"It was my own play *Twelfth Night* in which I had acted under the direction of George Baker at Harvard. Mr. Greet did Malvolio, the part Sam Eliot did for us, with much originality. You remember Ann Thorp and Helen Evarts were our leading ladies. In this case Viola Tree, Sir Herbert's buxom daughter, did the Viola. And the rest of the cast was perfection. It was certainly great credit to Ben Greet as producer.

"What a joy it was to hear the house, filled with poor people from the neighbourhood, splitting their sides over good clean fun, and to think of their taking back to the squalid places they inhabit the bright romance of *Twelfth Night!* I am satisfied my party enjoyed it. Mr. Greet had given me the best box in the house, but we did not go back to see him, chiefly because I know he does not like holding a reception after acting.

"I am leaving town now — as soon as I have seen Mrs. Burns and had lunch — for Magdalen. My month in London has been a rewarding one, and the term to come is to be the climax of my work on the dissertation."

9

LENT TERM, 1916

ONCE more I was come under the spell of those "most tuneable and melodious bells" which mark the quarter hours from the Magdalen tower, the tower begun building in the year Columbus discovered America and ascribed to Thomas Wolsey who was twice bursar during the period of its erection. Cardinals such as Wolsey and Reginald Pole — the former completed his studies at Oxford at the age of fifteen and the latter entered Magdalen as a gentleman commoner at twelve — reflected on my just hoping to get my degree as an undergraduate of Magdalen at the age of twenty seven. But I was satisfied to waive the prodigies of the past and to concentrate on my own present problems. The glamour of greatness which during my recent vacation in London had dazzled me a bit I was resolved to turn away from in order to accustom my eyes to the concentrated light of the student's lamp. I could almost hear Edward Gibbon advising me that although he never really studied while at Magdalen, he was able many years later to write history such as I was attempting to do for my thesis.

However, still dreaming of my exciting experience at *The Old Vic* my journal on January 21st noted, "A man asked me in Cloisters yesterday to show him where the Prince of Wales lived, this led to my asking him up to see my own 'cell.' He turned out to be a Mr. C. A. Barrett, in some way connected with theatrical producing. His father invented the grease paint used by actors in 'making up,' and he also wrote the well known book, *How to Make Up, by Harefoot and Rouge.* We had a long talk about the physical condition of the men who were coming back from the front, because he had made a special study of this. It would seem that although they are as a rule benefitted by the open air life and the regular wholesome diet, their nerves in many cases are disastrously affected.

"I later went to the Oslers where we talked more on this subject. They have not yet moved into the diningroom. Sir William was very pleased with an old set of Hooker which I had picked up. In the afternoon I took Phil Pye-Smith's photo in uniform down to 'Peter Martyr,' i.e. to Dr. Sanday, who lives — as I've probably told you — in the old reformer's house in the cathedral cloisters at Christ Church. Phil has improved so much by his military experience in France that Dr. Sanday did not recognize him from the picture. He recalled when staying with Dr. Pye-Smith about seven years ago, Phil had to be carried because he was so weak. Miss Hatch, who keeps house for Dr. Sanday, was there.

"Saturday Govy Hoffman, Hugh Terris, Peter Warren and myself went out on the river in canoes. It was rather fun going over places which are dry land in normal times, for the floods which come at this time of year through the Thames valley cover acres of the countryside. We started fooling, set my open 'brolly' sailing upside down and threw hats and sticks after it. Finally we were compelled to rush home dripping cold and take hot baths. Later we foregathered in Peter's rooms in the Grammar Hall to plan a reading party for the next vacation. He suggested his father's cottage on the edge of the Berkshire Downs but there is a chance of its being rented.

"I finished a short history of the American Church this morning and spent all afternoon in the Camera looking up books on the same subject. It is icy cold in the library, and I have caught a bit of it. I went to a Five O'clock lecture which Canon Scott-Holland gives once a week on the Gospels. He said the Gospels should be read with the understanding that when they were written there was a fully recognized creed which can be discovered in the openings and benedictions of the Epistles and in places where St. Paul appeals to a common ground upon which to base an argument. Also the Gospels are the close of the *old* rather than the beginning of the *new*. He is full of enthusiasm and is one of the outstanding personalities in Oxford today.

"I came back frozen. Had a friendly little fight with Peter — what we would call a rough-house. Dined in hall with the dim light of temporary candles which have been substituted for the electric lights because of Zeps. (It is said that at Oriel they have dispensed with table cloths because they reflect too much even the candle light.) Now I am off through the blackened streets to have another go at my history reading in the Radcliffe library.

"I received the newspapers, cuttings etc. It was good to read about the New York Charity Ball and get the Floor Committee badge. Wish I could have been there to wear it. What did Mother wear? Do write me if that business about the Queen and the pictures was to Mother's satisfaction. I ought to tell you that when the duchess showed the picture of the Victoria Home to Her Majesty, the Queen insisted she could clearly recognize Mother standing on the veranda. The figure was very small, as you know, and I had thought it was one of the inmates of the Home. But now you tell me it was Mother, I have great regard for the Queen's power of recall and keen observation.

"My I'm tired!" (Magdalen College, 23rd January 1916) "Just biked out to Clifton Hampden to lunch with Lord Aldenham. Walked with him through Nuneham Park — Harcourts not there.

"There were several interesting people at Lord Aldenham's besides his two daughters. A Mr. and Mrs. Gibbs who live near Dr. Longstaff at Putney Heath and a Mr. —, who had just come back from ten years in Australia. He told me a story which is rather a shocker, but well illustrates coarse and yet clever wit. One time when my friend, Sir George Reid, was campaigning in Australia, he stepped onto a platform before a rough audience of the opposition and was showered with vegetables and other missiles of a suggestive nature. The contention was over an Australian navy. Suddenly an egg hit him in the middle of his stomach, and, having paused to wipe his waistcoat, he exclaimed, 'Gentlemen, I expected to meet with hostile opposition, but I did not look for a navel engagement!' But this is nothing to some of the stories Sir George has told me of himself. Until recently he has been High Commissioner for the continent of the Pacific, but now he is to represent the St. George's Square constituency in Parliament. He is needed in the House because of his knowledge of Australia, but I can't even quote what Dr. Howard said on hearing he was to be represented by such a politician.

"Biking home I stopped in to see how dear old Mrs. Pochin was. She had the grippe. She says Lord Macclesfield is in Cairo and a rule preventing women going to Egypt keeps her granddaughter, the countess, here. Visited a short time and then back to Oxford just too late for chapel.

"They want me to go and sing for the wounded again, but no, this term from ten to ten is going to be nothing but solid work for me. Last night, however, the fellows dressed me in robes with a tea cosy for a mitre. Then with a long procession of tape-bearers before and aft, I made my official call on my tutor, Canon Brightman. The great authority on vestments, after a moment's genuine surprise, saw the fun of it and made us all sit down on the floor around the fire in his spacious study. We were then plied with sweets and allowed to play with wooden toys which latter are a hobby with him. We went away happier and wiser men."

A week elapsed before I found time to note down, "I went to the Oslers again for lunch yesterday. There was a doctor in charge of one of the neighbouring hospitals seated next to me at the table who was working out a new idea of preventing measles by innoculation. Also a girl who was studying something which nobody could understand, with the result that people thought she must be doing some deep research. For my part I don't think she is doing anything, and there seem to be a number of students of that sort here in Oxford.

"Sir William had just purchased all the collection of papers, clippings, etc. which had been preserved by the late Edward Dowden concerned with Walt Whitman. Dowden, a professor at Dublin, was one of Whitman's great friends and admirers. Contemporary newspaper accounts of the poet, magazine articles and pictures of his, a card of admission to an address given by him on the death of Lincoln, and many other valuable Whitmaniana. They could not have fallen into better hands, for Sir William delights in the get-atable preservation of literary and historic records. He showed me the books the old poet had given him when he, Sir W, was his physician in America. There was a picture of Whitman sitting in a dark room next to a window, working. Sir W said that was how he remembered him, sitting on the opposite side of the room from the door with a pile of newspapers knee-high which had accumulated over the years as he had read them and thrown them aside. In fact the only way to reach him was by a circuitous passage which he had kicked for himself along the wall.

"Sir William told me I must read Walton's *Life of Hooker,* but we found his copy had been sent to the binder's and therefore I sat down to the same man's account of Sanderson, for Sanderson had a lot to do with parts of the Liturgy. The family disappeared, but all sorts of people came in and interrupted me. Among them Dr. Mallock with a most interesting discovery he had just made. Finally I left a mark in my book and put it on a top shelf for later perusal. One always comes from the Oslers' with some definite addition to one's knowledge. One always feels impelled to bring something from one's searching to Norham Gardens in return.

"Teck and I called on Sir Herbert and Lady Warren for tea. Davison was there. You remember the account of him in the *Brooklyn Eagle.* Sir Herbert told me about an anthology of war verse which his friend, Robert Bridges, has just brought out. The poet-laureate has taken French and English poets and philosophers and placed them together so as to obtain a certain psychological connection which, Sir Herbert observed, does not appear at first. He said another American named Ogden had applied for entrance at Magdalen. He will probably have no difficulty in getting in, for the days of struggling ended when I finally broke the barriers. At that time there was a hope of everybody coming back from war in a few months. Now there is a danger of the college being deserted. We have only twenty undergraduates left.

"The study group this evening was more inspiring than usual. But it is pathetic to see how the fundamental to any religious faith — the belief in an intelligent God — is lacking with the average student. My liturgical work is making good headway."

This growing friendship between us American students and our Oxford instructors was to continue until in recent years a president of Magdalen would point with pride to more than two dozen American undergraduates resident in his college alone. A note from Sir Herbert Warren dated February 1st read, "Dear Langstaff, Will you give us the pleasure of your company at luncheon on Sunday next at 1.30 to meet Colonel and Mrs. Janes? Colonel Janes is commanding the Rgt whose officers are billeted in College."

It was on this occasion I heard of the Belgian professors who were holding forth in the New Lecture Rooms near Pembroke College. Some of these from the war-shattered Louvain University, the 'Oxford of the Low Countries' founded in 1425, and at one time numbering far more colleges than Oxford itself.

To these I referred on February 4th saying, "Certain scholars who might in normal times have sought the protection and inspiration of continental universities are now pursuing their labours at Oxford. Belgium has lost her universities for the time being. The French have become so skeptical of the value of university life — no matter how abbreviated — continuing in time of war, that they are sending a commission of professors from the Sorbonne to investigate the situation in Oxford. The American universities, which might well be a retreat for European scholars, are cut off by submarines and the troubles which hold people near their homes. These and other factors tend to draw the older scholars to Oxford and her sister university.

"Professor Santayana has just had tea with me. You remember I first came to know him in the house where I stayed before they admitted me to Magdalen, and since then we have been going on many long walks together. He is so keen and clear sighted; I wish he were still connected with Harvard. He admired a new tapestry I have bought to cover a long wall of my sitting room. It is a Louis XV hunting scene done by the Gobelin works in France which are now shut down. He also approved the plan of my dissertation. This latter is encouraging because my tutor, Canon Brightman, has a way of urging me to more definiteness by never letting me think he understands what I am driving at. It is a successful method, but it requires a lot of self-confidence on the part of the pupil.

"One rather interesting observation Mr. Santayana made was that when the war has taken away the false ideas about the altruism of the world in its far advanced state of civilization, we will come more to deal face to face with realities. This will show us the real state of our civilization, and we will see the necessity of sincere faith in God. He sees a significant religious wave coming. One can certainly feel the beginnings of it now here in England."

As I thought it over, what Santayana was foreseeing was not so much a resurgence of personal religion within the churches but rather a gradual swelling of the tide which was to mark a rising influence of religion in world affairs. This would be accompanied by minority oppositions to it. I saw temporal powers throwing up secular barriers to stem this rising tide of religion. But against this would come the strengthening and expanding of ecclesiastical structure and the overflow of religious consciousness in all parts of the world, carrying with it the ideals of freedom and the recognition of human dignity.

"Prince George and I have just been to lunch with Sir Herbert Warren and The Lady 'Pree,'" my journal recorded on February 6th. "We were asked to meet Colonel Janes, but a Major Atkinson and his wife were there instead. Major A is collecting data for the official history of the war. This, he says, will take years to write since some of the information at least could not be given to the public for twenty years from now. He is also bringing out Mrs. Humphrey Ward's new book, now appearing in the *Cornhill*, concerning life at Oxford in the Eighties when Mrs. W was a girl here.

"Well I remember Mrs. Humphrey Ward when she came to lecture in New York — the broad brim of her picture hat completely hiding her face as she looked down at her notes and then rising with the dramatic effect of a curtain as she looked up to speak to the audience. I had a talk with her after the lecture. Sir Herbert says her father, who finally ended up as a professor at Dublin, was constantly changing back and forth between the Anglican and Roman communions, but his wife remained always the same because — she explained — 'I might have gone over with Tom, but I could never have come back again with him.' But poor Mrs. Ward is headed for trouble with the more exact intimates of old Oxford. They are sure to be offended with the man she speaks of as having a large house in Holywell and holding several fairly paid positions and only receiving an income of 700 a year. Also the ices she speaks of being served on all the barges, and other little things with which no book on Oxford has ever succeeded in satisfying critics. As the major puts it, 'She has laid on the local colour with a trowel.'

"I questioned the major regarding the Compulsion Bill, to help me to reply intelligently to President Lowell's letter. For one thing, the major did not seem to think it involved any danger of getting malcontents into the army. What he felt the chief reason for men not wishing to enlist was that they feared, 'the other fellow would pinch their business.' This might happen if they took the *king's shilling* (now two and nine pence). If 'the other fellow' is compelled to go into service, everybody will be satisfied. But, he added, it ought to have come six months ago. Personally I don't think it would have been possible any sooner.

"Sir Herbert showed me the new anthology of which he had spoken. Mr. Bridges calls it *The Spirit of Man*. Sir H let me take

TELEPHONE:
KENSINGTON 860 & 867.

HYDE PARK BARRACKS,
S.W.

Sunday, July 23rd 1916.

My dear Brett.

Thank you very much for your touching letter and photograph. I ought to have answered you before, but somehow I could not do it.

I enclose a likeness of

Jimmy has gone down to Brest... I hope you had a good voyage. Stock goes over this week. I went to see Butler-Thwing and he is in hospital with in shoulder. to have can tell his people if you can then that he is up and about & looks fairly well

Yours ever
George Neath

Letter from H. S. H. Prince George of Teck (Marquess of Cambridge) to Brett Langstaff regarding undergraduates mentioned in the journal.

his copy for a bit and I have read part of it with much pleasure. It has been compiled within the last year and certainly it reflects the feeling of the war. In the Preface, 'the reader is invited to bathe rather than to fish in these waters,' and the selections from philosophers and poets are delightfully arranged for consecutive reading.

"This afternoon I went with Prince George to the Kempsheads — one of our dons — for tea. We had heaps of fun ragging each other. Perhaps we were a little too much, but nobody seemed to mind. We came away all knowing each other a bit better."

My intention to give the photographs of the home for aged British in America to Queen Mary had been thwarted because the Duchess of Teck had brought them back to me after showing them to the Queen. Thus my day's journal continued, "George told me that his mother was away in the country and would not see the Queen for some time, so I wrote to my friend, Mr. Wallington. I explained about my having two sets of pictures of the Victoria Home and asked him to advise me without troubling the Queen whether Her Majesty would like to have kept the pictures she had seen. This is his reply: 'Buckingham Palace, Feb. 5, 1916, Dear Mr. Langstaff, I have shown your letter to The Queen, and am desired by Her Majesty to ask you to be good enough to send the photographs here, as the Duchess took the copies of the same with her, after showing them to the Queen.'"

The 'comfortable house' at West New Brighton, Staten Island, which my mother as its first president opened in April 1915, was to be incorporated in August 1916 as the Victoria Home. At the time it was the only British home for old people outside the empire and would be followed by similar homes in Illinois, California and Florida. Years later, when the Victoria Home had been moved to Ossining-on-Hudson, a British queen was to grace it with a personal visit.

"There seems to be a sincere admiration felt by men of letters in England for their literary brothers in America. Sir Herbert at tea last Sunday in commending Lowell said, 'The only time I ever saw James Russell Lowell was after I had returned from a visit in America. When I told Lowell I had seen his house in Cambridge two weeks before, his reply was that he wished he had that same good fortune.'

"The arrangement about having a house for the coming vac

has been decided now. (March 1, 1916.) It is near John Masefield's cottage in Berkshire, some 16 miles south of Oxford, and since this poet is a close friend of the Warrens perhaps we shall see something of him. Mrs. Warren will come and a servant. Then there will be Peter, Govy Hoffman and Hugh Terris, of whom I have written previously. And now it is planned to ask a Balliol don, a Mr. Urquhart, to spend part of the time with us. This is usual on Oxford reading parties such as this. The house is fairly large and I think we will get a lot out of being together. I shall have plenty to do in finishing my dissertation.

"My work has been hustling this week. I set myself to have the rough draft done by March 5th, and I think this will be possible. That will mean that I have the Liturgy in the histories of England, Scotland and America written out, and the earliest texts of the liturgies in those countries as revised by the latest texts. Canon Brightman appears very satisfied with the way it is going.

"I don't see why this material I am getting together might not be published. Several of the men here have told me it should be. If this were to come about, although there can not be much financial return in such a venture, it will be of more value to me than a lot of money."

The following day I could write from Magdalen, "The members of the reading party of which I've been telling you have just had tea in Terris's rooms at the *House*. After we had settled things he took us around to see Ruskin's rooms and Gladstone's and the rooms which were used by King Edward VII, although he really lived in a house across the way from Christ Church.

"This morning Canon Brightman gave a breakfast party in his rooms in New Builders — six of us. These New Buildings were designed to be part of a great quadrangle which would have entailed tearing down the cloisters where I live. Fortunately only this one side was constructed because the money ran out. Brighters was in excellent form and gave us fish and eggs etc. From there I went to finish reading two tremendous volumes of American history in the 'Camera.' Now I shall try writing my own account from the notes I have been able to collect of references to the Communion Service."

After another ten days I wrote, "My work on this dissertation has kept me from doing anything lately to make letters interesting, but yesterday I did have a wonderful time. I went up to the Oslers'

for luncheon. I mentioned to Sir William about Father attending
the wealthy eccentric, Mr. Wynan of Baltimore. Sir W, while at
Johns Hopkins, had reason to know him well. He said Wynan was
an unusual man who — in spite of his gold-tiled residence in Newport — kept to himself. Sir W also had tales about Newport when
he was there with Weir Mitchell and Bancroft, the historian, and
others who frequented the resort.

"Do thank Mother for her letter and tell her I not only had the
Queen's pictures put in good order, but to insure their arriving in
the same condition I had them boxed as though they were oil
paintings. The shop that did it for me is now exhibiting the
Raemaekers cartoons which seem to me to illustrate the triumph
of the German spirit of brutality over the rest of the world — so
gross and disgusting are the drawings.

"While I was at the Oslers' Sir William said to me, 'You must
have your dissertation published.' I protested that I could not
afford it — because unless a book of this sort is published by a
Missionary Society or something of the kind, the author has to pay
at least part of the cost. This I know from the experience of two
of our best theological scholars here. *Foundations,* the most
popular theological publication that has gone out from Oxford in
recent years, Canon Streeter said cost him (I forget how much),
although it later paid tremendously. I shall go to the Press with
Sir W on Thursday and see how things stand. Sir W says that it
will cost half what it would cost in America, and the Oxford Press
also carry their books to America. He asked me what the title
would be, and now I think it over, this occurs to me: *Union among
Christians,* and on the title page: 'The Celebration of the Holy
Eucharist or the Administration of the Sacrament of the Body and
Blood of Christ Is the Principal Bond of Union among Christians.'

"I went to see Canon Scott-Holland to ask his advice. At tea we
talked of many things but regarding publication he said without
question I could proceed from my *B. Litt* to the *D. Litt* by sub-
mitting published works after a period of seven years according to
the university statutes. The dissertation I plan to submit for the
B. Litt after publication he felt would in the required time qualify
me for the higher degree. And he has followed my work closely
and heads the department which will eventually pass on my
receiving a B. Litt.

"One of the reasons for my choosing the history of the Communion Service as the subject for my dissertation was because I wished to discover for myself how this service — the subject of greatest controversy — had at the same time been the strongest bond between churches which use it for their most solemn form of worship. I am even more convinced that this Liturgy holds the key to the problem of Protestants vrs Catholics. I should like to devote my life to working it out. My thought of course had been that I would go into the ministry of the church, but if I could work in some organization planned for drawing the churches together I would almost prefer it. Even if I were ordained, still I would consider this my duty.

"I have told you about our going with Peter Warren to his father's house in Aston Tirrold, Berkshire. His father is the Administrator in charge of the military hospital at Corfu. This means that he comes under your *Serbian Relief* field. He is well known as an architect in London and has built several of the hospitals since the war began, here in England. Recently the Government sent him out to Corfu to have complete charge over the large hospital they are establishing there — over the con-struction and everything. His brother, as you know, is our college president, Sir Herbert. Will you do what you can to see that he is supplied out of your bounty? I know him, and if you knew him as well you would feel sure he would make the best use of any supplies you might send from America. His address as we received it here a few days ago is: Edward P. Warren Esq., F.P.O., W. 4, British Adriatic Mission, c/o G.P.O., London."

The Serbian Relief Society in which my mother was taking an active part was an expression of the sympathy felt in America. I had reason to know how that country was cruelly put upon by its enemy and weakly supported by its allies. Three months before my writing the above letter French troops had landed at Corfu to prepare for transferring thither the remnant of the Serbian army from Albania. It was referred to as 'an obligation of humanity.' To intercept this move Austrian submarines had been busy sinking what they could in the Adriatic. An Allied Squadron was being sent as a counter-measure necessitated by the submarine menace which had extended to the Mediterranean.

But my campaign was to be on the edge of the Berkshire Downs with all the dangers of distraction ahead of me.

On March 18, 1916, I wrote from Magdalen, "The last word of

advice my tutor had from Ruskin was, 'If you master ten years of
history, you have done a life work; not like that flea Buckle, who
attempted to write the history of European civilization.' Perhaps
Ruskin would call me 'a flea' for my present attempt. We had the
opinion of our tutors this morning in 'collecers,' and I find that
Brightman's idea that I was too ambitious has changed into one of
pleasure at the way my dissertation is shaping up.

"Sir William Osler took me to the Clarendon Press later in the
morning. He stayed long enough to show the head of the Press
that he was to take my job on and then left me there. I went over
my dissertation carefully with Mr. ———, who took every care in
telling me what best to do. You know my scheme. There are three
historical sketches of the part the Communion Service has played
in the histories of England, Scotland and America. Each of these
takes some twenty pages and forms an introduction to the text
of the Communion Service as used in the respective countries.
How to show the alterations made by reformers up to the present
day? In my dissertation as I have done it, the original texts are
typed in black, while the alterations are made in red, and what
has been left out by reformers is crossed out (//). What has been
inserted by them I have typed above the line in red. The two
colours would be impossible in the printing because as you know
the second impression for the second colour can not be depended
upon to print exactly where you wish it. So Mr. ——— advised
the method they had used in the Interlinear Bible. There would
be necessarily a great many footnotes to explain the changes made
in the revised texts. These footnotes would be where the main
scholarly value would lie — many of them in Greek or Latin. The
final volume would be cased in red cloth with gold lettering and
have the two colours on the title page.

"He said they are cutting down their printing now because of
lack of men caused by the war, and my having the opportunity of
getting it done at all is a great privilege and an indication of its
worth. I should be able to have the proof read by Canon Brightman, and he is the final authority on the subject of liturgies.
Moreover, its original arrangement and interesting reading matter
should give it a sale in America as well as over here. Shall I ever
have time in the future to do exhaustive research such as this?"

Concentrated as the last few months of my work were, I welcomed an occasional distraction when it seemed worth while.

Thus on March 19 I noted, "I went to see and hear G. K. Chesterton yesterday. He began by saying that as usual he would say nothing about the subject on which he had been scheduled to lecture — Soldiers and Songs. At this the ladies who composed most of his audience seemed highly pleased. He continued by observing that although Lord Byron had written a poem to show that the world was divided into bores and those who were bored, he (G.K.C.) felt sure that the world was divided into those who were bored at Byron's poetry and those who bored other people by reading Byron's poetry to them. He said the brilliancy of modern literature would not bear inspection, and in fact all modern literature was a joke. (This I take it did not include his own literary attempts.) He further told us that, 'Heigh noney O!' was

3. BUCKINGHAM GATE.
S.W.
9th. Jan. 1918.

Dear Mr. Langstaff

I will do my best with great pleasure to help you to obtain a mission as chaplain, which you desire. It seems to me that your ring been born as a British subject ought to be quite enough to set rest any difficulties on the score of nationality, and the Archbhop's letter ought to be enough for the Ecclesiastical authorities. will speak to the Archbishop about it and see what is best to be ne.

Your letter should have been answered sooner, but I have been der an overwhelming press of private and public work.

I am Very truly yours
Bryce

Letter from Viscount Bryce to Brett Langstaff regarding his application for a chaplaincy in the British army.

the best line that Shakespeare ever wrote, and the best English
song was 'The British Grenadiers' which excelled in its line, 'Fol,
dela, la.'"

Mr. Brightman, Delmar Banner and I had tea afterwards with
Hough in his rooms. Brighters in the course of our conversation
regarding churchmanship said he remembered Renan walking up
the High to St. Mary's like 'a toad on its hind legs.' After this
French orientalist whose '*Vie de Jesus*' continues to shock the
world, had heard the sermon in the university church, he remarked
to the preacher that they might have changed places. (This is a
twit on the broadness of the preaching.)"

From Magdalen College, 20th March 1916; "It must have been
shortly after Sir Clements Markham asked me to lunch with him
on Eccleston Square that he met with the accident you have
probably heard of. It seems it was his custom to lie in bed with
a book in one hand and a candle in the other and read until he felt
sleepy. One night about two months ago now, he woke to find his
bed in flames. His shouts enabled people to save him before he
was burned to death, but he died a few hours after from the shock.
How terrible to think that the two older men — Father Maxwell,
Superior of the Cowley Fathers, and now Sir Clements — both
of whom I came to know so well in the same house at Ewelme at
different times, have had so soon such unexpected deaths. They
both seemed so full of vigor, both explorers gone to new worlds.

"The night before last the President and Lady Warren gave
a 'little dinner' for the Bishop of Bristol, Nickerson. Mr. Gambier-
Parry and I were invited to meet him. In the course of dinner
conversation Mr. G-P said to the bishop in a depreciatory sort of
way, 'Yes, but a large part of your cathedral at Bristol is modern.'
The bishop's reply was immediate, 'And so are we.' He is a young
man and very progressive. I had a pleasantly instructive talk with
him on the mining district where he had been Suffragan Bishop
before. From what our Bishop Darlington, whom the bishop knew,
used to say of the mining conditions in Pennsylvania, I should
say the English miners are better off. He made a neat little sketch
of a miner's lamp for me.

"We also had a discussion as to the part the Communion Service
might play in the movement for church unity. He told me of a
growing custom in England of silent prayer-meetings where people
without surrendering their various religious convictions came to-

gether and prayed silently. He felt this was a step to the ideal of universal communion. He told me further of several meetings since the war started which gave evidence of the remarkable way the common distress is drawing people together in the fundamentals of faith. Combination services with dissenters — or non-Anglicans, as he called them — in which extempore prayer was offered even by the bishop. This was all very shocking to our hostess who is extremely 'high church.'

"Last night I was asked by Mr. Urquhart to dine at the high table in Balliol. This is the first time I have had such an honour, and at such a learned college too!! We congregated in the Senior Common Room, an institution not older than the 17th century, I'm told. The Master — corresponding to Magdalen's president — who holds the great Jowett's office with almost equal distinction, the two Picard-Cambridges, the Rev. Mr. Thompson — that is J. M. Thompson who recently ceased to be our Dean of Divinity at Magdalen —, Captain Von Stieglitz whom I saw a good deal of when he was recuping at Nuneham and several other officers who are stationed there in college with their men. We mounted a spiral stone stairway and reached the great hall through a little door at the upper end. There at a long table raised on a platform, we stood for grace. I was seated on the right of the Master facing the undergraduates in the hall. The thirty undergraduates made a sparse showing in so tremendous a room. Although Balliol was founded in the 13th century under the painful circumstances of expiating the soul of the late husband of Dervorguilla of Galloway, this hall and most of the other college buildings date only from the latter half of the 19th century, the last of which is comfortable and ugly.

"After dinner we took our napkins and descended to the Senior Common Room where we sat in a semi-circle with a little round table for each two persons. Then came nuts and raisins and ginger and fruit and port and smokes. One of the dons showed me a rare copy of the 1637 Scots Prayer Book, and I was able to tell him something about it. Mr. Urquhart took me back to his rooms where we pored over exciting books. His unusual display of undergraduate photographs indicate how popular he must be. They call him 'Sligger.' At ten thirty I came back to Magdalen."

The relation of dons toward their pupils which used to be strictly academic — Sligger being a rare exception — was now becoming more personal. Especially in the case of undergraduates who had made the 'supreme sacrifice' or were returned maimed for life, their memories or former associations were cherished in an almost deserted college community. And those who were going out to fight for their country and for a better world to live in, they went with an anxious prayer of hope from tutors who were in a position to appreciate the intellectual worth of their students.

In a comparable way there was a sympathetic remembrance on the part of those who had gone into military service, for dons or fellow undergraduates whom they had left behind in Oxford. The voluntary spirit was such — before the days of conscription — that to be turned down by the military and left behind at college was just so much 'bad luck.' It was in this spirit that my friend, Arthur Howard, wrote at this time from his home in Grosvenor Square, "Dear Brett, I have just got home for ten days leave, and have discovered your lovely present waiting for me. It is perfectly grand, but much too good — nevertheless many, many thanks.

"Edith tells me that old Hayward has been about. Is there any chance of finding him, or was he just on leave?

"Well, Goodbye for the present & let me know if you are coming up to town, as if not I could get down to see you sometime. Again many thanks, Yours Ever, Arthur Howard."

It was Ash Wednesday 1916 when my Magdalen journal noted, "Andrew Nugee, who went to the front from here and was reported in danger of losing the use of his eyes and one of his legs, came in the other day to see me. He looked as fit as could be. But then outward appearances are not the whole story.

"Last Sunday Peter Warren took me to call on his grandmother at Black Hall, an old residence here in the Giler (St. Giles' Street). There was a Belgian refugee visiting her who played superbly on a mellow old Bechstein.

"One of the historic things that has been going on in Oxford recently is the trial of conscientious objectors to military service. I went down and sat in the gallery of the court house to hear the cases of some of the men I knew. They are mostly undergraduates who resent the recent Compulsion Bill, some with high ideals, some admittedly cowards and some the sons of Cain who always object to everything. Among the first of these was Victor Murray, the general secretary of the Student Movement Christian Association, who besides having strong convictions against fighting is the last prop for the work of the Christian organization in the university. His influential letters and his rich personality commanded respect in the court, but they gave him only temporary leave from service.

"Then there came a perky little Jew who spread reams of paper out on the railing of the witness stand and stood there with a white orchid in his button hole, as irritating a sight as you can imagine. The Mayor and other Oxford celebrities (not including any of the University staff) went over this Mr. Kay's case. Finally they asked the military representative if he wished to say anything. The representative asked Mr. Kay whether he wished to answer questons or to make a statement, Mr. Kay chose the latter, and then the military representative disclosed the following facts: Mr. Kay's real name, which he had changed at the start of the war was Coberg; he had circulated a seditious pamphlet entitled SHALL BRITONS BE CONSCRIPT; and in short had identified himself with a small group of fanatic socialists. The military observed that on the whole Mr. Kay was not wanted in the army, and his case was referred to the civil court.

"The military representative was twitted, however, when he asked a theological student who had made an attack on war as murder, if he knew the text, 'An eye for an eye. . . .' The student asked him to complete the quotation. Then his cross-examiner confessing his ignorance, the student read at length from the New Testament Our Lord's own exposition of the text — 'But I say unto you that ye resist not evil; but whosoever shall smite thee on the right cheek, turn to him the other also. And if any man shall sue thee at the law, and take away thy coat, let him have thy cloak also.' This had such an effect that the court, which had poo-pooed the arguments about turning the other cheek, was rather flabbergasted at the direct words of Christ."

This change from what had seemed a voluntary crusade to what was apparently becoming a war of survival was getting to be more difficult for me who represented America on the side lines. Especially when I heard that recently a German torpedo had blown the bows off a French channel steamer, the *Sussex,* and killed several Americans who were on board. There would be another 'Note' from President Wilson on this atrocity which might pick up the American resentment over the *Lusitania* sinking. However, it was to be another year before the United States entered the war.

Further I was beginning to see that repercussions of the war were being felt in distant parts of the world which might make problems for my own country in the future. For example, the farewell speech of the Viceroy of India to the Imperial Council at Delhi as the newspapers quoted it seemed to carry a warning against Mrs. Besant's catchword, HOME RULE FOR INDIA. I recalled Annie Besant's influence even in New York as a theosophist vessel of spiritual enlightenment. Her propaganda publication, NEW INDIA, had been making trouble for some time. But people had confidence in Lord Chelmsford who was to be the new Viceroy.

The Viscount Chelmsford was among the distinguished inhabitants of my rooms at Magdalen. While an undergraduate he had been chosen president of the Junior Common Room. On his being appointed Viceroy we decided to congratulate him in the name of the J.C.R. To this he replied from Queen's Gate before leaving, "As an old President of the J.C.R. I very much appreciate your kind letter of congratulations & thank you sincerely for it." It was a satisfaction that Magdalen meant something to him in the difficult mission he was about to undertake.

10

EASTER VACATION AND DEGREE DAY

"THIS comes from FINCH'S, the Warrens' cottage in the country," my journal noted on March 23, 1916. "Thanks to the number of familiar pictures and descriptions of the Berkshire Downs with their dew ponds and curlews, not to mention the 'White Horse' on the chalky hillside, there is little need in my attempting to enlarge upon the glory of the rolling country. Suffice to say that my three companions and I left the historic streets of Oxford and bicycled down by the Thames past Abingdon to Wallingford. From there it is a short distance to the small group of houses known as Aston Tirrold. On the edge of this village stands this ancient brick cottage whose accumulated additions have developed it into a capacious dwelling. On the opposite side of the country road which leads past it to the hills is a trout stream, and there is nothing else between our narrow front garden and the open downs.

"Mr. Urquhart came to tea with me in Magdalen on the Tuesday before I came out here, and we talked over this projected reading party to which he is to contribute his stabilizing presence. A brother of one of the old Magdalen men whom I know also came. He had come up for Smalls. Also the son of the Grand Duke Michael came up for his entrance exams. He was a pleasing fellow, not at all 'Russian.' He and I agreed in a lot of things, especially in our dislike of mathematics. At the last moment it was found the suit he was wearing was not dark enough for the requirements so I fitted him out in mine. He was a friend of Teck's and put up in his rooms in the Cloister. There seems to be no reason why the Tsar's nephew should not sleep in the Queen's nephew's bed. At any rate this boy is known as Count Torby and he has a beautiful sister.

"On Wednesday we four, Hugh Terris, Peter Warren, Govy Hoffman and myself set up housekeeping in this picturesque house with its casement windows looking out over the rolling grass lands. A few minutes away is a round hill in a valley with great terraced steps on it sides. This was the site of an ancient Danish settlement whose chief, Brandebras, is buried in a tumulus on the top of Churn Hill. On Lowbury Hill, not far from this, is an old Roman fort guarding the Ridgeway, one of the oldest British roads in the country. The Romans were there for 300 years, and many interesting discoveries have been made on the site. Oyster shells which we find there are supposed to have been left by the Romans who counted them a choice delicacy. Another historic setting for my history writing but far different from my surroundings at Ewelme.

"Mr. Urquhart (pronounced Ercot) who was expected yesterday sends this letter from Balliol instead. 'Our dear old Master died suddenly this morning of heart failure, and naturally I can not get away till after the funeral. I suppose that will be Friday. I might be able to come that afternoon. Would that be convenient for you? He was a fine old man. I used to hope that he would be able to live out these critical times and link together the College of the past with that of the future. Many friendly greetings to the party, Yours ever, F.F.U.'

"We have set up a schedule for work hours and our exercise will depend largely on walking. The other day we walked to Blewbury, our nearest village. It is typical South England in concentration. You know the sort of thing; plastered cottages, irregular gables, chalk walls protected with thatch. We found an old man working in one of the many water-cress beds and bargained with him for some of his crop. We went on to examine the church. It is rather large for a village and dates back as far as the 12th century. One curious thing is an arrangement for running a curtain across the front of the altar. The iron rings are still in the walls on either side of the chancel. This is thought by the people here to have been a Lenten custom of veiling the altar in black, but I wonder if it might be connected with the Greek custom of shutting off the altar during the preparation for Communion before the actual beginning of the rite. There was also a niche in the wall supposedly where a rood screen may have been fixed at one time, but what it was really intended for we questioned.

"Another time we went in an opposite direction through the

fields about a quarter of a mile to a little brick house on the edge of an ancient moat. Here is where 'Philip the King' and other poems were written by the author of *The Salt Water Ballads*. John Masefield was not to be home until later, so we went on further in the cold rain and gathered some wild cress from the streams."

"We were eight for dinner tonight. (April Fool's Day, 1916.) Christopher Warren. Peter's brother, just arrived from the front. Also Sligger, alias Mr. Urquhart, who brought a friend from Balliol and told us of Strachan Davidson's funeral. You remember I told you of sitting next to the old Master, the successor to the famous Jowett, at the high table in Balliol. I was also placed next but one to him in the Senior Common Room after dinner so that I had the opportunity of conversing with him at length. There is a possibility of Mr. Urquhart being elected in his place but Sligger feels that in all probability A. L. Smith will be made Master of the college.

"The Masefields sent word for us all to come to tea today, but Mrs. Warren thought it would be too large a number of visitors for the Masefields' house and so took me off in the opposite direction to call on the Kenneth Grahames. Walking around the site of the Danish camp, Mrs. W and I came to Blewbury again. Here we found a little house more quaint than the others and, going in by the gate, we discovered a large ship's bell which hangs under a separate cover just outside the cottage door. This we struck with resounding effect. The boom brought out a maid who ushered us into a small livingroom. The walls of this room were lined with quantities of samplers. While we waited I had time to examine them. One extolling a political party, one declaring that although the maker of the sampler resigned the pen to men, her superiority with the needle was evident by the handiwork she had done. Above these samplers were dozens of glass rolling-pins gaudily inscribed with nautical — sometimes just naughty — sentiments. These sausage-shaped bottles were filled with rum in times gone by and presented to departing 'tars.'

"We hardly had time to inspect some of the other treasures of the collection before Mrs. Grahame entered the room. She was rather dishevelled and wore over her house-dress a heavy blue overcoat. After greeting us she went to a lounge and, making the excuse that she had tired herself in watching somebody unpack, she lay down and talked in a rather prim way. Her son, whom they call 'Mouse' — you remember how Kenneth Grahame personifies

The Park hotel
Keswick
Cumberland

10th June 1920

Mr Urquhart was with us in the autumn
& at Holywell. Mr & Mrs Bruce Warren
came & see us at Blenheim. I was to tell you
but it still seems very hard to write
such news. Sincerely yours E. Graham

Dear Mr Longstaff
Yr letters & envelopes were forwarded to

Kennetts here - where we arrived last Wed: He begs me
to answer it - because he has had cramp in his hand
& not enough his typewriter here finds it hard to write.
He wishes to say he is very interested in the

movement named by you for establishing the
children's library & would be glad to leave his name
included in the small advisory council as desired by
you. I don't know if you have come across that
"Cambridge book of Poetry for children" Edited & annotated
& made by him with much research & trouble
the regrets of the Cambridge Press- It would I think
please you, as there and though in it not otherwise
collected & some of them like the true children"

before he was most keenly interested. He always
thanked you "splendid" in yᵉ hon-work & was for
interested in the Magdalen - madein became
of you, when he was in for Mods: last march-he
& said there were some questions-the akin
about the mission of Magdalen & said he must go
& support it, & he much hoped you would come
& see him at Blenbury in the summer. Alas.

He was the most spiritual creature I have
ever known - & so full of fun & wit- Clear headed
& logical to a degree- He never held a superficial
view or said a superficial thought. His Store tutor
wrote " He was a very remarkable Boy. I never met
anyone of his age so well informed- he was
extraordinarily intelligent. he had very great gifts"
& the old Stow "Boys' mail" (who like all servants was
deeply devoted to him) said "He was so far above anything
that was not truly good". & there is out of hundreds
of tributes of love & honour - You have the power
of view of the learned scholar, & the humble servant
He was 20 on the very day that after a beautiful
service conducted by the Dean in the cathedral he

Pembleton, Oxon.

KENNETH GRAHAME (author) written for him by his wife regarding
recent death of their son, Alastair, 1920 (see index for references to
Oxford reading-party).

little animals — had come home disgusted with Eton. It seems the
first-year boys are made miserable with the fag system. They are
forced to serve the older boys at tea, and dare not roll up their
umbrellas, nor do a thousand other little things. The Grahames are
thinking of sending him off with a tutor until he is ready for
Oxford. Mrs. G also objected to the high-church notions which her
boy seemed to have acquired at school.

"As we rose to go I mentioned the fact that I had recently
purchased a rare sampler in Oxford and that Peter had given me
another. Mrs. Grahame's attitude changed at once. She rose from
the sofa with alacrity, threw off the rug which she had pulled up
from the floor to keep her warm and pleaded with us to see her other
samplers before leaving. She took us into a larger treasure room
also hung from ceiling to floor with samplers. Some of these went
a bit into the 1790s, but not many older than my 1801 sampler or
the one Peter had given me for my birthday. There were a few
other items of interest such as a miniature done by Napoleon's
second wife, and some rare pieces of china and glass.

"Mrs. G then took us into the drawingroom. Here is an original
sketch of Kenneth Grahame by Sargent, an original bit of poetry
illustrated by Blake and other relics of well-known people I should
have known. From there we went upstairs. In Mouse's room were
all his school treasures. Some original sketches which Robertson
had done of his life at Eton, funny watercolours. The signatures
of Punch's 'Round Table.' Mr. Grahame's room itself was quaint.
The doors were oak and very ancient. There they had the famous
cartoon which Sargent made of the 'Dreyfus Case,' presented
to them by the artist on their wedding day.

"Mrs. G promised to have tea earlier than their usual hour of six
if we would go out into the garden and wait. We had not more than
gone out into the unkempt garden when a large man in a very
black and white suit with a slouch-hat and stick came across the
grass to meet us. It was the author of 'The Wind in the Willows'
himself with his white hair and heavy moustache. Mouse was with
him. Mr. G took Mrs. Warren back into the house and I went off
with the son to explore a trout stream. He is a terribly lonely boy
for whom I felt an immediate affection.

"When we came back tea was not yet ready so Mr. Grahame
took me out to shut the 'barn.' It may well have been a barn in
days gone by but now it was furnished with all sorts of travel

treasures, bits of silk, old pieces of furniture, sketches, etc. Even Mr. G's precious books had been relegated to the ancient timbered structure which took on the air of a manorial hall. When the question arose of shutting out the sun by drawing a curtain across a large studio window cut in the side wall, or letting the books fade, Mr. G admitted he could not bring himself to keep the sunlight out. This seems typical of his character.

"In the course of an interesting conversation Mr. Grahame told me of a curious difficulty he had with his neighbour when they were living in London. The Grahames were enjoying the warmth of a new stove they had just installed with its back to the partition wall, when the neighbour in the adjoining house came in with a complaint that they were having trouble with their refrigerator which was on the other side of the wall. Since both the stove and the ice box were fixtures, it became a sore question which should take the trouble of moving his fixture. This was not the reason for the Grahames leaving the city, but rather it was on the advice of friends who urged that Mr. G should go into the country and devote himself solely to writing. Since coming to Blewbury, however, he said he had spent most of his time taking care of the house and garden with the result he had done no writing at all.

"When we were coming away the Grahames asked me to write Sir William Osler about their gardener whom they felt was dying at a hospital near Oxford. We thanked them for their tea and made our way back to Finch's."

My next letter from Aston Tirrold was merely dated "Another Day" and suggested the timelessness of the countryside. "Peter and I had a long visit with John Masefield this afternoon. He is a middle aged man with a moustache, rather light hair, with a soft manner, deep voice and full for manly gentleness. He is tall but slightly stooped and strikes one as having tremendous reserve. He read us some of Vachel Lindsay, whom he admires most among our present day American poets. It seems that after a tiring lecture recently in America three reporters cornered Mr. M. The first, who was a lady, said, 'Now, Mr. Masefield, please let me have a short story with plenty of pep!' The second asked, 'What do you think of the U.S.A.?' And the third put the question, 'What are your ideas about God?'

"Mr. M took us down to the edge of the moat which was probably used by the monks of old as a 'live fish pond' to supply their refectory table, and pointed out the part of the house which dates from the 14th century Benedictine order who are recorded as using the place as a recreation house for their brothers in Abingdon. But history seems poetry in this immediate area which was once the kingdom of the famous 'Old King Cole.'

"We asked the Masefields to come back with us for tea. They did, bringing with them milk — for we had run out of it — and apples and two grapefruit. These last had been given him by an 'American Millionaire,' when Mr. Masefield was leaving New York. I later found it was the same Thomas Lamont who had befriended my publication of *Harvard of Today*.

"Mr. M's trip to our country seems to have been a successful one. He lectured in Cambridge, Yale, Vassar and other girls colleges, as far south as Tennessee and as far west as Chicago. The commercial side of Chicago seemed to appall him, but he admitted

23 Wall Street.
New York.

April 24th, 1914.

J. Brett Langstaff, Esq.
Care The Harvard Union,
Cambridge, Mass.

Dear Mr. Langstaff:

I have gone through the "Harvard of Today" carefully, and think it is an excellent piece of work. I want to get a half a dozen more copies. Where can I secure these?

Very truly yours,

J. W. Lamont

THOMAS WILLIAM LAMONT (financier) who arranged for Brett Langstaff, although an undergraduate, to address the Associated Harvard Clubs meeting in St. Louis 1913.

he had always loved New York. He called it the most beautiful city in the world; especially the lighting effects at night appealed to him.

"He knew dear old Edwin Markham, who used always to be so good to me. He spoke of Markham's faculty for making speeches. Mr. Markham once told him of an incident which had happened to him many years ago in the West. One night in a saloon where he had put up, he was awakened by a noise outside his door and looking out discovered the landlord intoxicated and struggling up stairs. Suddenly he lost his grip on the banister, let himself go, and fell down to the bottom of the stairs. In the silence which followed Mr. Markham heard the landlord say, 'God help the sailors on a night like this!' Not bad, for the 'Man with the Hoe.'

"Peter Warren and I took Govy Hoffman's motor bicycle with his side car to Garsington near Oxford, where Mr. Morrell, Peter's uncle, has an attractive residence. Great stone gates, a long low house rather startlingly decorated, and further down the side of the hill a large pond which can be used for bathing.

"Mr. Morrell is a Liberal Member of parliament. Typical of the charming Englishman. While there I learned that the Cabinet had been set against the Dardanelles expedition, and in a three hours' speech Winston Churchill completely converted them to the idea of its possibility. This confirmed what I had heard before. Mr. Morrell seemed annoyed at the way the Conscription Bill had been put through. It was unfortunate, according to him, that men up to a certain age had not been conscripted, instead of the single-and-then-the-married-men method which is now being enforced with much dissatisfaction to all.

"Lady Ottoline Morrell (Cavendish Bentinck), his wife, is the half-sister of the Duke of Portland. She is a woman of natural charm but a woman upon whom personal eccentricities have laid a heavy veneer. A strangely alluring drawl, a well painted face, costume clothes of costly material — can you see her seated in a smart trap driving a high-stepping tandem through the streets of Oxford! We had lunch with them — Mr. and Mrs. John Peel were also there — played hare-and-hounds with the children, and (after some trouble with the bike) we had tea and came home in good style."

It was now April 6th and thanks to carefully guarded morning hours my work on the dissertation was going well. The regular afternoon walks and the relaxing conversations around an open fire in the evening kept us all healthy and happy. Occasional excursions abroad were welcome.

"I push-biked myself to Oxford and back yesterday," I wrote, "about forty miles altogether. It was a glorious blue-and-white day. I stopped at Nuneham Park and found that the kitchen was being made ready preparatory to the Harcourts' Easter visit. At Oxford I had lunch with Norman Nash in his digs in Ship Street. He has been rather laid up with colds and other things and does not seem entirely satisfied with his year at Cambridge. Burkitt, the scholar he especially hoped to read under, can be seen only at his house, for he is not now giving regular lectures. This made it difficult for Norman to get much from him. The lectures themselves are dry and solid. I fear Norman holds his American point of view too stubbornly to see the best side of these English colleges.

"After lunch I took Norman with me to the Oslers'. Revere was home waiting for a transfer from the Royal Ambulance Corps to the Artillery. One of the most tiresome parts of the Medical work seems to be the long periods of waiting when there are few wounded to take care of. The fighting is not constant enough to make the flow of patients even. Sir William and Lady Osler and three girls were there.

"After a little I came away with Sir William. I showed him the letters from the Kenneth Grahames' gardener, and he promised to look in to the case personally and write Mr. Grahame. We talked of the future Master of Balliol. J. A. Smith of Magdalen seems to have been thought of, but old A. L. Smith, Sir William says, is the guide and friend of more people outside of Oxford and can not be overlooked. It appears these college elections are done in close-corporation style by the dons. Sir W said, however, he hoped the time was coming when the graduates would be given more to say in the matter.

"I bought some postals with Magdalen pictures for Phil Pye-Smith's mother. She wrote asking for them and said that Phil was getting on well at the front. Arthur Howard had been home on leave, but my clothes were in the hands of the carrier who took my luggage from Oxford to Aston, for more than a week, and I could not go up to see Arthur as he suggested. I sent Lady Strathcona Josiah Royce's address on America's position in regard to Europe. It is strong.

"Going to Magdalen I fished out a will for Govy Hoffman from his room in the Grammar Hall, also measured my sampler in the hope of picking up an old frame for it. I biked home to Aston Tirrold via Clifton Hampden and dropped in at Lord Aldenham's. They are also to be expected at Easter. The floods in places are rather high, so that I was forced to go along through the fields to escape the rivers in the roads. When I came home it was just in time for tea, and I was exhausted. Mrs. Warren and Peter had gone to London with Captain Christopher to see the plays with Dorothy, the other member of the family — Mr. Warren being in Corfu as I have told you."

"Sligger, Govy, Hugh and myself — all went over to have tea with the Kenneth Grahames yesterday," I noted on the 10th. "I wanted especially to give them the result of the request they had asked me to make of Sir William. They were most grateful for what I had done.

"I questioned Mr. Grahame further as to why he could not find time to continue his writing. He said that he had received letters from men in the trenches asking for another *Wind in the Willows* and he had tried, but the truth was that now it took so long to get food and the merest necessities of life he was not left time for writing. I gathered that it was really because there was so little incentive in Blewbury — in London he had been one of a group of successful writers and artists contributing to Punch, the Yellow Plush and other periodicals — that he had lost the creative urge. He would live in Oxford if it were possible. Most of his writing in the past — when he was employed at the Bank of England — had been done after ten o'clock, after the family had gone to bed.

"Sligger and the others were highly amused reading the samplers. Here is one I might send home just at this time with appropriateness.

'Next unto God, dear parents, I address
Myself to you in humble thankfulness
    For all your care and charge on me bestowed
    The means of learning unto me allowed.
Go on, dear parents, let me still persue
These golden arts the vulgar never knew.'

"And this bit of purgatorial snobbishness.

'I dreamt that buried in my fellow clay
Close by a common beggar's side I lay.
    And as so mean an object shocked my pride
    Thus like a corpse of consequences I cryd.
Scoundrel, be gone and henceforth touch me not.
More manners learn and at a distance rot!
How scoundrel! in haughtier tones cryd he;
Proud lump of dirt, I scorn thy words and thee:
Here all are equal, now thy case is mine.
This is my rotting place and that is thine!'

"I missed the Communion Service at the little church in Aston here, and coming back met Sligger about to start off for Mass at

27th October, 1922.

Dear Mr Langstaff,

After nearly two years' wanderings, we have just arrived here for the briefest possible stay and general wind-up, before departing southwards again; and I have found awaiting me your kind letter of July from Italy, and the Lord Mayor's pleasant invitation for the function on the First.

First, let me congratulate you most heartily on so successful a close to your labours. There is singularly little in the nature of a permanent memorial to the genius of Dickens in existence. Many an intangible, though no less enduring monument — workhouse, prison, and other social Reforms, International Copyright and so on — but in stone, brick or marble i can really recall nothing at the moment, except a tablet or two.

Next, I want to beg you very kindly to hold me excused from attending the Meeting on the 1st November.

What with house-hunting, house-letting, packing, storing
and so on, every minute of the few days left us is more
than taken up, and I find it almost impossible to take
even an hour away from here. Were it really necessary
for me to be there, it would bo another matter; but I see
you have Henry Dickens and John Galsworthy, among (doubtless) other men of might, and I feel you are more than
amply provisioned. With the best of good wishes for a
most successful send-off, which indeed you are bound to
have.

                    Believe me,

                    Yours most truly,

                    Kenneth Grahame

KENNETH GRAHAME (author *Wind in the Willows,* etc.) written to
Brett Langstaff 1922, in reference to ceremonies at *The Mansion House*
presenting as a national memorial to Charles Dickens his boyhood home
in Somerstown, London.

Didcot. He suggested that I should go with him, and we biked off
together. We came to the camp which guards the large military
stores of Didcot and after some hunting found the hut where Mass
was said every fortnight. We went in past a temporary telegraph
office to a small room furnished with an altar, a tiny stove, some
benches and chairs, and a pile of things which had probably been
moved to one side for the occasion. There were about ten men,
two women and a child. A Tommy had warned us in a despairing
way that there was only a handful not Church of England in the
company.

"A loud genial voice — and the priest entered with a suit-case.
He laid his vestments out and, asking in a business-like way how
many were for confession, told them to follow him. He soon

returned with them from the Colonel's bedroom. Being so near I could follow the quickly spoken words of the service. It was the first time I had been able to make out the Latin as recited by a priest. The congregation certainly needs the tinkling bells and elaborate gestures to be able to find where the service has got to. After an exhortation to us, 'dear good Catholics,' to band together, he let us go."

Shut off from the rest of the world as my typing of the final draft of the dissertation demanded, I was nevertheless concerned with the course of the war. One of my immediate sources of information was through the Harcourts and now that Lent had passed they were coming down from London. On April 26, 1916, I wrote from Aston Tirrold, "After coming home from the Easter Service, I found your long letter waiting for me on the breakfast table. Also on the table Mrs. Warren had put a nest of Easter eggs with rings and little mottoes inside. I worked hard in the morning and in the afternoon started off on Arthur Howard's bike for Nuneham. Mrs. Harcourt had answered a letter with a wire to say she would be delighted to see me when they came down for Easter.

"I found Mrs. Harcourt in the smoking room with a bit of a chill. She had come down with Mr. H and the children for a week's rest. They had brought only a few servants and left the part of the house they did not need closed.

"Mrs. Harcourt had received a folder from a French Relief Society which seemed rather unusual and efficient. It is under the management of two influential Jewish French women, and purposes to appoint women guardians for the French war orphans, i.e. children whose fathers have been killed should be taken care of without removing them from their homes or former surroundings. Thus avoiding the impersonal character of an institution these children could be watched over and given advantages of which they would be otherwise deprived. On the American side it is patronized by Mrs. Whitelaw Reid, Mrs. Harriman, etc., and a few men including my Bishop Rhinelander.

"It seems the French societies have been federated. Mrs. Harcourt thought the requirement of having their accounts audited twice a year was too much to ask, but she agreed the accounts of such societies were apt to get muddled. The French upper classes have supported the war generously, but the rich middle classes including many of the bankers and controlling merchants have been sadly slack. This is not the case (I would say at least not now) with the English middle class. The French and other Latin people seem less generous in nature, certainly compared with the Anglo-Saxon.

"Mr. Harcourt came in from the garden, and the children came in from the roof of the house where they had been climbing on the balustrade. We talked not of the serious affairs of state which are now imminent, but of the more immediate affairs of family life which are getting more and more difficult. The taxes are cutting incomes in half. Mrs. Harcourt spoke of the responsibilities of the landowner to the tenants in England which is a marked contrast with the independence which the American landowner feels.

"We went out after tea. I wish I had the powers of description to tell you of the blaze of the sunset which lighted up the winding Thames in the valley, the formal terraces spread with flowered carpets, the soft green walks tunnelling through yew and holly and laden with the odour of box-wood. We threw crumbs to pheasants with gorgeous plumes and long tails sweeping the ground. I told Mrs. Harcourt how I had been persuaded by Sir William to have my book printed, how splendidly you had answered and said it should be done, and how I had written the Archbishop of Canterbury and received a reply expressing his interest in my work but saying that without some special reason he was bound to refuse appeals for prefaces and forewords. Someone said the archbishop was formidable but not brave. I told her I thought of asking Bishop Boyd-Carpenter because of the long talk I had had with him about my dissertation. (He married the Harcourts and Mrs. H said goodnaturedly that he always reminded her of the 'Bishop of Rumptyfoo.') Finally Mrs. Harcourt advised me to write my own 'Preface' rather than make the book seem to depend upon some distinguished authority's introduction.

"We crossed the terraces again in front of the house to the rock walk. Here where a rock garden borders one side of a long path edging the hill we found Lulu Harcourt with his weeding stick near the spot Edward VII had chosen to have a seat placed for him. On a clear day the king could have seen the spires of Oxford and reminisced about his undergraduate experiences — as I may do in years to come. The recent storm which brought down forty to fifty trees on less than a mile of road in Ewelme had wrought havoc also in Nuneham Park. Mr. Harcourt referred to the definition of dirt as earth in the wrong place. He enjoys poking around in his garden.

"We three walked together to where a small lake had been caught in a dell. This was a resort of weird wild fowl. There had been many flamingoes which had flown away or died. The Cabinet Minister had brought some crumbs for a pheasant whose nest he had had to remove because of the danger of foxes. Then back to the house. And about six thirty I left them as I might have left my own family. As I biked down the long drive to Culham, I started a herd of deer, an emu strode across the road, a kangaroo sat on his haunches in sympathetic amazement. Before the afterglow had died away I was home with our jolly little party at Aston Tirrold.

"You must know that after Sligger left (I meant to tell you he was a friend of our friend Sir Cecil Spring-Rice), I wrote to Professor Santayana asking him to spend a few days with us. He came and added his keen fun and Spanish courtesy to make things even more delightful. He had just sent his 13th book to the publisher, EGOISM AND GERMAN PHILOSOPHY. As we sat around the open fire in the lowceilinged livingroom he regaled us with intimate recollections of the famous schools of philosophers at Harvard in his day. William James, for example, was so given to being humorous that George Santayana recalled a Scotsman raising his hand in a lecture once protesting, 'But, Professor James, speaking seriously!' Whatever Santayana says (We call him 'Santy' for short) is apt and keen. He is a stimulating personality. We had him in his most whimsical mood making a Spanish omelet in our kitchen. With what nicety of precision every egg was cracked! With what critical taste each ingredient was added! The entire process accompanied with cutting comments which sent us into gales of laughter. And at last — what an omelet!"

"We have just been spending the afternoon at the Masefields'." This was written from Aston Tirrold on the 29th of April 1916. "Mr. and Mrs., their little girl and a mite of a sunny haired boy were all at home. Mr. M was suffering from a boil on the back of his neck. Nevertheless he had been to town going over documents of some sort — I think related to the Dardanelles. He may be writing about it.

"Mr. Masefield had chartered a small boat and he was allowed to go independently as an observer when the Dardanelles

JOHN MASEFIELD (Poet Laureate) written to Brett Langstaff 1920, mentioning "Govy" Hoffman (see index for references).

campaign was going on. The Turks are admired by the Allies, he assured me, because of the clean way they fight. He showed us maps of the trenches on both sides. Once he was within twelve feet of a Turkish picket, and the English soldier on duty refrained from firing, 'because it would have been too much like murder.' Masefield was himself under fire for two days at one time. He took us down to the moat to show us a model of his boat and describe the beach heads.

"Mr. M had talked with an English officer who had the experience of lying in a submarine at the bottom of the sea and hearing the German grappling hooks grating overhead. If they had found where he was his submarine would have been destroyed by their depth charges. Often times they waste bombs by mistaking dark weedy patches for submarines. To avoid repeating such mistakes they empty quantities of chalk into the water till the dark places disappear.

"He spoke of compulsion for service men on the sea. It would seem the law allowing men to be pressed into service for the British navy has never been repealed. It was a cruel, partial form of conscription, according to Mr. Masefield. He recalled that desertions from the navy, although punishable by death used to be constant. Nelson reported in one year 45,000 men had deserted. That would have been more than a third of the men in the service at that time. Lord Nelson added further, according to the record, that he could not see how it could be otherwise with the form of conscription used to get them in. If they did not hang a man for desertion, they flogged him on one ship after another until he was dead. Mr. M said that today floggings even for the smallest offence would not be tolerated. If a man were to be punished privately now some accusation of impertinency or mutiny would be made against him and he would be 'struck.' However, Mr. M had once seen two men have their faces thumped until they were actually jelly. (This probably during his experience when serving before the mast on a merchant vessel.)

"A black and white hen flew in at the window where a number of eggs had been placed along the sill. As it stood there cocking its eye in wonder at such a nest, Mrs. Masefield came along and observed she had recently gone out in the larder and found this hen on an open meal bag while at the same time the cat was busily lapping from the family milk pan. Poets' wives make strange housekeepers. Mrs. M and the children with Peter and Govy went up to the Badger Woods on the hill, but Hugh and I crossed over the moat to sketch the ancient monastic end of the house sheltered by an overhanging yew tree. Later we all joined Mr. Masefield again. Then, as tea was getting ready, he took us off to find white violets — some of which I enclose in this letter.

"To-morrow I go over to Ewelme to read the Lessons at the church. I will wear my Harvard hood which I have borrowed from Govy. I am getting more work done here than any vac before."

There was no question that we four undergraduates put in hours of work on our variously assigned studies but at the close of the day there was a natural reaction which expressed itself in hilarious skylarking. One of our nonsense projects was the damming of a brook which burbled along beside the road on which our cottage faced. In this John Masefield was our keen abettor. And years later he told of how one spring our dam had burst and flooded the village below.

Then there was the time when we endeavored to convince Govy Hoffman — who was studying the philosophy of mysticism — that ghosts really existed. As planned, Peter and Hugh had taken him for a walk on the Downs in the moonlight while I was left behind at my typewriter. It was agreed, however, that I was to circle around through the village and up into the hills to meet them disguised as a ghost. The disguise was a sheet hanging down over an inverted broom and so covering my human form as I held it high above my head. The fact that certain villagers — whom we thought would be asleep — had seen a ghost pass their windows added to the fact that three shepherds on the downs saw a ghost dash toward them through the moonmist — they having been mistaken by me for my three friends — created a legend of the Ghost of Aston Tirrold.

On May 2nd my letters were again coming from Magdalen College. "We ended our reading party by coming in to Oxford to see Peter Warren's sister Dorothy act in *Twelfth Night*, my old play which I had seen so well produced at the 'Old Vic' in London. After the performance we went around to Black Hall in the Giler where we had tea with Peter's grandmother in her garden. It is a stately old mansion in which this Mrs. Morrell's father had lived when he was president of St. John's College.

"After tea they dressed me up in a black velvet gown and made my face up with Dorothy Warren's theatrical outfit. I was supposed to play the part of an adventuress while Dorothy, dressed in some of my clothes, acted the part of a youth, victim of my wiles. Peter appeared in toga and headband to a classic rescue while Terris in 18th century get-up was introduced to romanticise the whole incident. It took so long to prepare our drama that our hostess insisted we come in to dinner as we were. We were all rather nonplussed, however, when we entered the formal dining-room and found Mrs. Morrell had as her guest a very sedate Roman priest."

Finally I could write from my rooms in the Magdalen cloisters, "My dissertation is shaping up nicely. The plan which is becoming fixed now is the following: I. A short introduction. II. The three liturgies from which the first English text comes, i.e. the Latin translation of the Greek Liturgy of S. Chrysostom, the Latin text of the Mozarabic use in Spain, and the Roman use as it was done in Sarum and most other places in England at the time of the translating. These in the Latin grouped in small sections for comparison, as 'The Lections'—taking in all the readings from the Epistles, Gospels and Old Testament. III. And third, the English text of the 1549 Book corrected in red ink to the present use of the Church of England, another of the same 1549 text corrected to the present use in the Church of Scotland (Episcopal), and a third corrected to the present use in the Protestant Episcopal Church in the U.S.A. And with these will go as footnotes the reasons for the corrections made by the revisors and other points which I may think valuable.

"As a final chapter of the dissertation I would like to set down a survey of the communion liturgy as it is used by the several nonconformist bodies and even add suggested changes in the liturgical text. This I may not have time or means to carry out. Perhaps you would help me by sending me the names and addresses of some of the representative men in each of the large Protestant churches in America. Then I could write them and ask the questions I wish to know in regard to their variations on the historic Liturgy. What denominations are Lyman Abbott and Henry Van Dyke? I know them through their having sent me contributions for the *Harvard Illustrated,* and Prof. McGiffert and Dr. Samuel Eliot I feel sure would help me because of my friendship with their sons. But maybe all this will have to be left for some other time."

There followed weeks of concentration on the composition of my final thesis when neither the war nor even the pleasant interruptions of my friends could divert my attention. Then, on the 23rd of May I wrote, "It seems a long time since I really sent a letter home, but I am sure you know it is only work that necessitated my neglect. The old dissertation, after two years hard work, is finished. I have had to do the whole thing by myself which has doubtless been good training for me. There have been discouraging times, but now that it is done, I feel positive that I have something worth while.

"I have just been talking with Mr. Hall of the Clarendon Press about the publishing. There seems no reason why I should remain here for the proofs which could hardly come to me for over a month after I hand them the copy at the end of term, about June 20. The Press is in the habit of sending proof to Harvard, and Mr. Hall assures me none of them have been lost during the war. In short, if there is no difficulty about getting permission of the Board to supplicate for my Degree (The Board meets on June 18), then after taking this B.Litt. on the next Degree-Day which should come a few days later, I will leave the better copy of my dissertation with the Press and bring the other back with me. The final revision before publication can better be done at home. All the wonderful times I am having here are not to be compared with the happiness I anticipate in being home with you.

"I went to the Oslers' Sunday for lunch and met a delegation of doctors which has been sent over by President Woodrow Wilson to inspect the hospitals etc. in the cause of preparedness. Doctor Ford, Dr. Pleadwell and two others. It seems as though the President is preparing to be prepared, in spite of his seeming slackness. I had taken the final copy of my dissertation with me. Sir William was enthusiastic, but it will be a different matter when a couple of liturgical specialists get scrutinising it through their microscopes.

"My tutor and I went for a fourteen mile walk. I would never have thought the little man's short legs could have made it. He will be sixty next month. And he nearly ran all the way. He said he wished he could make people act in their homes the way they made him act in church. He would have their tables built at an awkward height as altars are in most churches. He would make them go through all sorts of meaningless gestures and address people with their backs turned toward them. I can't quite get his honest opinion of my work. He really has let me go on by myself so much that although I have read the first draught to him once, I fear he has only a general idea of the contents. Dr. Scott-Holland, on the other hand, is most encouraging, and he is Chairman of the Board before which my dissertation must finally come."

On June 4, 1916, I noted, "These are anxious days waiting for the Public Examination on the 12th of this month and for the final decision on the 15th. Dr. B. J. Kidd, an eminent historian whose lectures on Church history are the best I have heard, writes thus; 'St. Paul's Vicarage, Oxford. June 1, 1916 — My dear Sir, The Rev. L. Pullan, of St. John's, and I have been appointed by the Board of Theology to consider your thesis for the degree of B. Litt; and I thank you for the copy that has reached me safely. I understand that you want to have the decision taken as soon as may be: and we, too, should like to be in a position to send in our Report to the Board of Theology, when it meets on Thursday, June 15th. In order that we may do this, it will be necessary to hold the public examination a few days before that date: & I am now writing to ask whether it will be convenient to you to have it on Friday, June 9th, or Monday, June 12th, at 5.30 p.m. in the undergraduates' Library, St. John's College. Please let me know which of the dates you prefer, and then I will have the statutory notice inserted in the University Gazette. I am, Sir, Yours most truly, B. J. Kidd.' This epistle was addressed to 'The Reverend J. B. Langstaff,' and I hastened to correct this mistake in thinking I was ordained."

The period between having completed one's work and standing by to hear the result would have been more trying if it had not been for unexpected diversions. The journal records, "There has been rather a lot of fun in college lately owing to the temporary residence of several old Magdalen men who had been wounded. H. O. Hopkins, an Australian, gave a theatre party and supper. Govy Hoffman's brother, Stoddard, who had been doing ambulance work, gave a large dinner party at the Clarendon Hotel. They made me get up and sing 'The Star Spangled Banner.' I don't know why I happened to learn the words of the anthem, so few people are familiar with them.

"Peter Warren gave a river party starting at six and punting down the Cherwell to the 'New Cut' where we ate. Then down further along the Isis. Miss Thornton, an army nurse, and a Miss Ward with her brother made up the party. The Wards' father is the late editor of the *Dublin Review*. The boy is not especially a friend of mine, but it is rather romantic to realize that he is a descendant of Sir Walter Scott's and that when he goes down he will go to Abbotsford. We came back about eleven. Also there have been little tea parties here and there. The Banners came up for a few days. Every afternoon we go up the river to the Cricket Grounds, play tennis and have tea. This is one of the most delightful experiences you could possibly imagine! The servants have brought out of somewhere an oversized cup for me because I drink so much of it.

"Yesterday was one of my red-letter days. Lewis Gielgud, whom I think I mentioned as a nephew of Ellen Terry, asked me to motor down with him and Stod Hoffman to Eton for the 'Fourth of June.' This is an important social occasion. It was not only generous of Gielgud because of the expense of the trip, but for an Etonian to show a man to his other friends at Eton is tremendous. I took the noon-day service at St. Mary's in Oxford first, and they kindly waited for me.

"We drove down the old Ewelme road with which I am so familiar. It was looking its best. The few dark rain clouds cleared away and left the country glistening and fresh. We crossed the river at Henley and finally drew up before the old buildings which recalled the day eight years ago when my tutor and I rushed about seeing the school for the first time.

"We went inside the chapel first. I don't remember having seen it before. The lofty roof and the great Burne-Jones tapestry behind the altar — which latter is repeated in Exeter College — are most impressive. From there we went out to the fields to see the people and watch the scratch games of cricket. There was to be no parade of boats, and the boys wore simply the regular top-hat and morning coat with no attempt at gala decoration. The original field where in normal times there would have been a spectacular match going on, was surrounded by men and women either lookin at a game which was being played or taking tea in a marquee

"When our host was encircled by his many friends Stod and I sometimes wandered off and left him with them. It was very, very interesting for me to see the type of Eton man in the surroundings which had made him. Suddenly Levett rushed up to me. Dear old Levett, I had not thought he would be there. He had a fellow with him who was in his regiment and who had a brother on the *Warspite,* which had been reported sunk in a battle just the day before in the North Sea. Levett and I had heaps to reminisce about and we went off by ourselves for some time. I joined Lewis and Stod in the marquee where I met Lewis's tutor. Everything at Eton seems to depend on the tutor a man is allotted, and this man was a splendid, youngish sort of healthy don. Lord Stanley, Derby's eldest son, whose rooms I have lived next to for the past two years, was back from the front on sticks. Count Torby, whom I told you came up for smalls, was floating about. And others whom I knew.

"After tea we came back to the Yard for 'Absence.' The Headmaster, Dr. Lyttleton, read the list of names from the chapel steps, and as each boy's name was called, the boy raised his hat in the air, and when he saw he was recognized put it on again and went off. This done, we went up stairs to the Upper Schools. Here all the men have their names carved on the walls when they go down. On the entrance door there was evidently an ancient record in large letters, HOWARD, and directly under it was Arthur Howard's name. A man can have his name placed with an ancestor's name if that should happen, otherwise he is placed in a long list carved by a professional hand."

What I was being shown — not as a tourist but as the friend of an Eton boy whose younger brother was to become one of the leading actors on the British stage — was an educational picture which to my American mind was outmoded. It did explain the crammers in Haslemere and the ingrained culture — sometimes mistaken for maturity — of men who had come up to Oxford from public schools such as Eton. I could comprehend better the loyalties of students at Harvard who had been trained at such schools as Groton and St. Paul's and other preparatory institutions modeled on the Etonian plan. But I was the product of Brooklyn schools well staffed and modern in every sense — although one of them, Erasmus Hall, was as old as any academy in colonial America — and I was not entirely convinced by what John Gielgud's brother was pointing to with pride and affection.

"The Headmaster's room at the top of the stairs with its pulpit backed by a great picture of a Greek theatre is a place for special examinations. Here was one of those whipping benches. It is made in the form of a mounting step, two steps high. On the first step the boy kneels and bends over the top step, his head hanging down and his hinder parts in favourable position for smiting. They showed me that bundle of twigs they call the birch. Of course this form of punishment is only for the younger boys, but thrashings are administered by monitors using light canes, for the older boys. To an American it naturally seems revolting. Personally I consider it barbarous. The long hall of the Upper Schools where speeches had just been made had had its walls carved with the names of such men as Pitt, Walpole, etc.

"Lewis then took us to the place he had lived in while he was at Eton. He was on the Foundation and thus lived in college. Upstairs overlooking the quad there was a long dormitory, in its English sense. Instead of all the beds being together as they had been originally, each boy had a cubicle with a curtained doorway. A corridor ran the length of the dormitory and in the centre was an open space forming a sort of common room with a round table and a large fireplace. The boys were housed here only for the first part of their residence and soon graduated to small rooms whose doors afforded more privacy.

"I met George Fortescue, just as we were leaving Eton. He is now helping to switch the search lights over London when the Zeps come. Finally we drove back to Oxford where I had ordered a general supper in my rooms. The day concluded with our all going off to the play as Peter Warren's guests."

A few days later the journal continued, "We are now busy planning about the dramatics traditionally produced at Magdalen when everybody's examinations are over. They will be held as usual at the top of the 'Kitchen Stair,' in the rooms occupied by Oscar Wilde when he lived as an undergraduate at Magdalen. Our Kitchen is said to be that used by a hospital founded 'for the relief of poor scholars and other miserable folk' as early as the year 1233. It is interesting to note that William de Waynflete — he had been headmaster of Eton when it was a new school — had written into the first charter for founding Magdalen the name spelled in the vernacular as 'Maudelayne.' This accounts for our pronouncing it today in this strange fashion.

"The plays will be Maurice Baring's two comic skits, *Ariadne* and *The Aulis Difficulty,* and also a third sort of farce we call *Pippa Passes* in which I am Pippa. This last is being written by Peter and Lewis Gielgud with unsolicited comments from Aldous Huxley and other literary minded undergraduates. Why they have put me down for the leading lady in two of the plays I am not sure, but since it does not interrupt my work I have agreed. We really take the acting seriously.

"James Street, the president of our 'J.C.R.', has just had an operation for appendicitis, but when I called on him at the Acland Home (our infirmary) it looked as though he would recover in time to be on stage with us when the curtain calls. I went from there with Windram to the Oslers'. Sir William told me that Phil Pye-Smith was struck with a bullet which cut the ligaments of his thumb so that he has temporarily lost the use of that digit. He is at a hospital in London and goes home every day. Lady Osler had seen Lady Strathcona and Mr. Howard at the station in London and they kindly had asked after me. She said Lady S was not looking well. With so much to worry her it is marvelous how she keeps up. Sir William has threatened to come to my public examination and ask about the baptism of Bishop White. The public is allowed to ask questions on points concerning the dissertation and I understand it does.

"At present time I am doing a bit of extra research to appear learned on the topic, 'The Liturgy of the New Testament.' I shall perpetrate this lecture at Keble College before a combined meeting of the Origen and Nicene Societies as a guest of D. C. Simpson, a don of much repute."

It was only later I learned that the battle in the North Sea to which my last letter referred was the Battle of Jutland, the first great naval engagement of the war, which had lasted from May 31 to June 1. I heard from home that the news of this battle, issued on Friday evening June 2nd, was so misleading that American papers like the *Philadelphia Inquirer* declared, 'The British decisively defeated.' But thanks to my friend Mr. McKenna and to Admiral Fisher, the British had built up their naval strength to such a point that it looked as though they had now dealt a death blow to Germany's High Sea Fleet.

It was the *Warspite* on which my friend's brother was stationed which the Germans persistently claimed to have sunk. But on Sunday, the day of my writing, the British Admiralty issued notice that this was untrue because the ship had now "returned to harbour." To settle this matter, I heard at the Oslers', a representative of the Associated Press of America was invited to interview the captain of the *Warspite*. Captain Phillpotts' observation was, "I am not surprised that there have been reports that the *Warspite* was sunk, as from our position, between our Fleet and the German battleships, our escape from such a fate was simply miraculous. Several times we disappeared from sight in the smoke and spray." He said that after two hours engagement the steering gear of the *Warspite* went wrong and she ran amuck among the enemy. Six German battleships concentrated their fire on her but she remained in action without a single vital injury."

President Lowell wrote me from Harvard on June 7th, "Evidently the first news of the battle in the North Sea gave the public a shock, but from that they recovered quickly when the real news came in. Now comes the death of Earl Kitchener. I suppose he had had many trials, disappointments and failures during the war, and it is sad that he should have been lost."

Sir William Osler had asked me to write Lowell regarding an item he felt the Harvard library should have and the president had replied that he was "very sorry to say that our Library does not feel able to purchase the Greek manuscript about which you and Sir William Osler wrote me. I suppose the Library, like most of us, must cut its cost according to its cloth."

To this President Lowell had added, "I am glad to hear that the Oxford Press is to print your dissertation on the liturgies in English. It must be a great gratification to you to have it appear in book form. Your account of the people you have been seeing intimately makes me feel what a very interesting time you must be having, for which I am very glad. England is always an interesting country, and this is a marvelously interesting time to be there."

Finally on June 18th my letter from Magdalen read, "I have been having a relapsed feeling after hearing the decision of the Board of Theology in favour of granting me a degree. But many things have been happening.

"Our little cousin, the Marquesa de Barrio, has come back from Spain. I asked her to come to Oxford last Sunday, which happened to be her birthday. She brought with her a step-daughter, Miss Taylor. I had invited Peter Warren, Hugh Terris and Victor Murray to meet her at lunch and a few minutes before lunch Gilbert Elliott arrived from Paris, rather unexpectedly. To make the number even I asked Delmar Banner to join us. You can imagine what a jolly party Estelle would make any gathering, especially a gathering of young college men. After lunch, which wound up with a birthday cake for the beautiful marquesa, I sent them up the tower and around the colleges sightseeing because Miss Taylor had not been to Oxford before. There followed a grand tea party to which all the other men came. Our guests did not get away till about eight that night.

"Gielgud, Warren, Banner and myself went to London for wigs to use in the little plays we are having at the end of term, and Estelle asked us to dinner and the theatre. There were two other men besides her two 'babes' — as she calls her daughters — and Miss Taylor. The dinner was at the Savoy in luxurious style, where Estelle has had a suite for eleven years. Afterwards we had a dance and Peter and I arrived home (his home in Bedford Square) about two in the morning.

"While I was in London I took tea with Lady Strathcona and heard from her that Uncle Gari and his bride from Bath have given birth to a daughter. Lady S had been the first also to tell me they were engaged. The Howards' new house — just completed building in Green Street, Park Lane — is even more spacious than the Grosvenor Square residence. Here I met Sir William Peterson (Principal of McGill University) and Lady Peterson, whose son I had come to know before. I also lunched with the Pye-Smiths and found Phil in splendid shape. His wounds leave no trace."

My last letter from Magdalen College was a long one dated 27th June 1916 urging my parents in New York "not to worry about my sailing home on the Canadian Line. When so many of the men are risking their lives, it ill becomes me to go too far out of my way to be safe. But I do not feel that I am doing anything in the least hazardous by not coming on one of our American ships.

"The performance of our traditional 'Kitchen Stair' plays was entirely satisfactory. Oscar Wilde had a pair of rooms at the top of the Kitchen Stair. They were large and divided by heavy portieres. The smaller room served us well enough as a stage because the stage-setting was simple drapery effectively lighted. The audience crowding the larger room numbered many of prominence, old and young, standing and sitting everywhere. Maurice Baring's *Aulis Difficulty* was solved in 'Agamemnon's Tent' with Gielgud, Warren, Banner and Chrussachi. His *Ariadne in Naxos* found me as Ariadne in my 'boudoir" with Henry Fraser, Jimmy Street and Govy Hoffman, as Dionysus. Our original melodrama was finally titled *The Winning Stroke* patterned on Thomas Hardy's *The Dynasts* and adding to our cast Stod Hoffman, Charles Jury, Victor Murray and Purdon Hough. There was no entrance charge but our audience was 'invited to contribute at the close of the performance to Mr. Sidney Ball's *Fund in Aid of the Serbian Refugees in Oxford.*'

"The demand for seats was such that we had to have a matinee and evening performance. The plays themselves were well received, and between performances the cast combined to have our special guests for tea in the Junior Common Room. The point I had in mind all through, of cheering the dons and undergraduates until the end of term, was accomplished for everybody seemed gloriously happy.

"One of the many amusing incidents was this. The line of my part as Ariadne seemed to drag a bit in rehearsals until it was suggested I copy the exaggerated accent and affectations of the Lady Ottoline Morrell. When the curtains parted and I was discovered lying on a couch in classic wig and female attire, toying with grape leaves twined around the head of 'Govy' Dionysus, to my horror I beheld in the front row the Lady Ottoline herself. Immediately after the final curtain John Masefield came around and reproached me for seeing too much of the Duke of Portland's sister. And when I confronted the Lady herself at tea she asked me pointedly where I found my accent, drawling in her alluring way, 'Now we see what lurks behind these calm exteriors.'

"Sir Herbert Warren was so intrigued in the afternoon that he insisted on coming a second time, in the evening. The audience was of course far more distinguished than the cast. The Marquesa de Barrio had driven down from London and took the Masefields back in her motor as far as Cholsey. Perhaps this is the last of the jolly time because the long continuance of the war is wearing down the thrill of voluntary adventure with which it started, and in its place is coming the spirit of conscription and all the deadening restrictions of big military business.

"Shortly after the Board's decision regarding my degree Professor Santayana took me up to the Robert Bridges' place on Boar's Hill. It is a picturesque residence fitting a poet laureate with its terraces looking down toward the spires of Oxford. Mr. Bridges was greatly concerned about the hood which was to be given me. He said he preferred it to all his other hoods, but that he had substituted his own shade of blue for that usually used by the tailors. He then sent for Mrs. Bridges' sewing basket and, gathering all the bits of blue silk it contained he thrust them at me with the admonition that I would have to go to China to find the proper shade which would combine them all.

"We talked of many things. When Bridges talks he barks, and his tall bent figure and shaggy grey hair lend a naturalness to his gruffness. When I told him I came from New York, he said the only Americans he cared for came from the South. When I found that he knew nothing about America really, I suggested in a modest way that perhaps he might find a visit to the country interesting since it was, after all, a sort of development of English culture. 'Well,' he growled, 'It may be a development of English culture, but I'm not proud of it!' I soon found that he was very much cut up by the war. He is one of the few I have come across here who think we Americans ought to come in on the side of the Allies, but he didn't say so exactly. He was just generally sour and pessimistic about conditions. However, he did come to our plays and the lovely Mrs. Bridges and (I think) their two daughters.

"In a few days the ceremony of my degree day will have passed. It is the prerogative of one's scout at Magdalen to put the new hood over one's head and arrange it properly before returning to the assembled representatives of the University for inspection. No college servant could deserve it more than my scout, Hunt, who after taking care of a long succession of the sons-of-the-great or the since-great, took me on with equal devotion. How much Oxford undergraduates owe to their scouts will probably never be set down. And remember, Hunt's interest in me was as the interest of a groom in a race horse. He knew what I should be fed and how I should look when I went out to compete with other undergraduates. He did his best to see that I did my best. And when Degree Day comes it will give him satisfaction to see his horse win. It will then remain for him to pack my things and send me home.

"There are certain usual exchanges of signed photographs among more intimate friends and a schedule of flying visits of goodbye, but in a few days it will be the ocean to Montreal and then the train to home where I wish I were at this very moment. Along with his signed picture George Teck gave me his Eton prayer book and hymnal with his name stamped in gold on the cover."

Before I set sail for my overseas homeland I was informed that there was a small package following me from house to house as I made my farewell visits. No one had presumed to open it, but, as they inscribed one forwarding address after another they could not help but notice that it bore the imprint of the royal seal and for those few who might ever have seen it the package was addressed to me in the handwriting of the Prince of Wales. When it finally reached me in New York I opened it to find a picture of the Prince of Wales in his footer togs which I had sent to him in France as a token remembrance of our beagling. With it in the folder was the following letter all in the Pragger's own handwriting.

"H. Q. 14th Corps — B.E.F. — June 29, 1916

"Dear Langstaff, Many thanks for your letter; I return the photograph signed as you asked. It's kind of you to suggest sending me a copy but I have some!! Well do I remember that day's beagling last Nov!! I wonder when I shall get another day? I was also delighted that they gave George a commission in his father's regt. as he was so keen!! I'm very glad to hear you think the beagles will be able to carry on another season by which time one can only hope the war will be nearing its end: but who will be master? My congratulations on getting a B. Litt. & I wish you the best of luck on your return voyage to New York!!

"I remain, Yours sincerely, Edward."

* * *

Thus it was I returned to New York with my Oxford degree. Then, on January 12, 1917, in the Chapel of the General Theological Seminary — in the presence of my former instructors and fellow Theological students — wearing the blue and white hood over my cassock and surplice, I knelt before the altar and was ordained *Deacon* by the statesman-bishop, Charles Henry Brent.

He had chosen me as chaplain to carry his pastoral staff in the
Vatican at a conference called at that time by Pope Benedict
XV to bring an end to the World War.

And so, farewell, dear friend;
Who e'er my reader be
Who hast made friend with these
Who once befriended me.

— J. B. L.

INDEX OF PARTICULARS